HATE CRIME POLICY AND DISABILITY

"For the first time, this book effectively combines the historical context of activism, political obliviousness and a need for recognition of the victims of these heinous crimes."
David Wilkin, The Open University and Disability Hate Crime Network

"Compelling and rich in evidence, this timely new book challenges us to question prevailing assumptions about Disability Hate Crime. Essential reading for anyone seeking to develop fresh ways of thinking about and responding to an urgent set of problems."
Neil Chakraborti, Professor of Criminology, University of Leicester

"Grounded in interviews with disability activists, policymakers and practitioners, this book highlights the limited recognition of targeted violence that is part of the lived experience of people with disability. Taylor acknowledges ableism as a foundational enabler of such violence."
Barbara Perry, UNESCO Chair in Hate Studies, Ontario Tech University

"Taylor draws on his unique experiences as a policymaker and scholar to help us understand the true nature of Disability Hate Crime and why it really matters. Essential reading for anyone interested in ensuring justice for disabled people."
Joanna Perry, Independent Consultant (Hate Crime) and former Hate Crime Advisor, OSCE, Warsaw

"Taylor has been at the centre of Disability Hate Crime policy development for some years. He is ideally placed to describe this journey and, most importantly, the action that is still needed to provide equitable rights and protections to disabled people."
Paul Giannasi OBE, National Policing Advisor for Hate Crime, HM Government

HATE CRIME POLICY AND DISABILITY

From Vulnerability to Ableism

Seamus Taylor

First published in Great Britain in 2024 by

Bristol University Press
University of Bristol
1-9 Old Park Hill
Bristol
BS2 8BB
UK
t: +44 (0)117 374 6645
e: bup-info@bristol.ac.uk

Details of international sales and distribution partners are available at bristoluniversitypress.co.uk

© Bristol University Press 2024

British Library Cataloguing in Publication Data
A catalogue record for this book is available from the British Library

ISBN 978-1-5292-1787-2 hardcover
ISBN 978-1-5292-1788-9 paperback
ISBN 978-1-5292-1789-6 ePub
ISBN 978-1-5292-1790-2 ePdf

The right of Seamus Taylor to be identified as author of this work has been asserted by him in accordance with the Copyright, Designs and Patents Act 1988.

All rights reserved: no part of this publication may be reproduced, stored in a retrieval system, or transmitted in any form or by any means, electronic, mechanical, photocopying, recording, or otherwise without the prior permission of Bristol University Press.

Every reasonable effort has been made to obtain permission to reproduce copyrighted material. If, however, anyone knows of an oversight, please contact the publisher.

The statements and opinions contained within this publication are solely those of the author and not of the University of Bristol or Bristol University Press. The University of Bristol and Bristol University Press disclaim responsibility for any injury to persons or property resulting from any material published in this publication.

Bristol University Press works to counter discrimination on grounds of gender, race, disability, age and sexuality.

Cover design: Liam Roberts
Front cover image: Giorez

To my Anam Cara, Kleber Alcantara Pereira
and to the memory of my parents,
Eamonn and Bridie Taylor.

Contents

List of Figures and Tables   viii
List of Abbreviations   ix
About the Author   x
Acknowledgements   xi

1   Introduction   1
2   Fifteen Cases of Disability Hate Crime   21
3   From Hate Crime to Disability Hate Crime   41
4   Agenda Triggering   65
5   Agenda Development   89
6   Towards Agenda Institutionalization?   116
7   The Problem with the Current Agenda: Focus on Vulnerability   144
8   An Agenda Item Yet to Fully Speak Its Name: Ableism and   168
    Disability Hate Crime
9   Conclusion   193

Appendix: Research Design and Methods   206
Bibliography   219
Index   244

List of Figures and Tables

Figures

1.1	Window of opportunity	10
4.1	Diagram of Phase 1 developments	87
5.1	Diagram of Phase 2 developments	115
6.1	Diagram of Phase 3 developments	143
8.1	Ideologies of ableism and disablism	189
8.2	Disability Pyramid of Hate	190
A.1	Sample analytical memo	218

Tables

6.1	Principal offence category by hate crime strand, 2018–19	121
A.1	List of key informants	207
A.2	Headline details of Disability Hate Crimes cases analysed	212
A.3	Codebook\\Phase 1 – generating initial codes (open coding)	214
A.4	Codebook\\Phase 2 – axial coding (developing core categories)	215
A.5	Codebook\\Phase 3 – focused coding	217

List of Abbreviations

ACPO	Association of Chief Police Officers
CJA	Criminal Justice Act
CJS	criminal justice system
CPS	Crown Prosecution Service
DHC	Disability Hate Crime
DPP	Director of Public Prosecutions
DRC	Disability Rights Commission
EHRC	Equality and Human Rights Commission
EU	European Union
HMCPSI	Her Majesty's Crown Prosecution Service Inspectorate
HMI	Her Majesty's Inspectorate
HMIC	Her Majesty's Inspectorate of Constabulary
HMIP	Her Majesty's Inspectorate of Probation
IAGs	Independent Advisory Groups
IPCC	Independent Police Complaints Commission
LGB	lesbian, gay, bisexual
LGBT	lesbian, gay, bisexual and transgender
MOJ	Ministry of Justice
NGO	non-government organization
OCJR	Office for Criminal Justice Reform
ONS	Office for National Statistics
OPM	Office for Public Management
RNIB	Royal National Institute of Blind People
UN	United Nations
VIA	Values Into Action
WHO	World Health Organization
WPR	what's the problem represented to be?

About the Author

Seamus Taylor is Head of Applied Social Studies at Maynooth University where he teaches social policy and researches hate crime. Seamus brings over 25 years of policy and practice experience to the field of hate studies. He was previously Director of Equality and Diversity at the Crown Prosecution Service (England and Wales) where he led on community-informed policy making on hate crime. Earlier he served as Director of Strategy at the statutory Commission for Racial Equality where he led on the responses to the Stephen Lawrence Inquiry in terms of setting agendas on addressing racist and religious crimes and on the public sector duty to promote race equality. Seamus serves as Independent Chair of the CPS London Hate Crime Scrutiny and Involvement Panel and was awarded a CBE in 2010 for his work on advancing equality in the legal system in England and Wales. Seamus was educated at University College Dublin, Goldsmiths College, University of London and at Lancaster University.

Acknowledgements

While writing this book, although a solitary act, I never felt alone as so many people supported me throughout and now is the time to say thank you.

I primarily wish to thank Professor Paul Iganski for all you shared and taught me about the craft of writing. I am forever in your debt.

I want to thank Joanna Perry, Paul Giannasi, Baljit Ubhey, Mick Conboy, Ken Macdonald QC, Keir Starmer QC, Peter Lewis, Siobhain Barber, Simon Cole, Katharine Quarmby, Lord David Blunkett, Anne Novis, Ruth Bashall, Simon Green, Kirsten Hearne, Stephen Brookes, Mark Brookes, Jenny Offord, Neil Crowther, Conor Ryan, Caroline Ellis, Sinead Glancy, Professor Nathan Hall, Dr David Wilkin, Ben Meehan and Mike Smith. Your advice and support at different stages in the journey to this book has been invaluable. A very special thanks to Dr Lucy Michael for reading through the complete draft and for your feedback, advice and support. It was excellent.

I want to thank my interviewees in the research underpinning this book for your valuable insights and I hope this book does justice to your contributions.

I want to thank my friends, Julian, Breege, Maura, Anne, Roxanne, Valerie, Geoffrey, Suresh, Niall, Declan, Val, Bruna and John R for your encouragement. All your support has kept me going. I also want to thank my wider Taylor family for your support.

I want to thank my Maynooth University colleagues, Maurice Devlin, Ciara Bradley, Rory Hearne Brian Melaugh, Niamh Flanagan and Tonye Benson Olatunde. A very special thank you to my colleague, Joe Larragy, who has given me very sound advice at every stage of this book project. Your advice has been invaluable. I also want to thank Maynooth University more widely for significant support over the years of working here.

I want to thank Freya Trand and Rebecca Tomlinson at Policy Press for your enthusiasm for this book from the outset and your encouragement along the way. Thank you.

I dedicate this book to Anam Cara, Kleber Alcantara Pereira and to the memory of my parents, Eamon and Bridie Taylor, who taught me so much about the fundamental claim on respect and dignity that resides in all people.

1

Introduction

Key points

Twenty years ago, Disability Hate Crime was unheard of in England and Wales. Disability Hate Crime is today a significant criminal justice concern. This book addresses how Disability Hate Crime moved from invisibility to policy action.

This chapter sets out the book's themes which focus on:

- the contributions of activism, politics and policy making to the Disability Hate Crime policy agenda;
- the challenges of a pervasive focus on vulnerability in Disability Hate Crime;
- ableism as a prejudicial ideology fuelling Disability Hate Crime.

This chapter introduces the book's organizing and analytical policy concepts of the problem stream, the policy stream, the politics stream, problem representation and problematization as they apply to Disability Hate Crime.

Overview of the book's themes

Disability Hate Crime is a new crime category for very old behaviour. Targeted harassment, hostility and violence towards disabled people is age old. At varying times, it has included banishment, incarceration, abuse, enslavement and murder. This targeted harassment had a high point of hate in the Nazi era mass murder of disabled people. While this history of hate exists, Disability Hate Crime as a distinct policy domain is a peculiarly modern 21st-century response to this behaviour. Twenty years ago, Disability Hate Crime was unheard of in Britain. Today it is a significant criminal justice concern.

This book addresses how and why Disability Hate Crime developed as a criminal justice system policy and practice concern. The development of Disability Hate Crime in the criminal justice system in England and Wales is charted and analysed. In doing so this book provides the first comprehensive account of this issues development. The book analyses the contribution of activists, politicians and policymakers, and criminal justice system practitioners to this area of hate crime development. I focus on the challenge posed by the pervasive view of disability targeting in crime as vulnerability targeting – and point to ways through this challenge. I also focus on the under-recognition of disability prejudice and link this to the fuelling ideology of ableism. These twin challenges of an over-focus on vulnerability and an under-focus on ableism are significant and give to Disability Hate Crime both unsettled and unsettling features. Notwithstanding these challenges the book concludes on an optimistic note. Progressive legal policy change together with a critically reflective approach could enable Disability Hate Crime to transition from unusual business to usual business within the criminal justice system into the future.

Setting the scene: Disability Hate Crime public milestones

There are a number of significant public milestones on this policy journey from the invisibility of Disability Hate Crime to significant institutional actions being undertaken, and these are identified and critically explored throughout the book. I examine how these relate to hate crime more widely and explore the journey from hate crime to Disability Hate Crime. Here I identify the main lines of inquiry that the book addresses. First it is helpful to set out the context in which Disability Hate crime first emerged.

In 1997, the Labour Party General Election Manifesto contained a pledge to create new offences in the area of racist crime. This marked the initial step in the creation of, first, racial, and, second, religiously aggravated offences. A Labour government was duly elected and, although not the first hate-related legislation, it is then that hate crime began to be recognized as entering the criminal justice policy domain in England and Wales. For the next five years, hate crime was officially regarded as concerned with, first, racist and, latterly, racist and religious crimes. A catalysing event with far-reaching impacts was the publication in 1998 of the independent inquiry into the handling of the racist murder of Stephen Lawrence (Hall, 2013; Giannasi, 2015a). Although some advocated an extension to include disability and sexual orientation as strands within hate crime, there was no serious debate on these issues at this time (Labour Party, 1997; UK, Home Office, 1997a; UK, Home Office, 1997b; Law Commission, 2013).

In 2003, another significant, but less noted, development occurred. Baroness Scotland QC, then a Home Office Minister, introduced an amendment in the House of Lords to the Criminal Justice Act (CJA) 2003, which was the Labour government's flagship legislation for criminal justice reform. This amendment provided for sentencing enhancement in cases where hostility on the grounds of disability or sexual orientation (later amended to include transgender identity) was a factor in crime – it became Section 146 of the Criminal Justice Act (2003). Baroness Scotland indicated that the government was 'guided by the evidence' in relation to targeted crimes experienced by disabled people and gay people (Hansard (HL) 5 Nov 2003). Although not specific hate crime legislation and less than the racist and religious crimes provisions, Section 146 was constructed as government recognition of Disability Hate Crime and Homophobic Crime (Bacchi, 2009; Hall, 2013).

Section 146 of the Criminal Justice Act (2003) was not enacted until 2005 and the policy domain on Disability Hate Crime in terms of police and prosecution policies and monitoring only became effectively established from 2007. Both prior to and after 2007, there was a significant increase in policy, activist and independent sector activity in the years up to 2010 (Mind, 2007; Scope, 2008; ACPO, 2010; CPS, 2010a, 2010b, 2010c; UKHMG, 2009-10). These activities and public milestones included:

- Early ground-breaking and agenda setting work of the then Disability Rights Commission (DRC) followed by DRC agenda setting reports which flagged targeted disability harassment as an issue.
- Publication of non-government organization (NGO) reports highlighting issues of deinstitutionalization for disabled people and highlighting issues of harassment of disabled people in the shift to community living (VIA, 1999), both prior to and after 2007.
- Implementation of the Disability Equality Duty from 2004, with disability equality schemes required from all public bodies in 2006 and that required for the first time public bodies including police and prosecution services to involve disabled people in identifying criminal justice priorities to promote disability equality.
- Establishment of a Disability Hate Crime Network in the NGO sector in 2008, a coalition of activists seeking to secure an effective criminal justice system (CJS) response to Disability Hate Crime.
- Promotion by the Association of Chief Police Officers (ACPO) and adoption of a common definition of monitored hate crime by the CJS in 2007, which included Disability Hate Crime as a category of officially monitored hate crime for the first time.
- Publication of ACPO hate crime manuals and guidance (2005, 2014).
- Publication of government hate crime action plans (2009–10, 2010, 2012a, 2016).
- Keynote speech by the Attorney General in 2007 recognizing hate crime impacting diverse groups including disabled people.
- Keynote speech by the then Director of Public Prosecutions (DPP) in late 2008 acknowledging and challenging the criminal justice system's neglect

of Disability Hate Crime and calling for a priority focus on Disability Hate Crime across all CJS agencies.
- An NGO report that charted significant failures by the CJS to respond appropriately to Disability Hate Crimes, including murders (Scope, 2008).
- Report of an Independent Police Complaints Commission (IPCC) inquiry into the deaths of a mother and her disabled daughter in Leicestershire (IPCC, 2011), known as the Pilkington Inquiry.
- Research commissioned by the Equality and Human Rights Commission (EHRC) into targeted violence experienced by disabled people in 2009 (EHRC, 2009), which delineated the nature and range of targeted disability violence.
- Launch of a formal statutory inquiry by the EHRC into disability related harassment in 2010 (EHRC, 2011a).

In 2010, following the general election, the Conservative–Liberal Democrat coalition issued its first Equality Strategy, which contained a commitment to improve the recording of Disability Hate Crime (UK Government Equalities Office, 2010). Subsequently, the Labour Party pledged that a future Labour government would create specific disability aggravated offences (Liam Byrne MP, Labour Party, September 2013). This became the Labour Party position at the time of the 2015 general election.

Alongside these activist, policy and political developments, the criminal justice inspectorates began to publish inspection reports on the response of the CJS to Disability Hate Crime. Early inspection reports were highly critical of criminal justice system performance (HMCPSI, HMIC, HMIP, 2013, 2015), although a later inspection report noted improved performance (HMCPSI, HMIC, HMIP 2018). The Law Commission also published a first report on the possibility of extending the racially aggravated offences provisions to cover Disability Hate Crime (Law Commission, 2013) but did not consider themselves in a position to do so at that time given the terms of their review. More recently in 2018 the Law Commission embarked on a fundamental review of hate crime legislation including the provisions in respect of disability hostility and published a comprehensive consultation report on hate crime law (Law Commission 2020) that directly addresses the challenges in ensuring an effective legal response to Disability Hate Crime. It now stands alongside the work of Walters et al (2017) as the most comprehensive overview of the hate crime legal landscape in England and Wales. Also, the Crown Prosecution Service (CPS) reviewed its public policy statement on Disability Hate Crime, and published a revised policy statement (CPS, 2015–16, 2017).

Taken together these are some of the public milestones on a journey to increasing focus on Disability Hate Crime, if not quite parity of provision with other forms of hate crime, in England and Wales. In a sense, there has been a significant flurry of activity on the Disability Hate Crime agenda, reflective of the relative adolescence of the hate crime domain in Britain compared to its increasing maturation in the US (Iganski, 2010). In the space of 20 years approximately, Disability Hate Crime appears to have journeyed from invisibility to significant institutional action within the criminal justice system in England and Wales. In this book we follow the policy journey informing these public milestones. I chart and analyse the emergence of the issue of Disability Hate Crime, its relationship to other forms of hate crime, the issues it raises, and the development of activist, political and, in particular, policy responses to this issue in England and Wales.

My interest in researching and writing this book

My interest in this topic ignited when I was involved in the development of hate crime policy and practice as Director of Equality and Diversity at the CPS of England and Wales from 2004 to 2009. During this time, I contributed to a review of the CPS' racist and religious crimes policy, a review of the homophobic crimes policy to also include transphobic crime, a review of the violence against women strategy, the development of a CPS Disability Hate Crimes policy and the development of a policy on crimes against older people. This gave me a clear overview of the range of areas that the hate crime agenda addressed and the nuances within them. At this time, there was growing activism around Disability Hate Crime as well as the political developments described, and a sentencing uplift provision in place, thanks to Baroness Scotland's amendment. I sensed that the emerging policy area of Disability Hate Crime might challenge how the criminal justice system constructed hate crime overall. There was also a pervasive construction of disabled people as vulnerable. This seemed likely to present challenges within a focus on Disability Hate Crime.

As I became immersed in the policy responses to Disability Hate Crime, I was increasingly prompted to reflect on the processes of defining and constructing social issues as social problems, the problematization and problem representation of social issues (Bacchi, 1999, 2009), how issues gain policy agenda status (Lister, 2010; Kingdon, 2011) and the contribution of different actors to policy making. I began to wonder if I was involved in a policy making process that was socially constructing a new crime category for what might be very old behaviour (Quinney, 1970; Best, 1999; Hall, 2013). If so, how and why had this happened? Was this an issue before its time in 2003, and was this an issue whose time had come in 2007? This reflection led me to embark on the research underpinning this book.

While there were increasing accounts of aspects of Disability Hate Crime in England and Wales, there were very few as I embarked on this research that analysed policy development on Disability Hate Crime. Some accounts highlighted aspects of the contribution of the disability movement, while others highlighted shortcomings in the CJS response to Disability Hate Crime (Scope, 2008; Quarmby, 2011). Critiques of the construction of Disability Hate Crime focused in particular on the issues raised by a perceived conflation of issues of vulnerability and hostility (Roulstone and Sadique, 2013). There were some accounts that began to profile the features of disability hostility and targeted violence experienced by disabled people (EHRC, 2009). More recent accounts covered aspects of the development of the CJS' response to Disability Hate Crime (Giannasi, 2015a) and the location of the Disability Hate Crime issue in an international context (Sin, 2014). More recent and compelling accounts focus on victimization of disabled people who have experienced hate crime in the context of austerity cuts (Healy, 2020) and a significant analysis of everyday experiences of disability hostility on public transport (Wilkin, 2020), and in both instances the inadequacy of the policy responses to disabled peoples' experiences of Disability Hate Crime are well highlighted.

The most comprehensive account to date of the development of Disability Hate Crime policy per se is that of Mason-Bish (2009). She explored the development of a hate crime policy domain in Britain in terms of race and religion initially, its expansion in terms of sexual orientation and disability and, finally, its exploration in terms of age and gender. It was the first attempt at a comprehensive account of hate crime policy development in Britain. However, as Mason-Bish pointed out, this was not 'the definitive account of how hate crime policy developed but rather I have identified important areas for future research' (Mason-Bish, 2009, p 63). Her contribution was not able to examine the full range of factors that may contribute to the development of hate crime policy, and she identified her limited engagement with wider political and legal factors and a lack of consideration of the role of discrimination legislation on the development of policy as limitations in her research. In a study focused on the establishment, expansion and exploration of the hate crime policy domain overall, there was a constraint on what could be addressed in detail in relation to each hate crime strand. In recognizing this, Mason-Bish identified the gap that this book seeks to address by augmenting and building on her work. It 'is difficult to examine the development of every area of hate crime policy because each victim group actually warrants a study on its own' (Mason-Bish, 2009, p 62). This forms the starting point for this book.

Evidence presented in this book

This book draws on two key pieces of work. First, it draws substantially upon an original research study I undertook in England and Wales between 2012 and 2018, and second, it draws on a subsequent analysis I conducted on developments between 2018 and 2020.

The underpinning research comprised:

- Fifty-five in-depth interviews with key informants in activism, politics and policy making. Interviewees ranged from disability activists, through to interviews with national leaders in the police, the prosecution service, the judiciary, the House of Lords, the House of Commons to senior members of the Cabinet.
- Analysis of 548 Disability Hate Crime cases (leading to 15 case studies) through unique access to the CPS case management system. Analysis of these cases highlight the challenges of a focus on vulnerability and the non-recognition of disability prejudice and ableism in Disability Hate Crime cases.
- A critical analysis of key policy documents on the topic of Disability Hate Crime.

The appendix of this book provides details the research methods used in the underpinning research study which informs this book.

Organizing concepts used in this book

The central organizing concepts in this book are informed by the work of Kingdon's (2011) policy streams approach and by the work of Bacchi (2009) on problematization and problem representation in policy making.

Kingdon's ground-breaking model of public policy conceives of the public policy environment as comprising three streams. These are:

1. A problems stream – a stream in society in which a range of issues exist only some of which become recognized by government as policy problems and policy issues. Some of these issues are defined as problems to be addressed. For issues to be addressed by public policy, they need to go beyond being conditions and become problems meriting agenda status. They need to be regarded as legitimate problems warranting the attention of public policy and lending themselves to a policy response. Factors that can influence whether problems succeed in securing policy attention include the results of monitoring of indicators, feedback to government, the place of values in problem definition and 'focusing events' such as a crisis that can have a significant impact, particularly if they fit with pre-existing views of a problem.
2. A policy stream – a stream in society around and within government in which policy development is undertaken by key actors including, on occasion, 'policy entrepreneurs' who may be policy officials, activists, politicians or combinations of all three. Kingdon suggests that, in public policy, the policy solution can already exist in terms of a policy approach and a problem is more likely to secure agenda status if it can fit with this policy solution. It is in this context he talks of solutions seeking problems

as well as problems seeking solutions, with policy entrepreneurs, on occasion, playing key roles. Policy entrepreneurs can be civil servants, activists/pressure groups, or politicians. They are keen to progress their issues on the policy agenda. These actors may seek opportunities that combine problem and policy concerns and political interest in addressing the issue. Factors that may influence whether an issue becomes a policy issue include judgments about 'technical feasibility' or 'fit' with a wider policy approach and values, efficiency and equity.
3. A politics stream – a stream in which politicians champion a particular policy issue, programme, or approach that can be informed in part by earlier developments in the policy and problems streams, including 'feedback' and 'spill overs' from earlier policies. Influential factors may include election results, public mood, opinion polls, changes in political administration, or ideological shifts.

Kingdon uses the three streams' metaphor to convey how problems, policies and politics can exist, flow fairly independently and in parallel for much of the time. At critical junctures, the three streams can flow closer together, converge and, in converging, create a 'window of opportunity' through which a new policy can emerge through a coupling of problems and politics and a new policy agenda is set and institutionalization of a policy area progresses. The policy streams model of policy making has been applied over the past 30 years to numerous case studies and to both small-scale studies and large-scale policy shifts. It has been applied to an analysis of the development of American disability policy in the late 20th century (Switzer Vaughn, 2003) and in criminal justice studies in both British and US contexts (Jones and Newburn, 2002, 2007).

In particular, use has been made of Kingdon's emphasis on the influence of factors such as key indicators, focusing events, feedback to government and wider value congruence in issues moving from being a condition among many to a problem selected by government as meriting specific policy attention, There is, however, a sense where he may under-expose a key element in the problem stream: the process of problematization, i.e. the process through which an issue becomes problematized as something requiring policy attention and how that problematized issue becomes represented as this particular problem and not another representation of the same issue. Kingdon acknowledges that policy problems go through a process of problem definition, but sometimes in ways that do not render them sufficiently critical. He can neglect the critical construction of problems in his model of policy making. Thus, while this model has been very valuable as both an organizing and analytical framework for understanding the emergence and development of Disability Hate Crime policy, some adaptation was necessary, and this was informed by the ground-breaking analysis of policy making by critical social constructionist Carol Bacchi (1999, 2009).

Bacchi has developed a framework for analysis of public policy, theoretically underpinned by critical social constructionism, known as 'What's the problem represented to be?' (WPR). It involves asking the following questions of any public policy:

- What's the problem represented to be in a specific problem?
- What assumptions underlie this representation of the problem?
- How has this representation of the 'problem' come about?
- What is left unproblematic in this problem representation? Where are the problem and the policy silences? Can the problem be thought of and represented differently?
- What effects are produced by this representation of the problem?
- How/where has this representation of the problem been produced, disseminated and defended? How might it be questioned, disrupted and replaced? (Bacchi, 2009)

Central concepts in Bacchi's WPR approach are those of problematization, problem representation, policy and problem silences, and competing policy and problem representations, policy disruptions and replacements. For Bacchi, problematization and problem representation are the overarching concepts that ground the analysis and to which her other concepts relate. She defines problematization as referring to how something is put forward as a problem, an issue to be addressed. Problematizations of issues contain 'implicit representations of the character and causes of problems' (Bacchi, 2009, p 277). Inextricably linked to this is the concept of problem representations – these are the implied 'problems' that sit within how an issue is problematized linked to public policy (Bacchi, 2009). With Bacchi's analytical framework to support our analysis of Disability Hate Crime, we see how targeted hostility based on disability – an age-old problem – can be viewed through different lenses. It has been variously named, if at all, as abuse, a motiveless crime, as senseless crime neglect, a failure of care and most frequently (although problematically) today as crimes against vulnerable people. Over the past 20 years its problematization has presented in a new way as Disability Hate Crime. Bacchi's WPR framework also usefully addresses the issues of policy-problem silences, helping us to understand what goes unrecognized in problem representations and how problem representations of the same issue can compete with one another as different policy issues.

Taking Kingdon's policy streams model (Kingdon, 2011) together with Bacchi's WPR approach (Bacchi, 2009), I devised an adapted organizational and analytical framework that better fits this book's themes. I have replaced Kingdon's problem stream with an activism and problematization stream

Figure 1.1: Window of opportunity

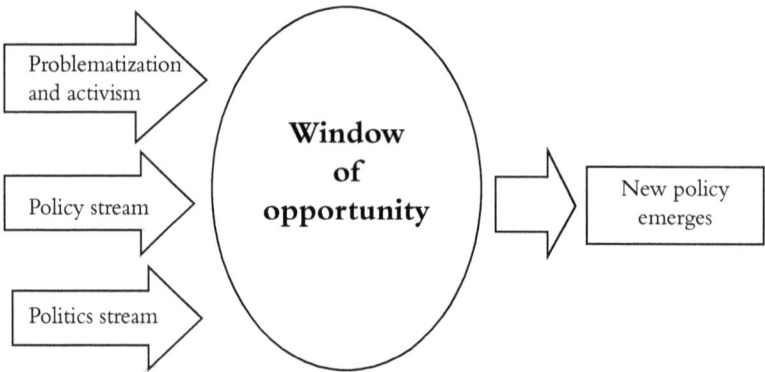

that I think has particular value in analysing social policy formation such as Disability Hate Crime. Diagrammatically, this adapted organizational and analytical framework would be represented as in Figure 1.1.

This adapted policy streams approach is used throughout this book and informs the titles and organization of the chapters which follow. It provides an organizing and analytical lens rather than a complete conceptual framework.

Introducing central analytical concepts used in the book

As well as being informed by organizing concepts from the policy studies literature, there are two central analytical concepts drawn from a critical engagement with the disability studies and wider equality studies literature that inform this study: vulnerability and ableism.

Vulnerability: a concept subject to critical interrogation

The term vulnerability is a term that has entered the public policy discourse nationally and internationally in recent decades. It has also entered academic discourse in recent times (Brown, 2014a; Fineman, 2008, 2010, 2017, 2020; Butler et al, 2016). With notable exceptions there has emerged an uncritical embrace of vulnerability as if it is a helpful categorization of groups of people for policy purposes (Roulstone et al, 2011; Brown, 2014a; Thorneycroft, 2017). Various groups are today constructed as vulnerable for policy purposes. Groups of people constructed as vulnerable include women, Black and minority ethnic people, LGBT people and invariably disabled people. The vulnerability label as used in public policy discourse can be well intentioned and applied by policymakers in uncritical ways as a shorthand for protective policy and service measures these groups may need. It implies that these groups need to be 'looked after' in policy terms rather than people who are rights bearing citizens. This vulnerability focus can reflect at best a paternalistic attitude on the part of the state. Groups of people who have campaigned for decades for recognition within equality and human rights policy frames are being reframed as vulnerable. This slip in state policy making from the focus on rights bearing minorities experiencing inequality to the vulnerable to be looked after is a slip from the structural to the individual that can be regressive in its impacts on both individuals and social groups.

In considering the use of the term vulnerability in public policy including in the law it is worth considering the etymology of vulnerability. The term vulnerability has its origins in the Latin words *vulnus* and *vulnare*, which is to carry a wound and to be wounded. This begs the question of public policy as to whether we risk constructing women, Black and minority ethnic people, LGBT people and disabled people as inherently wounded and that public policy can at best mitigate those wounds? This book seeks to shift and raise our gaze from the so called vulnerable or wounded to the wounding society that structurally and situationally positions some groups at greater risk of marginalization, exclusion, and social and physical wounding including the risks of hate crime.

Disabled people interviewed for this research unanimously rejected their categorization as vulnerable for policy purposes. It is a deficit concept that neglects personhood, and human and collective agency. If there is a prevalent view on the part of policymakers of the benign application of the vulnerability categorization, there is an equally prevalent view of its malign impacts held by disabled people. In an age that purports to afford a basic respect to people's self-definition in terms of identity it is striking that 'progressive' public policy continues to ignore disabled people's rejection of the vulnerability categorization and categorizes disabled people as vulnerable regardless of disabled people's rejection of this categorization.

While some authors point to the universality of vulnerability in the human condition (Fineman, 2008, 2010, 2020) – and indeed this perspective has much to offer – it does not adequately address the full range of issues raised in applying the vulnerability concept to all groups of people at this time. Indeed, Fineman does acknowledge that much of the use of the vulnerability categorization in public policy is problematic and flawed (Fineman, 2017). Given the particular history of disability discrimination, the geographies of disability segregation, the enduring legacy of a denial of personhood and human agency leading to the current required focus on independent living and rights for disabled people, a categorization as vulnerable fundamentally jars with this wider civil rights journey. In this context this book takes a critical perspective on the categorization of disabled people as inherently vulnerable for public policy purposes. This critical interrogation of vulnerability in hate crime policy forms a central focus of the analysis in this book. It features throughout the text and is considered in particular detail in Chapter 7.

Ableism: under-recognized and under-applied

The term ableism is increasingly but not yet widely used in the social sciences and even less so in policy and public discourse. Prejudice and discrimination experienced by disabled people goes under-recognized and, as a result, is often not responded to. Academics, activists and policy officials today readily speak about racist crime, homophobic crime and antisemitic crimes and, in doing so, recognize and emphasize a link between hate crime and the underpinning prejudicial ideology that drives the relevant biased criminal behaviour. There is no such ready recognition and emphasis on the link between Disability Hate Crimes and the underpinning prejudicial ideology of ableism.

This book argues that pervasive non-recognition and under-developed understanding of ableism as akin to racism, homophobia and antisemitism is fundamental to the limited policy and practice progress made in relation to Disability Hate Crime. In this context ableism, to paraphrase Wilde, is the prejudice that is yet to fully speak its name.

Ableism, as used in this book, refers to a prejudicial ideology that naturalizes and normalizes an able-bodied norm and, in doing so, inferiorizes disabled people who are constructed as deviating from that able-bodied norm and that corporeal standard. This book conceives of ableism as a prejudicial ideology equivalent to racism, sexism, ageism, homophobia and transphobia. Ableism embeds an ableist normativity in society that serves to diminish disabled people's identity and lives. Ableism has manifestations and impacts in terms of the advantages experienced by able bodied people, a society constructed around able bodied privilege. Ableism equally has manifestations in terms of the disadvantage and discrimination experienced by disabled people at structural, cultural, institutional and individual levels.

Ableism, disablism and the Social Model of Disability

A key framework for analysis and action on disability equality over the past 50 plus years has been the development and promulgation of what is termed the Social Model of Disability. The Social Model of Disability emerged in Britain in the 1970s. From the outset it questioned the dominant medical and welfarist/charity approaches to disability, which had constructed disabled people as largely individual tragic subjects who needed welfare, care and protection. The Social Model challenged society to distinguish between impairments and disability. In doing so, the Social Model positioned disability as a social consequence of barriers facing people with impairments at a physical, attitudinal and institutional levels. It is a powerful rallying model and has helped shift the policy gaze from the individual disabled person to the disabling society.

However, the Social Model of Disability is not a theory of disability oppression and discrimination that can be compared to those theories of oppression developed to understand, for example, racism. Its leading architects, including Oliver and Barnes (2012), are very clear that they intended it as a simple yet powerful heuristic device that can contribute to understanding and action in countering aspects of disability discrimination and not a coherent theoretical model.

This book acknowledges the very significant contribution of the Social Model of Disability in its powerful critique of the dominance of the medical–welfarist model, which has held back progress on rights, equality and justice for disabled people. The book is, however, drawn to the developing analysis of disability disadvantage, discrimination and oppression in terms of the concept of ableism, which locates disability discrimination within a wider identity inequalities frame of understanding alongside analysis of racism, sexism, ageism, homophobia, transphobia and other prejudicial ideologies that diminish people's identities. This book is influenced by the seminal work of Nario-Redmond, Kumari Campbell and other scholars such as Goodley on this topic.

At this point it is important to distinguish between the terms ableism and disablism as used in this book and why ableism is the preferred concept used here. Both ableism and disablism are terms found in critical disability studies literature. Disablism features in a relatively small body of literature (Miller et al, 2004; Kumari Campbell, 2008, 2009; Goodley and Runswick Cole, 2011; Goodley, 2014) and ableism even less so (Kumari Campbell, 2008, 2009; Goodley, 2016; Nario-Redmond, 2019). Disablism highlights attitudes and practices which diminish and negate impairment, and which leads to an undervaluing of disabled people and to discrimination experienced by disabled people. In a sense, proponents of disablism take disability as a given rather than as a social construct. In contrast ableism views both disability and ability as social constructs that should always be critically interrogated. In an approach that foregrounds understanding through a lens of ableism there is not only an asking of the question, what does it mean to be able-bodied, there is also a need to ask how do the privileges of being able bodied come about, how are those privileges held it place and what are the consequences for those constructed as disabled? Ableism shifts our gaze to the ideological production and embedding of able-bodiedness and how ableist normalization and normativity leads to disability disadvantage and discrimination at individual, institutional, cultural and structural levels.

Locating the understanding of disability discrimination within the wider ideology of ableism places the understanding of Disability Hate Crime within an equivalent frame of understanding of racist hate crime within racism, homophobic hate crime with homophobia, transphobic hate crime within transphobia. It better positions Disability Hate Crime to take up its place in the hate crime domain. Barbara Perry identifies common theoretical threads in accounting for hate crime including how dominant ideologies contribute to the dehumanization, demonization, stigmatization of identity-based groups and how in this context of ideological inferiorization it then becomes 'very easy to justify their victimization' through hate crime. Without the framework of understanding provided by ableism as a fuelling prejudicial ideology the vital link in understanding individual hate crimes is too easily lost, the hate crime can be lost and justice denied. It is for these reasons that this book is located within and draws upon the concept of ableism.

The legal framework and domain in England and Wales

I describe here the legal framework on which this study is based, and which continues to govern the area of Disability Hate Crime. The named provisions have recently been combined into a single Sentencing Act 2020, without any amendment or review. There has been no substantive change to the wording of these provisions, other than their titles.

In its reviews of hate crime legal provisions in England and Wales, the Law Commission (2014 and 2020) provides an overview of the law on hate crime. They identify three main sets of legal provisions.

Aggravated offences involving racial or religious hostility

These are separate racially or religiously aggravated variants of what are existing base criminal offences. The base offences for which there are aggravated variants are: malicious wounding/grievous bodily harm; actual bodily harm; common assault; criminal damage; fear or provocation of violence; intentional harassment, alarm or distress; harassment, alarm or distress; harassment; stalking; putting people in fear of violence or serious alarm or distress.

An offence can be racially or religiously aggravated on the basis of either demonstration of hostility or based on a hostility motivation. The Law Commission says these offences were included because they were the most likely offences to involve racial hostility. These aggravated offences were introduced initially in terms of racial hostility in the Crime and Disorder Act 1998. Religiously aggravated offences were added to the Crime and Disorder Act through the Anti-Terrorism, Crime and Security Act, 2001. There are no aggravated offences in respect of disability hostility.

Enhanced sentencing provision in certain areas of hate crime

In the Criminal Justice Act 2003, one Section (Section 12) deals with the sentencing regime in England and Wales. Section 12 includes two sections – Section 145 and Section 146 – dealing with enhanced sentencing in respect of crimes aggravated by hostility or what is popularly termed 'hate crimes'. Section 145 deals with racial and religious hostility for any offences not covered by the list of aggravated offences mentioned. It requires a sentencing court to take racial and religious hostility into account at the sentencing stage. Section 146 deals with hostility based on the grounds of gender identity, sexual orientation or disability. It requires the sentencing court to take into account hostility based on gender identity, sexual orientation or disability at the sentencing stage. The sentence passed and the reasons for the sentence, including any enhanced sentence, must be stated in open court. In terms of this research study, it was first with an analysis of the emergence of this Section 146 provision of the Criminal Justice Act 2003 and, second, with the development of policy and practice in this area of what has become termed Disability Hate Crime that the research for this book was concerned. Section 146 has become Section 66 of the Sentencing Act 2020, but there has been no substantive change to the wording of the previous Section 146. I continue to refer to it as Section 146 through the book, to reflect the legislative position of the time.

The stirring up offences

The stirring up offences are also referred to as *Incitement to Hatred provisions*. They constitute a quite separate set of offences from the aggravated offences and from the sentencing enhancement provisions. Incitement to Hatred offences were first introduced in England and Wales in the Public Order Act (1986) in respect of racial hatred. Offences in respect of incitement to religious hatred and sexual orientation were added in 2007 and 2010 respectively. The Incitement to Hatred provisions are not the same across the protected characteristics. The provisions are 'stronger' in relation to racial hatred than in relation to religious hatred or sexual orientation hatred. They exist to address behaviour intended to or likely to cause others to hate entire protected groups (Law Commission, 2014).

While these constitute the main elements in the hate crime legal provisions in England and Wales, there are others, including provisions to address 'racialist' chanting at football matches and murder tariffs in hate-related murders (Hall, 2013). It is within this legal architecture outlined and policy domain that this book's themes are explored and developed.

This summary provides the legal architecture for the hate crime domain in England and Wales today. It is an uneven set of legal provisions constructed over time in response to events, activism, politics and policy making. What is striking is that there is no reference to the term 'hate crime' within the legal provisions. It is equally striking that this patchwork of legal provisions has given rise to the construction of a very active criminal justice policy domain entitled hate crime, such that it is accepted by activists, politicians, policy officials and practitioners as a legitimate arena for engaging in policy and practice developments (Iganski, 2010). As this book is being written the Law Commission is undertaking a comprehensive review of these existing hate crime legal provisions in England and Wales with a view to making recommendations to government to amend some of the current legal provisions, extend some of the legal provisions to other equality grounds such as gender, and to help remedy some specific challenges in addressing Disability Hate Crime. These specific issues are considered further in Chapters 6 and 9 of this book.

Overall aims of the book

The aim of this book is to provide the reader with an analysis of how and why Disability Hate Crime emerged and developed as part of the criminal justice system hate crime domain in England and Wales over the past 20 years. In addressing this aim the book analyses:

- the contributions of activism, politics and policy making to the Disability Hate Crime agenda;
- the challenges posed by a focus on vulnerability in Disability Hate Crimes;
- the challenges posed by the non-recognition of ableism as a fuelling prejudicial ideology driving Disability Hate Crimes;
- building on this analysis the book then outlines policy relevant recommendations that can better embed Disability Hate Crime within the hate crime domain.

Chapter overviews
Chapter 2: Fifteen Cases of Disability Hate Crime

This chapter builds on the introduction to aid understanding the book's themes and makes the phenomenon of Disability Hate Crime real through profiling 15 cases. These are drawn from unique access to CPS case files, together with cases from the voluntary and independent statutory sectors. Cases are set out in terms of context, what happened, response and outcome. Cases range from disability harassment, through targeted abuse and enslavement to murder. They provide vivid if shocking accounts of the nature and range of Disability Hate Crimes. The response to the cases by criminal justice agencies provide insights into the construction and indeed rejection of Disability Hate Crime by police, prosecutors and judges indicating how their decisions can fail to deliver full justice for disabled people. The case analyses illuminate the challenges of an undue focus on vulnerability in Disability Hate Crime together with the challenges of non-recognition of disability prejudice and the underpinning ideology of ableism, and how both impact the delivery of justice for disabled people. The cases outlined are drawn upon in the later chapters.

Chapter 3: From Hate Crime to Disability Hate Crime

This chapter considers the topic within hate studies and disability studies, together with the limited scholarship on Disability Hate Crime. It also locates the book in relation to policy studies. It highlights how race, religion and ethnicity once established as the anchoring provisions of hate crime law posed challenges for the inclusion of 'newer strands' such as Disability Hate Crime within the hate crime domain. It highlights the existence of two policy paradigms addressing disabled people, namely a welfare, care and protection paradigm and a rights and justice paradigm. It notes a policy-practice gap in criminal justice policy between a rights and justice espousal and a predominant practice focus on welfare, care and protection. It questions the implications of a continuing prevalence of a welfare, care and protection approach for the establishment of Disability Hate Crime in the hate crime policy domain. Through this contextualization this chapter identifies the topics explored in subsequent chapters.

Chapter 4: Agenda Triggering

This chapter analyses how and why Disability Hate Crime first emerged as and when it did in the early 2000s in England and Wales. The focus is on agenda triggering, a term coined here to refer to that early point in the policy process when an issue is first initiated rather than when the policy agenda and the domain becomes fully active. This chapter provides the first significant account of the history of policy making on Disability Hate Crime in England and Wales. It analyses the part played by activists, the then Disability Rights Commission, a government minister, and how together they seized a window of opportunity, the passage of the Criminal Justice Act 2003 to enact a legal provision addressing disability hostility or what has become popularly known as Disability Hate Crime. It illustrates how at different stages in this policy making process, different policy actors were ascendant. In the very early stages activists and politicians were ascendant and policy officials largely acted on political instruction. This ascendancy while central at this policy triggering stage was not to last as Disability Hate Crime moved on to become a policy agenda.

Chapter 5: Agenda Development

This chapter analyses the policy activity, activism and problematization processes that moved the Disability Hate Crime agenda from legal statute to a substantive policy agenda and active policy domain. It analyses how it shifted to become an issue driven by policy officials, spurred on by activist critique with politicians playing a lesser role. This chapter analyses the influence of the disability equality duty in spurring further development of the Disability Hate Crime agenda. It highlights the significance of the CJS in adopting a shared definition of monitored hate crime, which included Disability Hate Crime.

This chapter also analyses how policy-practice gaps together with individual case failures were highlighted by disability activists, which led to further action to embed Disability Hate Crime within the hate crime domain. Linked to this, the chapter analyses the significance of a Disability Hate Crime focusing event, the Pilkington case, a murder–suicide in Leicestershire in the development of the Disability Hate Crime agenda. Finally, the chapter analyses the impact of campaigning research and other reports from the NGO sector in contributing to the development of the Disability Hate Crime agenda.

Chapter 6: Towards Agenda Institutionalization?

This chapter analyses the extent to which Disability Hate Crime has become institutionalized within the CJS in terms of policy and practice. The focus is on analysing the extent to which Disability Hate Crime is routinized with shared definitions, shared discourse, shared ways of recording and shared ways of responding across the CJS. Analysis points to limited institutionalization having taken place. The chapter analyses how the differences in manifestations of disability hostility have raised the dilemma of disability difference and how that is viewed as a challenge to institutionalizing the agenda.

The chapter also analyses the findings of the EHRC formal statutory inquiry into disability related harassment and concludes that this formal inquiry acted as a challenge to existing CJS responses to Disability Hate Crime and as a call to institutional action. The final part of this chapter analyses the limited engagement of the judiciary with the Disability Hate Crime agenda. It highlights the judiciary's intensified desire to focus on disability vulnerability alongside very limited engagement with disability hostility. It notes the important role played by the judiciary elsewhere in enlivening hate crime laws and as meaning makers on hate crime. This stands in contrast to the limited engagement by the judiciary in England and Wales and concludes that such engagement is integral to institutionalizing Disability Hate Crime.

Chapter 7: The Problem with the Current Agenda: Focus on Vulnerability

This chapter analyses the challenge posed by vulnerability targeting in Disability Hate Crime. This vulnerability focus is central to the unsettled and unsettling agenda that is Disability Hate Crime today. Challenges to progress lie not in the nature of disability hostility but in the limitations of the current legal and policy framework. This chapter analyses some of the cases profiled in Chapter 2 and concludes that an undue focus on vulnerability in Disability Hate Crime occludes a recognition of and due focus on disability hostility. Vulnerability has become the master stereotype of disability in public policy and as a consequence vulnerability floods the disability experience. This focus on vulnerability has led to serious justice failures for disabled victims of hate crime. Analysis concludes that a way forward is not to hermetically seal off vulnerability targeting from hostility targeting in disability targeted crimes. A way forward is to regard vulnerability targeting as potentially a bias indicator for Disability Hate Crime and to interrogate vulnerability targeting whenever it arises for a possible hostility dimension. Vulnerability targeting and hostility targeting should not be viewed as opposite sides of the same coin, rather as the same side of the hate crime coin. Vulnerability targeting may simply be a variant of hostility targeting.

This chapter's analysis has implications for how the legal system considers hostility in targeted crimes. It notes how in England and Wales the law focuses on hostility motivation or hostility demonstration. This captures some but not all targeted crimes. It does not capture crimes committed against a disabled person 'by reason of' their disability, that is a discriminatory selection that can include perceived disability vulnerability.

Chapter 8: An Agenda Item Yet to Fully Speak Its Name: Ableism and Disability Hate Crime

This chapter analyses non-recognition of disability prejudice and ableism and analyses how these non-recognitions affect the development of Disability Hate Crime policy and practice. It explores whether the competing paradigmatic accounts of disabled peoples' experiences in terms of welfare or rights again occlude recognition of wider disability prejudice and ableism. This chapter analyses a number of the Disability Hate Crime cases profiled in Chapter 2 that involved disability prejudice and found a non-recognition of prejudice in these cases, which led to significant failures to deliver justice in Disability Hate Crime cases. This chapter charts and analyses disabled people's experiences in England and Wales within a profile of group disadvantage and discrimination and its recognized link to institutional discrimination while simultaneously noting the non-recognition of ableism. This is analysed and the under development of a theory of disability discrimination (beyond the social model) is noted and stands in contrast to developed theoretical accounts of racism, heterosexism, antisemitism and islamophobia. This lack of focus on wider disability prejudice and ableist ideology matters in the delivery of justice in cases. The chapter concludes noting the developing scholarship on ableism and how its development can in time aid the delivery of justice in Disability Hate Crime cases.

Chapter 9: Conclusion

This chapter concludes the books consideration of Disability Hate Crimes emergence and development – and concludes that Disability Hate Crime is an unsettled and unsettling agenda within the hate crime domain. This chapter reminds the reader of the features of a settled policy agenda, namely a policy domain with shared definitions, shared ways of responding, shared discourse on the problem, a diminution in the need for strategic action over time, an embedded taken-for-granted approach and a predicted area of practice that has become routine business for the CJS. Against these features this book has found that policy and practice on Disability Hate Crime displays an unsettled approach with limited policy institutionalization. This chapter also concludes that Disability Hate Crime is an unsettling agenda. It disrupts prevalent constructions of 'the problem' of disability as a welfare issue and seeks to replace these with a construction based on justice and rights. It questions understandings of disability prejudice and ableism and unsettles understandings of hostility in hate crime. It questions the uncritical use of the vulnerability categorization in crimes experienced by disabled people. It pushes at the boundaries of possibility in the hate crime domain. While it disrupts prevalent constructions it is yet to replace them. Thus, it is an unsettling policy agenda. The unsettled stage of this policy agenda's journey to institutionalization is linked to its unsettling features.

The book concludes that there is a need to move beyond the dual problematization of disability targeting in crime as an issue either of vulnerability targeting or of hostility targeting. Vulnerability targeting and hostility targeting must always be interrogated together in Disability Hate Crime cases in order to settle the agenda.

2

Fifteen Cases of Disability Hate Crime

Key points

This chapter sets out and analyses a range of Disability Hate Crime cases. It makes the phenomenon real through an analysis of the empirical data in actual cases. This chapter interrogates how the recognition of Disability Hate Crime and application of penalty uplift affects the outcomes of criminal justice proceedings. Fifteen cases of Disability Hate Crime are reviewed to interrogate the impact of the Disability Hate Crime framework, the recognition (or non-recognition) of disability hostility and the way in which this affected case outcomes. The chapter examines what types of cases attract uplift, the impact of penalty uplift at court on sentences and the implications of the different understandings of the Disability Hate Crime approach drawn upon in policing, prosecution and judicial sentencing.

Introduction

This chapter illustrates the application of the Disability Hate Crime approach in prosecutions. Here 15 cases of Disability Hate Crime are reviewed to interrogate the impact of the Disability Hate Crime legal framework, the recognition of disability hostility and the way in which this affects case outcomes. The cases are introduced with the facts drawn from case files and revisited in later chapters where the implications are drawn out in the analysis.

The success of cases being prosecuted as Disability Hate Crimes, and the sentencing enhancements given (if any), is a unique way to interrogate the key concepts involved in this study. For the research, case files were reviewed in depth to explore how the police, the CPS and judiciary understood and used the Disability Hate Crime lens to deal with cases of violence and harassment against disabled people. I set out to look at a range of cases that feature in Disability Hate Crime with variety in the base offence (for example, harassment, assault, sexual offences, murder and so on) and spread across the range of offences. The variety of cases presented here are selected to provide a rich understanding of the range of possibilities in the prosecution of Disability Hate Crime. I present them here, grouped by outcome, to highlight some of the commonalities and differences with how they proceeded through the criminal justice system.

The cases were accessed via the CPS case management system. Upon request, the CPS provided a table of all 548 cases flagged to Disability Hate Crime in 2013–14. An initial review of 405 of those cases produced only three where disability hostility was taken into account by the court at sentencing stage, reflected in the penalty handed down and recorded on the Hearing Record Sheet. On consideration of all 548 cases, six such cases were identified. A further six cases were identified in which the application of the Disability Hate Crime framework could not be considered successful. A further three cases were accessed via NGOs, public reports and inquests from the independent statutory sector.

The victims and perpetrators have both been anonymized, as have the locations in which they occurred. There are two exceptions to this; the Pilkington case, which is easily recognized in its facts due to extensive media coverage, and the murder of Brent Martin. The facts of each case are drawn from original case files to which I was given access. While I had additional access to the files of each case, only facts already in the public domain are reproduced here. The case of the murder of Brent Martin discussed may be recognizable to some readers because of the response by disability organizations at the time to its occurrence and the criminal justice response. Facts here on this case are drawn from case files and from a book by Quarmby (2011).

The 15 cases include those officially recorded as crimes and those that were 'no-crimed'. Police forces record some cases initially as crimes that are subsequently judged by police not to meet the threshold of a criminal offence. The recording of these incidents is described as being 'no-crimed'. The Home Office Counting Rules (HOCR) set out circumstances under which a crime report may be 'no crimed'. These include situations where a crime is considered to have been recorded in error or where, having been recorded, additional verifiable information becomes available that determines that no crime was committed. 'No crimes' relate to crimes already recorded and are therefore distinct from 'incident' reports that are not recorded as crimes in the first place.

Cases with successful sentence uplift

In the following five cases, Disability Hate Crime was successfully prosecuted with reference to Disability Hate Crime by the CPS and, in court, recognized by the judiciary. Enhanced sentencing was given and recorded:

- ongoing neighbour harassment of disabled man on social housing estate by a mother and son, with abusive language;
- ongoing harassment of two learning-disabled men in supported housing scheme by local youth;
- abusive behaviour towards learning-disabled man by neighbour, with abusive language;
- common assault of disabled wheelchair user, with abusive language;
- harassment and abuse of disabled man in his flat and on street by able-bodied associate, with abusive language;
- common assault of disabled man in a homeless hostel, with abusive language.

In all of these cases, the facts include targeted abuse of disabled persons, at their homes or in the street. Some perpetrators were known to the victim, others were not. Not all of these cases had witnesses but all included abusive language together with the base criminal offence.

The Downtown case

Andrew Bates moved to live in a social housing estate in a large town, which I call Downtown, in 2012. Soon after arriving, he began to experience problems with a neighbour, Barbara Crawley, and her nine-year-old son, Len.

As a child, Andrew had been involved in a car accident, which left him with an impaired walk. Barbara and Len mimicked Andrew's walk when they met him. Barbara lived opposite Andrew and allowed her son out into the road to cause nuisance. She encouraged him by laughing at his behaviour towards Andrew. Len would verbally abuse Andrew, calling him "fucking retard" and "spasy cunt", and saying "ha, you can't fucking walk". False calls of emergency services and pizza deliveries to Andrew's home also began at that time, believed to be linked to this harassment by the Crawleys.

One evening Andrew went onto his doorstep to smoke. Standing at her door, Barbara smirked and feigned a 'wobbly legs' walk. Andrew, fed up with the abuse, shouted across the road at Barbara, asking why she did not leave the estate because everybody was "sick of her behaviour". Other neighbours came out and also shouted at Barbara. Before she went indoors, she shouted at Andrew, "You need to fucking learn to walk, you do."

A few weeks later, Barbara confronted Andrew, threatening, "Watch what happens to you if I get evicted … I'll be back and I'm going to blow up your car." She added, "You can't even fucking walk." Andrew contacted the police to report the threat and three witnesses came forward. Barbara denied the targeted hostility. She alleged she was the victim because the neighbours had ganged up on her.

This case was flagged by the police and the CPS as involving 'a vulnerable victim' and as a Disability Hate Crime. The accused, Barbara, was charged with harassment without violence. At sentencing, the judge accepted the disability hostility aggravation and sentenced her to 5 months' imprisonment, suspended for 12 months. This included a sentence uplift from three months to five months for disability hostility aggravation.

The supported housing case

Martin Taylor and Richard Franks lived in supported housing in a rural town with access to 24-hour telephone support. Martin has learning and physical impairments. Richard has a learning disability and a mental health disability. After moving into the bungalow, Martin and Richard were approached by four young men, Wallet, Wilkins, Menton and Warnock. When Martin and Richard refused them entry, the harassment started. Initially the police view was that Martin and Richard were over-reacting 'due to their vulnerability'. Police advised them to stay indoors and not to confront those responsible.

Over a six-month period, Martin and Richard reported harassment, criminal damage, alarm and distress on 16 occasions. These included: windows being smashed, damage to their electricity box, attempted break-in, stones thrown at their windows, verbal abuse and harassment in the street based on disability, individuals seeking to render the CCTV camera inoperable, individuals approaching the bungalow door wearing face masks, banging on the door and throwing food at the door.

From the outset, the case was identified by the CPS as involving both 'vulnerable victims' and Disability Hate Crime. The victims' perceived vulnerability informed the advice given not to engage with the defendants. When the police finally interviewed Wallet, Wilkins, Menton and Warnock, the accused admitted the incidents. They also admitted their behaviour would cause harassment, alarm and distress.

Because there were no witness statements, impact statements were presented in court, strengthened by housing staff statements and CCTV evidence. At sentencing, the prosecutor brought Section 146 of the Criminal Justice Act 2003 to the judge's attention. The judge accepted that disability hostility aggravation applied to all the defendants. Sentences varied slightly among the defendants. The most severe comprised a youth referral order for 12 months, which included a 6-month uplift due to disability hostility.

The Valetown case

Will Hawkins is a young man who has cerebral palsy and lives with his parents in a Welsh town. At the time, he attended college and travelled there each day from home. Will had been subject to harassment involving hostile name-calling on numerous occasions in the past from a neighbour, Howell

Ewing. This hostile name-calling and harassment made Will nervous and wary of going out, and it affected his self-esteem.

One afternoon Will was dropped home by his friend's mother, Diana. As they approached Will's home, they saw his neighbour, Howell Ewing, outside his house. Ewing was staring at the car. Diana noticed that Will appeared scared getting out of her car. When Will left the car, he heard Ewing mimicking his speech and as he walked to his home, Ewing shouted "mong". Will did not reply, but once indoors, he began crying and told his parents about the incident. Having tolerated the targeted abuse of their son for years, Will's parents decided to report the incident to the police.

The police and the CPS identified this as a Disability Hate Crime from the outset. The police interviewed Will, his parents and his friend's mother, Diana. They secured an impact statement from Will and his parents. It conveyed how, following this and earlier abuse, Will was wary of leaving the house in case this neighbour was outside. On occasions, he was very upset, including following the recent verbal attack, when he was shaking and refused to go to college, unless his parents could collect him. The statement conveyed his fear of repercussions from this man and the negative impact on his identity as a disabled person. His parents' positive attitude towards Will's impairment had previously helped Will, but now his confidence was eroded, saying he was not good enough, that he must be "one of them (a 'mong')" because that was what his neighbour called him.

During a police interview, the defendant denied calling Will a "mong". He stated he did not see Will that afternoon. He acknowledged there had been previous disputes with these neighbours, and he did not engage with them. He said he did not know Will had cerebral palsy. He just thought "there was something wrong with him".

In court the defendant pleaded not guilty to the charge of use of threatening, abusive, insulting words/behaviour to cause harassment, alarm/distress. He was found guilty after trial. The prosecutor raised the issue of disability hostility at sentencing stage. The sentence comprised a fine of £1,250 and a four-year restraining order not to approach Will Hawkins. The sentence included a penalty enhancement for disability hostility.

The spitting cyclist case

Lenny Judd is a disabled man who lives in a northern English city and uses a motorized wheelchair. His friend, Mike White, is also a disabled man who uses crutches to walk. They knew each other through attending the same day centre. They sometimes met in the street and chatted on days when they were not going to the day centre together.

Mike was on his way to the day centre when he stopped for a chat with Lenny. A young man was cycling towards them. When he was a few feet away, he stopped and made a noise in his throat. He then spat into Lenny's face, the spit landing on Lenny's left cheek. The young man shouted at Lenny, "You're a fucking mong", and cycled off.

Both men were shaken up and outraged that someone would deliberately spit and abuse someone in a wheelchair who was unable to defend himself, and whose friend was also, in this situation, unable to defend his friend. Both viewed this as a targeted act. The men reported this incident to the police, and it was flagged as involving 'a vulnerable victim'. The CPS also flagged the case as a Disability Hate Crime.

The defendant, Brian Flint, denied the charge of common assault. He stated that, as he was cycling past the two disabled men, he sneezed because the sun was in his eyes, and this was why his spit landed on Lenny. He mounted a defence on that basis.

The defendant was found guilty after trial. The judge accepted the relevance of disability hostility and passed a sentence of eight weeks and a two-year restraining order preventing contact with the victim. The judge stated that if this had not been aggravated by demonstration of disability hostility, the sentence would have been a community penalty.

The visiting mates case

Mike Butler has cerebral palsy, causing an impaired walk. Mike also has learning difficulties. At the time of this case, he lived in a flat in a large southern town and was close to his mother, Dawn, who lived nearby. Sometimes, friends, 'mates' and associates came to visit at Mike's flat. Mike felt more comfortable with some of these friends and less comfortable with others who visited his flat.

One evening, Mike was at home with a friend, Roger. Linda Tynan knocked on the door. Mike did not want her to come in. Two weeks earlier, she had been abusive to Mike and his mother, Dawn, in Mike's flat and was arrested on suspicion of assaulting Dawn. Mike's friend, Roger, told her to go away. She did but returned later when Mike was on his own. She kicked the door. Mike was afraid of her. Tynan and her boyfriend, Rick Drury, began banging on the door.

Mike phoned another friend, Des, and told him what was happening. Des was concerned for Mike's wellbeing. He knew that Linda verbally abused Mike and called him "spacka", "peg leg" and "fucking spacka" in the street or when she did not gain entry to his flat. Des and his father-in-law, Brian, came to Mike's flat. Mike was pleased they came as he was scared. At this stage, Linda Tynan and her boyfriend had left. Des, Brian and Mike agreed to go to Tynan and Drury's flat together and request that they stop coming to Mike's flat, harassing him and calling him abusive names. Upon arrival, Tynan appeared at her window, shouting "You fucking spacka, you fucking little peg leg. I'll beat you up like I done your mother the other week."

As this happened, her landlord, David Deasy, was driving past and witnessed what occurred. He reported that Linda was hanging out her window, shouting at three men. He informed Linda that he was recording her behaviour including shouting "fucking spacker head" towards Mike Butler. Deasy contacted the police and gave them the recording. A day later, Linda Tynan was arrested on suspicion of harassment with the intention to cause fear of violence.

While en route to the police station, Tynan commented, "Who the fuck am I supposed to have harassed? It better not be some spacka cunt." When this was read to the defendant during questioning, she admitted saying it. When asked what she meant by "spacka", she gave the victim's name. She said she was a nice person and would never call him "spacka" to his face as she would not want to hurt his feelings. However, there were witnesses to her regularly calling Mike "spacka". Mike said he did not know what "spacka" meant but he knew Linda called him these names deliberately because he had a "bad leg and a bad arm".

During interview, Linda Tynan stated that anyone who would call a disabled person those names would be nasty and admitted the language was offensive. The landlord's recording, the two witness statements and the text of her verbal abuse was put to her. She still denied she made abusive comments to Mike. She did say, however, she had drunk wine on that day.

This case was identified by the police and the CPS as involving 'a vulnerable victim' and a Disability Hate Crime. At the sentencing hearing, the judge accepted the relevance of disability hostility, and it was taken into account. Tynan was found guilty of harassment without violence and sentenced to 15 weeks' imprisonment, including three weeks uplift arising from Section 146 aggravation. A quarter of her sentence was suspended for 12 months.

The homeless hostel case

Eddie Thorne had a stroke in 2011 and has impaired mobility. He now has severe epilepsy, is partially sighted and walks with a crutch. At the time of the case, Eddie lived in Home House, a hostel in a city in the east of England. He moved there six weeks before the attack.

From his first day in Home House, Eddie was harassed by another resident, David Torsey. One morning, David Torsey verbally and physically abused Eddie in a corridor at Home House and demanded a lighter. Eddie refused, as Torsey was abusive towards him previously. Torsey called Eddie a "spastic", an "invalid" and a "fucking bastard". He raised his fists towards Eddie. Eddie raised his crutch to ward off the defendant, but he grabbed it from Eddie's hand and used it to hit Eddie repeatedly. Without the crutch, Eddie fell over. As he beat Eddie, the defendant threw the crutch to the floor, calling Eddie a "spastic" and shouting, "I don't care if you're disabled" and walking away. Staff helped the victim and called the police.

The police and the CPS identified this as a case involving a vulnerable victim. The CPS also identified this as a Disability Hate Crime. The charge was actual bodily harm.

The judge found the defendant guilty of common assault. The judge imposed a barring order on the defendant for 18 months, placed him on probation and placed a restraining order on him not to contact the victim. The issue of disability aggravation was reflected in the sentence imposed. The specific uplift element was not explicit in the sentence details available.

Disability Hate Crime rejected by the court

In two of the cases identified as unsuccessful, Disability Hate Crime was recognized by the CPS but rejected by the court in favour of other approaches.

- attack on a learning-disabled man in a skate part in Middletown involving abusive language;
- Sunset View care home – targeted ill-treatment of learning-disabled residents revealed by undercover reporter.

In the first case, the judge rejected the Disability Hate Crime approach in favour of viewing the case as 'an attack on a vulnerable victim'. In the second, the Disability Hate Crime approach was rejected by the judge in favour of Mental Health Act offences.

The skate park case

Fred Soames was a 29-year-old learning-disabled man living in a Midlands city. He had physical and learning impairments. Fred lived with his mother and frequently went for a walk in the local skate park, sometimes alone and sometimes with his mother.

On one evening walk alone in the park, a group of young people began verbally abusing him and swearing. Fred remonstrated with them and became upset. A short time later, three young men came into the skate park in a van. Eddie Jenkins, the accused, approached Fred with a second man. Eddie proceeded to assault Fred by punching and kicking him, causing bumps, cuts and bruising over his body. Fred got away and, although injured, was able to get home.

Fred told his mother who contacted the police. Fred was able to identify his attackers because one of them had assaulted him previously. He was able to identify the second man through a social media account. The police and the CPS identified this as a case involving a vulnerable victim. The CPS also identified this as a Disability Hate Crime.

The main defendant, Eddie Jenkins, admitted travelling with others to the park and that one of these males assaulted Fred but refused to name the others. He admitted punching the victim twice about the head and shoulder. Jenkins appeared in court on a charge of common assault. The other defendant received a police caution. The judge found Jenkins guilty of assault and sentenced him to eight weeks' custodial detention in a young offenders' institution, and he was not to contact Fred Soames for two years.

The judge did not accept the disability hostility aggravation raised at sentencing. He stated this was not a Disability Hate Crime and that he knew what type of individual the defendant was. He said the defendant knew the victim was a vulnerable person (that is, a disabled person) and there was a previous incident where this defendant targeted a vulnerable victim (that is, another disabled person). He indicated that this was an attack on a vulnerable person and 'not your argument' of hostility. No penalty uplift was applied.

The Sunset View care home case

Sunset View was a care home providing residential care for learning-disabled adults in the South West. It was owned by Towerhouse Ltd, and the Care Quality Commission had expressed concern about the low training threshold in another of their homes, an issue that also featured in Sunset View. The people living in Sunset View had been placed there through families and Adult Social Care in neighbouring local authorities, and they required continuous support.

In late 2010, a former nurse at Sunset View, contacted a TV station as a whistleblower and raised concerns about the care provided. Nothing had been done about concerns he raised internally. The TV station decided to undertake an investigative programme. Over two months, an undercover reporter who secured a job there as a care worker, used a hidden camera to record what took place in terms of care practices.

The undercover reporter/care worker recorded a range of ill-treatment and abuse of the learning-disabled residents by 11 care workers. The behaviour included assault, bullying, potential asphyxiation, physical ill-treatment, unnecessary restraint and verbal abuse including goading a resident into jumping out a window, as their "life was useless anyway". The police obtained the programme footage ahead of the broadcast and placed the staff on bail; they were questioned again once the programme material was further analysed.

Both the police and the CPS identified this as a case involving vulnerable victims. The CPS also identified this as a case of Disability Hate Crime. However, the focus was placed on prosecutions under the Mental Health

Act. Such prosecutions were considered appropriate given that the TV material showed physical ill-treatment that could amount to ill-treatment under the Mental Health Act.

Video footage constituted the primary evidence and was put to the defendants in police interviews. Defendants accepted the video footage as largely accurate. However, they questioned the interpretation of their actions as offences of ill-treatment.

Section 127 of the Mental Health Act created offences of ill-treatment or wilful neglect of patients. It includes deliberate and reckless conduct that amounts to ill-treatment. Once this set of offences were deemed appropriate, it guided the prosecutions. The various aspects of ill-treatment listed earlier featured in the defendants' interviews and then at court in early 2013, the defendants were found guilty of offences including ill-treatment of residents of Sunset View. The prosecuting counsel opened and closed the case by identifying this as a case motivated by disability hostility.

As a result, six staff were jailed, the longest sentence being for a period of two years; five staff were given suspended sentences. Convictions included ill-treatment, abuse and wilful neglect of disabled residents of Sunset View. The judge did not respond to the issue of disability hostility in sentencing and sentenced solely in relation to ill-treatment under the Mental Health legislation. However, in a media statement after the trial, the prosecuting lawyer and police lead officer referred to the case as a Disability Hate Crime.

Disability Hate Crime flagged but not raised in court

In two of the cases identified as unsuccessful, Disability Hate Crime was flagged in the course of investigation but not raised in the prosecution of the case:

- husband abused wife with vascular dementia; and
- church warden's targeted abuse of two disabled churchgoers.

In the first case, while Disability Hate Crime aspects were initially identified, the case had multiple identifications as domestic violence and involving a vulnerable victim. When the case came to court, disability hostility was not raised.

In the second, Disability Hate Crime aspects were also initially identified, but the focus was on victim vulnerability, and disability hostility was not raised in court.

The domestic violence case

June Smith was in her mid-70s and diagnosed with vascular dementia. She lived with her husband, John, in London, who, together with social services, provided her daily care. They had four adult children (Trevor, Ivor, Linda and Roger). Trevor lived at home but was out at work each day. When they were growing up their father was abusive towards their mother and sexually demanding of her. They recalled her standing up to him when she was younger and in good health.

As June's condition deteriorated, Trevor and Ivor were concerned about their father's treatment of her. They were not happy with their father's explanations of bruising on June. They were also concerned about their father's verbal abuse of their mother. Trevor and Ivor installed a wall clock CCTV security camera in the living room facing the sofa that June sat on. This was done without their father's knowledge. One month later, their concerns were confirmed. The recording showed verbal and physical abuse of June by her husband. The sons confronted John that his abuse had to stop or they would go to the police. They did not say they were recording his actions. John did not deny abuse but stated that he was frustrated. They arranged daily help from social services. However, the CCTV recordings showed that the abuse continued for another four months, at which time the sons reported their father's behaviour to the police.

The recording showed John's using abusive language, calling June a moron, a cunt, mimicking her diminishing use of speech, slapping her on the face and shoulder, pushing her into chairs, prodding her with a walking stick, threatening to deprive her of food and cigarettes if she would not partake in sexual acts, forcing her to partake in sexual acts despite a possibly reduced capacity to consent, throwing clothes at her, stomping a walking stick in front of June while verbally abusing her. The recordings showed a change in John's tone when Trevor was at home, with his father becoming quieter and calmer. When confronted again by his sons, John did not deny mental, verbal, physical and sexual abuse of his wife. Yet, he gave police a 'no comment' interview.

This case was identified by the police and the CPS as a case involving 'a vulnerable victim' and as a case of Disability Hate Crime. It was additionally identified by the CPS as potentially a case of domestic violence and a crime against an older person. The CPS and the police jointly came to the view that June would not be able to give evidence, given her deteriorating health condition. It was decided the CCTV recording and the sons' evidence would constitute the primary evidence.

The prosecutor regarded the case as involving a particularly aggravating set of offences: (a) domestic violence of an older woman by her husband, which was ongoing, despite her deteriorating state; (b) Disability Hate Crime based on review of the CCTV where husband John appeared to enjoy his power over her and abusing June's frailty. John pleaded guilty in court. John was sentenced to six weeks' custody (suspended for six months) and £165 in costs. There was no consideration of the disability hostility dimension at the sentencing stage.

The church warden case

Bridget Coulter has a hearing impairment and uses sign language to communicate. Denise Nichols has a learning disability, is a single parent and, at the time of the case, lived with her mother. Bridget and Denise regularly attended an Anglican Church in rural England for many years. The defendant, David Seery, had become involved with their church more recently as deputy warden.

Denise Nichols got to know David Seery through the church. One day David came to Denise's home and offered to move rubbish for her. While in her home, he made inappropriate comments to Denise. She asked him to leave, and he 'launched' himself towards her and began kissing her. She described how she felt violated and angered by his actions.

In the same month, the defendant offered to drive Bridget home from church one Sunday. On the way, Seery stopped his car and made inappropriate sexual remarks to her. He started to touch Bridget on the breasts and between the legs and persisted for some time. Bridget pushed him away, got out of the car and walked home. While in the car, he also asked Bridget for money. She gave him £10 and then another £20 when she met him later at evening service. Later that night, Bridget told her mother and was upset. Subsequently, the local vicar and the police were informed.

The police and the CPS identified this as a case involving two vulnerable victims. While video interviews indicated that the defendant's actions caused great distress to the victims and while both were assessed as vulnerable, they were considered capable of giving evidence with the support of special measures, including a video link for one and a sign language interpreter for the other.

The CPS identified this case as a Disability Hate Crime. The prosecutor identified how the defendant exploited his position as church warden to gain the victims' trust. This was considered a targeting/ grooming of these victims based on their disability akin to 'mate crime' cases (often involving exploitative fake friendships). The victims were regarded as providing credible evidence and the case was strengthened by having the two complaints. In addition, another witness indicated that the defendant could behave in sexually inappropriate ways. The issue of disability hostility aggravation was not raised at sentencing stage.

In court, the defendant pleaded guilty to the sexual offences in relation to both victims. Seery was given a 12-months suspended sentence, required to attend a sex offenders' programme, was placed on the sex offenders' register, given a restraining order and was placed on a tag for six months.

Disability Hate Crime not recognized at all

It is striking that two of the most serious crimes were not recognized at all as involving disability hostility. Two of the cases identified in this research as Disability Hate Crime were not flagged at any stage of the investigation or prosecution:

- enslavement of young disabled woman and exploitation over many years; and
- murder of a learning-disabled man with mental health difficulties.

In these cases, the identification of 'vulnerable victims' was key in the investigation of the crimes involved. No aspects of Disability Hate Crime were identified, despite both being targeted at selected disabled people. The murder case, although it occurred in 2007, is a notable example of the failure to recognize Disability Hate Crime and is included here for illustrative purposes.

The enslavement case

Fatima Saeed was born in Pakistan and brought to England aged nine by her neighbours, the Siddiqui family. She was given a false passport that indicated she was much older and sponsored by the Siddiqi family as a family help. She has a range of physical impairments and is deaf. Furthermore, Fatima had not been taught to read or write but had developed her own basic sign language.

Fatima lived with the Siddiqi family for 15 years. Living in the same house was the father, Khalid (aged 80), his wife, Leyla (aged 65), and their daughter, Mussarat (aged 45). Fatima was kept in a cellar accessible under the stairs and bolted from outside. In the cellar was a single bed, an ironing board and an iron. She lived there unnoticed by public authorities.

Trading Standards officers investigating counterfeit football shirts sold online searched the Siddiqi home. During this, Trading Standards officers noticed Fatima entering the cellar. They established that she was deaf and without speech. Through basic signing, Fatima was able to convey that she was 25, had been in the country a number of years and was unpaid domestic help. Police were informed but not concerned at this stage.

Further investigations uncovered an online sales account linked to a clothing business in Fatima's name. The officers returned to the address and arrested her. The bank account in Fatima's name was also in the joint name of Leyla Siddiqui. Fatima was used as part of an attempt to launder monies obtained fraudulently from customers online. Investigations revealed this family was involved in complex fraud.

In interviews, Fatima was able to indicate that she was taught her name by the family and made to write her name onto documents. Fatima was de-arrested and a specialist sign language interpreter was engaged. She was placed in safe accommodation while attempts were made to build a relationship of trust. She revealed how she was kept in the cellar and allowed out to cook, clean, wash cars or pack goods for sale online. Fatima indicated she had been regularly physically assaulted by members of the family. The interpreter and a specialist intermediary met with Fatima over a three-month period for 11 video interviews. Fatima revealed how, from an early age, she had been sexually assaulted including raped within this family.

The police and the CPS identified this as a case involving 'a vulnerable victim' with emphasis placed on Fatima's vulnerable status. This was understandable given the supports required to communicate with and enable Fatima to give best evidence. There was no identification of the case by the police or by the CPS as a Disability Hate Crime.

This case took significant time to bring to trial. There was an approach adopted involving close collaboration between police, the CPS and social services. The sentences imposed included: false imprisonment, placement on the sex offenders' register and community orders involving unpaid voluntary work. There was no consideration of disability hostility aggravation at sentencing stage.

The murder of Brent Martin

Brent Martin was a 23-year-old learning disabled man with mental health difficulties who moved to live in a Northumbria town in 2007. He had recently been discharged from hospital. Brent was subject to harassment from a young age linked to his impairments. He was, in his mother's words, 'a softie' and described as 'slow'. This harassment resulted in him moving to a special school out of mainstream education. Brent had a breakdown as a teenager, which his mother linked to a targeted assault. His health deteriorated and he was placed, aged 16, in compulsory detention in a mental hospital. After seven years, he was released in the summer of 2007. He was discharged with limited transition planning. It was agreed he would live with his sister upon discharge. However, he shortly moved to live with his mother.

Brent was given £3,000 approximately upon discharge, which was due to him from accumulated benefits. He was assessed as low risk for self-harm, self-neglect, exploitation and violence. These assessments were questioned when Brent was murdered within three months of release.

Evidence indicates that Brent was keen, if not desperate, to make friends, and he used his £3,000 to socialize with a group of young men. He struck up an acquaintance with Tim Carey, Vince James and Nick Niland (anonymized) in the few weeks before his death. He was bullied into giving his money away and, by the time he was murdered, he had virtually given it all away.

One evening, the defendants went looking for Brent to get money from him. When they met, Brent bought them a bottle of vodka and had £5 left. The defendants, all trainee boxers, decided to attack Brent and see who could knock him out. The person who knocked him out would get his last £5. Over the space of a few hours, they punched and kicked Brent into unconsciousness and attacked him while unconscious. The final assault involved punching to the head, body kicking and banging the victim's head against a parked car. Brent never regained consciousness and died three days later in hospital.

This case was not identified by the police or by the CPS as a Disability Hate Crime. The police investigating officer was reported as saying, "There is no motive for the assault but children often bully people with learning difficulties on the estate where Brent died."

The defendants were convicted of murder and obtained sentences ranging from 15 to 22 years. The judge commented on the sadistic nature of the murder and the "extreme vulnerability" of the victim. No mention was made of disability hostility, while a witness told the court that Carey, one of the defendants, said "I'm not going down for a muppet."

'No-crime' cases

In the final three cases presented here, Disability Hate Crime was not considered despite the victims being targeted as disabled people. The incidents were initially recorded as crimes, but later judged by police not to meet the standard of criminal offences. They were recorded as 'no crime':

- neighbours' dispute which evolved into targeted disability hostility;
- a case categorized as noise nuisance; and
- sustained harassment of family with disabled children culminates in murder–suicide, Pilkington–Hardwick case.

These cases resulted in no prosecutions. Advocacy and liaison were employed to address the first case, and the last was classified as a series of anti-social behaviour incidents.

The last of these cases, the Pilkington–Hardwick case, occurred in 2007, earlier than the other cases. It is of note because of the profile the case gained and is included here for illustrative purposes. It illustrates starkly the non-recognition of Disability Hate Crime. A report was published on it by the IPCC in 2009 and it continued to the be the subject of debates on Disability Hate Crime until 2013.

The neighbours' dispute case

Linda and John lived on a housing association estate in a Welsh city with their daughters, Ceri (aged 12) and Kathryn (aged nine). Both daughters had been diagnosed as autistic. Linda had a difficult relationship with her neighbour, Peggy, over the years. They frequently rowed with each other. Given recent developments, Linda had contacted a hate crime helpline advocacy service for support.

In recent years, Peggy had begun to target Linda's daughters and sought to draw them into what was a neighbours' dispute. She began to cause noise nuisance targeted at the children when they went to bed. She knew that if the children were kept awake at night, their autism would be aggravated in subsequent days. Peggy targeted the children through standing under their bedroom window, shouting verbal abuse including "spacka" and "mong".

Linda phoned the hate crime helpline and said she wanted "this behaviour to stop". The helpline ascertained that this case, originating as a neighbours' dispute had taken on a disability hostility dimension.

Linda was referred to the Helplines Advocacy Service, which seeks to provide support and mediation in appropriate cases. The Advocacy Service established that Linda was in contact with her housing association, her council and local police regarding the problem. The housing association supported Linda to gather evidence of the harassment of her children.

Linda was hesitant about pursuing mediation. The agencies were concerned that the dispute had gone on over time, and the resentments accumulated could militate against a mediated solution. Linda was adamant that she just wanted the behaviour to stop. The Advocacy Service believed that mediation was worth pursuing and, if it did not resolve the situation, then a firmer option could be considered.

Contact was made with Peggy to explore mediation. In the aftermath, the harassment of Linda's children stopped. When last contacted, Linda was not wholly satisfied but relieved that the harassment had stopped. The Advocacy Service felt this was for now 'a good outcome'. Linda did not get her day in court, but she secured an end to the harassment. She had built relationships with support agencies, should she need to use them in future.

This was a 'non-crimed' disability hate incident in that it did not enter the criminal justice system as a Disability Hate Crime for prosecution and a resolution was secured.

The noise nuisance case

Tom lived in a council apartment block and was experiencing noise nuisance from his neighbours. Tom experienced epilepsy and the noise from some music his neighbours played loudly triggered his epileptic attacks. He asked his neighbours, "If you really don't mind, if you're playing that music, can you play it really quietly because there is something about it that triggers my epilepsy." Instead, his neighbours turned up the volume when they played this music. He felt it was as if they had power over him now that they knew how this affected him. He reported it to police. The responding Police Community Support Officer (PCSO) dealt with the case as noise nuisance, and it was not dealt with as a crime. No disability aggravation was considered.

This case came to light during a training delivered to a Safer Neighbourhood Team, including police, council and NGO staff, by a London-based NGO for disabled people. The Hate Crime Awareness Training included Disability Hate Crime. An objective was to get participants to reflect on how to recognize and respond to Disability Hate Crime in their work. During the training, this PCSO reflected on the noise nuisance case, and upon reflection, he identified this as noise nuisance involving disability aggravation. He now viewed the case as one demonstrating hostility through deliberate targeting. Although this originated as noise nuisance, he saw how it morphed into a Disability Hate Crime where people exploited the situational vulnerability of their disabled neighbour.

The Pilkington–Hardwick case

Fiona Pilkington was a 38-year-old mother of two children, Francecca Hardwick, then aged 18, and her younger brother, when she died in October 2007. Fiona and her son had mild learning impairments while Francecca had profound learning impairments.

Fiona lived on a mixed tenure housing estate in Bardon Road, Barwell, Leicestershire, for many years, initially with her partner and children. Recently, her mother came to live with Fiona. Barwell and Earl Shilton are among the most deprived neighbourhoods in Leicestershire and contain a number of anti-social behaviour 'hot spots'. The police identified anti-social behaviour 'hot spots' close to but not including Bardon Road. It was thus not included in proactive policing responses (IPCC, 2011).

Fiona and her disabled children experienced anti-social behaviour and targeted disability harassment over a ten-year period approximately. As the principal contact for the family and local agencies, Fiona made clear her children were disabled and targeted on this basis. Yet, state agencies seldom met the children.

On over 30 occasions, Fiona reported incidents of ableist verbal abuse, her children being called "mong", "spastic", "freaks", "Frankenstein", "perv", "nutcase", "spazzo" and "lunatic". Both children were also subject to bullying and harassment at school. This often took place in the context of other targeted hostility including window breaking, damage to the family's car, damage to the family's garden and, on one occasion, taking the boy captive, locking him in a shed and holding him at knife point. He spoke of his fear that the local youths who did this were going to "kill him".

Fiona reported these incidents to the police and was frequently able to name the youths involved, as was her mother. Fiona's diary entries express her frustration with the lack of police and other official responses to the harassment. In a letter to her MP in 2004, she wrote, 'I really am getting to the stage where I am at a loss as to what to do about most things.' Three years later, with little official response to the family's experience, she wrote to her son: 'The street kids are still being intolerable ... the street kids, well, I have just given up ... I am just not cut out to take this much harassment' (IPCC, 2011).

The bodies of Fiona and her daughter, Franceccca, were found in a burnt-out car in a lay-by near Earl Shilton in October 2007. An inquest in September 2009 concluded that Fiona unlawfully killed her daughter and died by suicide herself. The inquest concluded that Fiona intended to cause her own death due to stress and anxiety regarding anti-social behaviour issues and her daughter's future. It also concluded that responses of the police and the council to the family's reporting of incidents contributed to the two deaths based on the failure to prioritize and to link the numerous incidents reported (IPCC, 2009).

Over the years of harassment, incidents were dealt with as isolated and in an unstructured approach. There was no serious attempt to link incidents and appraise the extent and nature of the targeted harassment that the family were experiencing. Arising from this, most incidents were closed soon after reporting and noted as 'anti-social behaviour'.

There was no identification by the police or other agencies of the incidents as hate incidents or crimes despite the police having a hate crime policy in place since 2004. The area did not incorporate national guidance on hate crime until late 2007.

The anti-social behaviour categorization became the frame for interpreting what happened. As the IPCC noted, police involved did not distinguish between general anti-social behaviour and targeted harassment of this disabled family. As a consequence, they failed to consider the family's treatment as Disability Hate Crime.

Latterly, this case led to a critical inquest into the deaths, which linked the lack of appropriate response by local agencies to the two deaths. It led to an IPCC inquiry into the police handling of the family's contact with the force over 11 years and it triggered the EHRC to proceed with an inquiry into disability related harassment.

Conclusion

In presenting the facts of these cases, an opportunity is taken to outline some of the common patterns determining the application of a Disability Hate Crime approach, the identification of disability hostility, and the prosecution and sentencing outcomes that follow.

Analysis of these cases highlighted not only the role of awareness among police, prosecutors and judiciary but the importance of manifest demonstrated hostility, visibility and 'fit' with an already embedded concept of hate crime in the criminal justice system which has developed from manifest racist hostility. All of those successfully applying the Disability Hate Crime approach involved the use of disability slurs on or around the time of the offences by the perpetrators. Successful cases involved strangers and neighbours, and sometimes fake friends ('mate' crimes), but not family or carers. Most tended to occur outdoors or in visible public places.

Cases that are considered 'unsuccessful' here, in that they did not apply fully or at all the Disability Hate Crime approach to prosecution, also have some identifiable patterns. These incidents were more likely to have occurred indoors, without witnesses. They often involved abuses of trust and occurred in an asymmetrical power relationship, including where the victim was reliant on the care of the abuser. Most often they did not involve manifest demonstration of the hostility at the time of the offence. However, they did often involve egregious violence, indeed some far worse than those recognized by the court as Disability Hate Crime.

In grouping the cases as I have done so, the patterns are seen more clearly, and we can proceed to examine the development of Disability Hate Crime as a policy domain in light of what these cases reveal about the assumptions employed by criminal justice professionals in investigation and prosecution. Different criminal justice officials shared different understandings of what constitutes Disability Hate Crime, in particular the judiciary. The judiciary are important meaning makers on hate crime. This is illustrated by the decisions made particularly in the cases where the CPS identified Disability Hate Crime, but the judges involved opted not to take that approach in the sentencing of the crime. For example, in the skate park case, the judge said it was not Disability Hate Crime because the victim was attacked due to their vulnerability, not hostility on the part of the defendant. In the case of Brent Martin's murder, the judge viewed it as a senseless attack on "a very vulnerable victim", not a particular hostility on the part of the defendant. To a very real extent, criminal justice officers, police, prosecutors and judges find what they go looking for in these cases. A dominant interpretive framework influences what they look for, what they find and what they conclude.

Hostility manifests in different and varied ways, and the framework that is applied by criminal justice professionals constrains the nature of what is seen, recognized and responded to in the investigation and prosecution. Interpretations of the Disability Hate Crime approach vary across and between practitioners, but even when applied fully, produces differentiations between what is recognized and what is not. For criminal justice practitioners, investigation outcomes are often determined by what is looked for, so while flagging a case early as Disability Hate Crime can help, what is found will also reflect the expertise and understanding of the criminal justice practitioners who apply it. Additionally, these cases show the importance of a shared understanding of disability hostility across the different criminal justice institutions. For example, as police and prosecutors became increasingly alert to a Disability Hate Crime lens, the judiciary continued to come to these cases overwhelmingly using a lens of vulnerability. Unless and until they share understanding of Disability Hate Crime, there will be a persistent problem in successfully prosecuting these cases.

3

From Hate Crime to Disability Hate Crime

Key points

This chapter traces the journey from hate crime to Disability Hate Crime through an analysis of the relevant literature including policy related documents that construct and reference Disability Hate Crime. It considers the origins and evolving conceptions of both hate crime and Disability Hate Crime, the construction of disability in public policy and the construction of disability within hate crime policy. It is only recently that disability hostility has begun to be recognized as Disability Hate Crime, and it is a contested, contentious and ambiguous concept. Nonetheless, it is now recognized as a 'social fact' with an active policy domain and set of policies and practices. A review of the key academic literature on Disability Hate Crime and its relationship to hate crime literature in general is set out, as well as a review of the significant literature produced by the independent statutory sector, the community sector and by individual authors. Here is set out the critical consideration of the journey from hate crime to Disability Hate Crime that follows, and that is concerned with how Disability Hate Crime policy and practice emerged and developed and equally on seeking to explain why it emerged as and when it did in England and Wales.

Introduction

This chapter traces the journey from hate crime to Disability Hate Crime through an analysis of the relevant literature including policy related documents that construct and reference Disability Hate Crime. It considers the origins and evolving conceptions of both hate crime and Disability Hate Crime. It considers the related issue of the construction of disability in public policy, including criminal justice policy, and, within this, considers the construction of disability within hate crime policy. Consequently, the chapter identifies lines of exploration that inform the book and that are kept under active review in subsequent chapters.

Wider context

While targeted harassment and violent discrimination towards minoritized groups has existed in almost all societies throughout history, the construction of such behaviour as hate crime is relatively recent (Iganski and Levin, 2015). Indeed, it might be argued that, strictly speaking, there is no legal category of hate crime in England and Wales. However, as indicated in Chapter 1, there are specific aggravated offences and sentencing uplift provisions that can be applied to cases involving targeted hostility; there are also Incitement to Hatred offences. This contrasts with the US where some federal and state statutes carry 'hate crime' in their title.

Notwithstanding this, there is an active policy domain on hate crime in England and Wales, developed initially in the early 2000s. Indeed, '"hate crime" has been wholeheartedly adopted by the criminal justice system in the United Kingdom' (Iganski, 2010, p 351). Hate crime is now an established policy domain, an identifiable field in which ongoing policy developments take place (Mason-Bish, 2009). Hate crime has been appropriated by identity politics movements and criminal justice agencies as a policy domain within which claims for recognition are framed and responded to. There are varied views as to what forms of targeted hostility might be included in hate crime in terms of its adaptability (Iganski, 1999; Chakraborti and Garland, 2012; Dimock and Al-Hakim, 2012). There are also varied views as to what is meant by hate crime. At one reading, hate crime is an ambiguous, contentious and contested concept. At another level, it has proven to be an evolving, dynamic concept that is the basis of an active policy domain. Significant knowledge, policy and practice developments are occurring in this context of ambiguity, adaptability and contestation.

The concepts of disability and disabled people have also been ambiguous and contested over time. Evidence points to a range of debates and factors influencing how disability is addressed in public policy, including criminal justice policy, with the definition of disability a significant consideration. Is it conceived of in terms of a medically defined impairment – the so-called Medical Model of disability? Is it defined as a social rights issue focused on tackling barriers to equality at various levels – aspects of which are termed the Social Model of Disability (Barnes and Mercer, 2003; Mercer and Barnes, 2010)? Or is it defined as some combination of functional impairments made more problematic by negative social attitudes and barriers (Shakespeare, 2017)? Evidence points to the historic dominance and legacy influence of the Medical and Welfare Model of disability, which has led to the construction of disabled people as vulnerable and in need of care and protection. This has given rise to a 'paternalist policy heritage', focused on welfare, care and protection (Braddock and Parish, 2001; Borsay, 2005; McDonnell, 2007; Roulstone and Prideaux, 2012) as opposed to an equality, rights and justice focus that the Rights-Social Model of Disability advocates and with which Disability Hate Crime resonates with its focus on justice and equality. Evidence from the research underpinning this book and elsewhere shows that the prevalence of the medical, care and protection approach has filtered into the criminal justice system and that its influence may have hindered the fuller development of an equality, justice and rights approach (EHRC, 2009; EHRC, 2011a; Mason-Bish, 2009). This is evidenced through the proliferation of criminal justice policies responding to vulnerable victims, alongside a single policy responding to Disability Hate Crime.

The experience of targeted hostility is one continuing thread in the experience of disabled people throughout history (Sobsey, 1994; Evans, 2004; Sherry, 2010; Quarmby, 2011). Accounts point to varied, complex experiences in disabled people's lives (Braddock and Parish, 2001; McDonnell, 2007) and chart hostile experiences from harassment to assaults, murder and mass killings (Sobsey, 1994; Evans, 2004; Sherry, 2010; Quarmby, 2011). Recent systematic reviews found that disabled people are at a higher risk of violence than are non-disabled people (Hughes et al, 2012; Jones et al, 2012; Emerson and Roulstone 2014). This is borne out by the World Health Organization (WHO), which identified disabled people as a group more at risk of violence than people without disabilities (WHO, 2011, p 59). In the British context, analysis of the Crime Survey data for England and Wales for 2015–18 estimates an average of 51,000 incidents of disability motivated crimes per year, significantly less than but second only to racist crime estimates at 101,000 per year (Home Office, 2018). Alongside this, there were just 579 Disability Hate Crimes recorded by the CPS in 2018–19. Indeed, there is a significant gap between disabled people's experience of targeted crime and what is reported and responded to as Disability Hate Crime. This is the gap between targeted victimization and the construction of targeted victimization as Disability Hate Crime or not.

Responses to the experience of disability hostility have varied over time from condoning, ignoring and facilitating such acts to expressions of concern and outrage. It is only recently that such hostility has begun to be recognized as potentially crime, and, much more recently, that it has begun to be recognized as Disability Hate Crime. As with hate crime, Disability Hate Crime is also a contested, contentious and ambiguous concept. Nonetheless, it is now recognized as a 'social fact' with an active policy domain and set of policies and practices that this study analysed.

Taken together, Disability Hate Crime and hate crime meet as already ambiguous concepts in the contested terrain of hate crime theorizing, policy and practice. Indeed, it is remarkable how much policy and practice on Disability Hate Crime has taken place and is advancing in these contexts of ambiguity and contestation.

Given the origins of the hate crime domain with its early focus on racist and religious crimes, its expansion to embrace Disability Hate Crime is at one level remarkable. Grattet and Jenness (2001b) analysed the development of hate crime provisions in terms of a 'core' and 'second tier' of protected statuses. They identified race, religion and national origin as 'core' protected statuses, and disability, gender and sexuality as 'second tier' protected statuses. They argue that civil rights advocacy 'solidified a trio of statuses – race, religion and ethnicity as the anchoring provision of all hate crime law' (Grattet and Jenness, 2001b, p 672). They argue that Disability Hate Crime, as a 'second tier' protected status, has been recognized more recently, with disability recognized as a 'legitimate axis' around which hate crime occurred (Grattet and Jenness, 2001b, p 671).

This book now turns to a critical consideration of the journey from hate crime to Disability Hate Crime, with a view to locating this study within existing hate crime studies and identifying the lines of inquiry that informed the research underpinning this study.

Conceiving and defining hate crime

A feature of the hate crime literature is the attention given to defining hate crime (Herek and Berill, 1992; Lawrence, 1999; Iganski, 2002; Levin and McDevitt, 2002; Perry, B., 2001, 2003, 2009a; Jenness and Broad, 2005; Hall, 2013). Hate crime has become a widely used term in western societies, including in academia, policy discourse and the media. However, it has a varied level of shared meaning and, according to Iganski (2010), ambiguity. It has been noted that, perhaps arising from this ambiguity, many academic texts start with a chapter exploring and defining the concept of hate crime (Iganski, 2010, p 353).

Origins of the phenomenon of hate crime

While many scholars recognize that hate crime is a recent social construct in response to the recognition of targeted violence based on identity and linked to the rise of identity politics (Jacobs and Potter, 1998; Jenness and Broad, 2005, 2007; Hall 2013), it is also recognized as a response to contemporary manifestations of a long history of targeted violence (Herek and Berill, 1992; Turpin-Petrosino, 2009). It reflects a recent problematization of long-standing violent discrimination. In a sense, it is the social construction or reconstruction of very old behaviour in a relatively new crime category (Quinney 1970; Best, 1999; Hall, 2013).

It is recognized in some scholarly literature that, in western societies, there is a continuum of discrimination for identity based social groups including disabled people (Young, 1990; Hollomotz, 2013). This continuum is seen to range from the 'softer' end of jokes, stigma, ridicule, through social exclusion, marginalization, discrimination in employment and service access and provision to harassment and violence. This range of prejudicial discriminatory behaviour is also described in academic literature as a 'Pyramid of Hate' (Levin, B., 2009, p 5). This pyramid builds upwards from a base of prejudicial attitudes, through acts of prejudice and discrimination to acts of violence and, ultimately, genocide (Levin, B., 2009). The explanatory power of Levin's framework, itself informed by Alport's earlier work on prejudice (Alport, 1954), is evidenced in a range of contexts including the Holocaust in the 20th century. It provides a framework for understanding the experience of disabled people during that period (Alport, 1954; Evans, 2004).

Significance of post-World War II rights settlement

Evidence indicates that, post-World War II and in recognition of the magnitude of the issues raised by the Holocaust, a new human rights and equal opportunities architecture was gradually developed (McLaughlin, 2007). This found expression in the establishment of the United Nations (UN), the European Convention on Human Rights and, over time, their various conventions, institutions and committees in areas of racial, religious, gender, age and disability discrimination. Much of the contemporary western concern with issues of rights, equality and diversity, including hate crime, owes its origins to this post-World War II rights-related architecture (Freeman, 2002; Donnelly, 2003; Clapham, 2007; Hanimaki, 2008; Neier, 2012 Shelton, 2013; Weiss and Daws, 2020). In the latter part of the 20th century, these were supplemented with the increasing development of the European Union (EU) and the development of the Organization for Security and Co-operation in Europe (2017). In each of these contexts, as well as domestically, activity on disability equality has lagged, sometimes by decades, behind activity on other equality strands, in particular race, religion and gender (Roulstone and Prideaux, 2012).

Emergence of contemporary concern with hate crime

As mentioned earlier in this chapter, contemporary concern with hate crime appears to have first emerged as a criminal justice challenge in the US in the 1980s, influenced by the earlier black civil rights movement in particular (Jacobs and Potter, 1998). Given a key part of its origins in the civil rights movements and its transition into the policy arena (Jenness and Broad, 2005), hate crime has been an area where activism and policy activity often preceded academic scholarship. That said, significant scholarship is underway, with some more recent scholarship considering Disability Hate Crime specifically and/or reconceptualizing hate crime overall (Herek and Berill, 1992; Lawrence, 1999; Perry, B., 2001, 2003, 2009a; Iganski, 2002, 2008, 2010; Levin and McDevitt, 2002; Jenness and Broad, 2005; Levin, B., 2009; Mason-Bish, 2009; Sherry, 2010; Walters, 2011; Chakraborti and Garland, 2012; Hall, 2013; Roulstone and Mason-Bish, 2013; Iganski and Levin, 2015; Ogden, 2016; Schweppe and Waters, 2016: Healy, 2018; Wilkin, 2019).

Writing hate crime

Broad strands of hate crime scholarship have emerged over time: a legal scholarship literature, a social problems literature and a social movements literature. Much theorizing today cuts across this broad-brush heuristic framework, and this study draws upon work within and across these areas of scholarship. Some recent scholarship appraises established theoretical perspectives (Walters, 2011; Hall, 2013). Others who seek to reconceptualize hate crime and its traditional focus on identity groups argue that it should operate within a framework that can encompass targeted crimes based on identity groups, difference and vulnerability (Chakraborti and Garland, 2012).

Given its recent origins as a multidisciplinary area of scholarship, it is not surprising that defining and delineating hate crime has been a central preoccupation of much of the literature on hate crime in the 1990s and early 2000s. And, given a key origin in the early US civil rights movement, it is also not surprising that much of the early significant scholarship defined and delineated hate crime in terms of the features of racist crime and homophobic crime to a lesser extent. Significant definitions include those of Lawrence (1999) in the area of legal scholarship, Herek and Berill (1992) in terms of social movement scholarship, Perry in terms of public criminology and sociological scholarship (2001), and Grattet and Jenness (2001b) and Jenness and Broad (2005) in terms of social movement scholarship and policy studies scholarship. Levin and McDevitt's (2002) contribution in terms of the social problems literature on hate crime is also significant. Their approach finds an echo in the more recent work of Sherry on Disability Hate Crime (Levin and McDevitt, 2002; Sherry, 2010).

In earlier writings, Lawrence (1999), Herek and Berill (1992), and Perry (2001, 2009a) tended towards conceiving of hate crime in terms of stranger crime, public space crime and crimes targeting people with a shared group identity/membership and reflecting significant societal divides/fissures. Much of this literature is written from a 'classic' racist crime or homophobic crime perspective. While the existence of Disability Hate Crime is not rejected, it is either not mentioned (Herek and Berill, 1992; Perry, B., 2001) or it is located at the margins of the hate crime phenomenon (Lawrence, 1999). There have been exceptions, notably Grattet and Jenness (2001a) and Sherry (2000a, 2000b, 2003, 2004, 2010), the latter almost a lone academic voice on the subject for many years.

The earlier academic notion of hate crime as outlined appears to be reflected and more prevalent in the early criminal justice sector policy and practice definitions and developments of hate crime in England and Wales. The first mention of Disability Hate Crime in police literature was in 2005, although it was 2007–08 before steps were taken to monitor it (ACPO, 2005; Home Office and ACPO, 2008). The CPS literature first mentions Disability Hate Crime in the 2006 CPS Single Equality Scheme, setting out a commitment to put in place the then 'Disability Crimes Policy' by 2007 (CPS, 2006). There is no mention of Disability Hate Crime in the Judiciary's Equal Treatment Bench Book (Judicial Studies Board, 2008) or strikingly in their more recent edition (Judicial College, 2018). Yet, these publications emerged in a context where a sentencing uplift provision had been put in place for crimes aggravated by disability hostility since 2003.

Identity politics and disability hate crime

As indicated earlier in this chapter, the origins of the phenomenon of hate crime owes much to the early civil rights movement in the US, and its spawning of identity politics first in the US and latterly through movement diffusion and transfer its influence on identity politics in Britain. Identity politics is a term that has evolved over time but is broadly taken to refer to a social movement politics whereby people relate to others as members of social groups based upon identity characteristics such as ethnicity, religion, gender, sexuality, gender identity and disability (Jacobs and Potter, 1998). The identity based social movements arising from this politics are referred to as the race equality movement, the LGBTI + movement, the women's movement and, in this instance, the disability movement. There are scholars who advocate for the acknowledgement of the contribution of identity politics and the specific equality movements to advancing specific strands of identity inequalities (Young, 1990), and critics of these social movements contributions (Jacobs and Potter, 1998). There also are more recent scholars who focus on reconsidering identity politics and its contributions (Alcoff, 2006; Siebers, 2006).

Critics argue that the hate crime movement owes its origins not to any significant prevalence of hate crime, but, rather to society's heightened sensitivity to prejudice and to society's emphasis on identity politics (Jacobs and Potter, 1998, p 6). In this book I first identify the disability movement initiatives including agenda triggering and agenda setting publications that can be viewed as arising in this context of identity politics, and, second, go on in the book to explore the contribution of these publications and this disability movement activism–identity politics in influencing disability hate crime emergence and development (Jacobs and Potter, 1998; Hall, 2013). In doing so I tend to use the language of disability movement rather than disability identity politics, as disability movement was the term used by disability activists interviewed for this research. No respondents involved in disability activism in the research underpinning this book identified themselves as engaged in identity politics while many identified as engaged in a disability movement.

Some early community sector disability movement publications dealt with targeted harassment and violence experienced by disabled people. These emerged at a time when hate crime was being defined academically and surfacing as a policy domain in England and Wales. As an example, Mencap's 1999 report, 'Living in Fear', framed the experiences of disabled people in the UK in terms of 'bullying'. There is no mention of hate crime. However, crime, while scarcely mentioned, is a critical consideration of the experiences identified by respondents who indicated targeted crimes based on disability. This targeting includes reports of damage to property, assaults and disablist verbal abuse. Most interviewees (88 per cent) reported an experience of bullying in the previous year, while 32 per cent reported weekly experience of bullying (Mencap, 1999). There is no evidence that this report informed policy debate on hate crime in the early years after publication. However, it was referenced by the government some 12 years later in the government 'Hate Crime Action Plan' (HM Government, 2009). From 2007 onwards, however, Mencap increasingly adopted the language of hate crime in its literature (Mencap, 2007).

Another early community sector report was 'Opening the Gateways' by the Values into Action (VIA) charity in 2002. This is the first community sector publication pinpointed in this book as identifying hate crime as an experience of disabled people. Uniquely, it also recommended that hate crime legislation address disabled people's experiences (VIA, 2002). It built on earlier VIA reports from the mid-1990s through to the early 2000s, which addressed the closure of residential institutions for learning disabled people and the shift to increased community living. In charting this shift, because of which over 60,000 learning disabled adults moved to live in community settings, VIA identified community-based disability harassment as a risk in managing this transition to increased community living. Over time, VIA's representation of the problem evolved to describe the issue as hate crime (VIA, 2002). However, these ground-breaking reports were not acknowledged in the early academic or policy debates and developments on hate crime.

With the exceptions of a few scholars in the US – Grattet and Jenness and, particularly, Mark Sherry and Barbara Faye Waxman – the international literature in academia, the policy domain and, indeed, the community sector in the mid-1990s and early 2000s was silent on the issue of Disability Hate Crime. Faye Waxman highlighted, as far back as 1991, how hostility and hatred were the unacknowledged dimension in disabled people's experiences in the US, when she proposed that disability be included as a monitored characteristic in the US Hate Crime Statistics (Faye Waxman, 1991). Yet the notion of hostility and hatred towards disability was not easily accepted in the larger hate crime domain in the UK. Indeed, Sherry, whose work dates back to 2000 (2000a, 2000b, 2003, 2004, 2010, 2020), said that, for a significant period of time, the prevalent response to his research was one of disbelief, the view being that people tend to be sympathetic and show pity towards disabled people. It was only with the later emergence of Disability Hate Crime as a policy concern in Britain that his work has gained wider acknowledgement (Sherry, 2010).

Both Sherry and Faye Waxman question whether the early adoption of vulnerability as central to the framing of disabled people's experience of hate crime has particularly posed challenges for the recognition of Disability Hate Crime. In a British context, Mason-Bish (2012) goes further, asking whether the development of the Disability Hate Crime approach has in turn particularly posed challenges for how we conceive of hate crime overall, because of the contrast with dominant definitions of 'classic' racist crime and homophobic crime.

In this context, the Law Commission's 2013 consultation paper, 'Hate Crime: the case for extending existing offences', was a first significant policy review and consideration of the issues (Law Commission, June 2013). It questioned whether there should, in the future, be disability aggravated offences akin to racially aggravated offences. However, the document could only consult on a replication of the existing racially aggravated offences regardless of their appropriateness to Disability Hate Crime. This again raised a question as to the prevalence of a particular conception of hate crime and its implications for Disability Hate Crime.

Given the prevalent view of hate crime that informed early academic and policy work, how and why did Disability Hate Crime emerge as an area of policy and practice within the criminal justice system of England and Wales? How did that prevalent view contribute to the non-recognition and under-reporting of Disability Hate Crime? And how did the emergence of Disability Hate Crime affect that prevalent view of hate crime in turn?

Disability, societal and public policy responses

Just as there is a body of writing on conceiving and defining hate crime, there is likewise a body of literature on defining disability. That literature includes historical analyses of disability and societal responses (Foucault,

1997; Braddock and Parish, 2001; McDonnell, 2007; Quarmby, 2011), as well as contemporary attempts to define disability (Barnes and Mercer, 2003; Shakespeare, 2006, 2017; Oliver and Barnes, 2012). What almost all these accounts point to is that, over time, disability in Britain and the US has 'existed at the intersection between the particular demands of a given impairment, society's interpretation of that impairment and the larger political and economic context of disability' (Braddock and Parish, 2001, p 11). While acknowledging the stubborn fact of impairment, there is a shared understanding of the significant social basis of disability.

The literature portrays both a complex varied set of experiences by disabled people and the existence of targeted hostility as one continuing thread within these experiences (Sobsey, 1994; Braddock and Parish, 2001; Evans, 2004; McDonnell, 2007; Quarmby, 2011). This continuing thread of violence was evidenced in ancient Greece and Rome, in banishment and torture in the Middle Ages, in institutional abuse in the 19th century, in mass killings in the mid-20th century in Nazi Germany, in ongoing institutional abuse and in what is now described as Disability Hate Crime (Faye Waxman, 1991; Sobsey, 1994; Evans, 2004; Quarmby, 2011; Mason-Bish, 2013). The literature also highlights a 'marking out' of disability over time (Braddock and Parish, 2001; Borsay, 2005; McDonnell, 2007). Authors highlight a close link between disability and poverty, social exclusion and marginalization (Quinn and Redmond, 2007; Oliver and Barnes, 2012; Roulstone and Prideaux, 2012). This can be traced back to the Elizabethan Poor Law and before (Borsay, 2005; Roulstone and Prideaux, 2012).

Elsewhere, there are bodies of work on various aspects of disabled people's experiences in relation to public policy. These include works on disability and poverty (Palmer, 2011), disability and the labour market (Blackabay et al, 1999; Grewal et al, 2002), disability and education (Haines and Ruebain, 2011), and disability and healthcare (DRC, 2006). These studies tend to convey a profile of disadvantage and discrimination in discrete aspects of disabled people's lives.

There are few studies that have looked specifically at disabled people's experience in terms of disability related oppression, disablism or ableism (Abberley, 1987a, 1987b, 1999; Miller, Parker and Gillinson, 2004; Kumari Campbell, 2008; Koppelman and Lee, 2010; Nario-Redmond, 2010, 2019; Watermeyer, 2013; Iganski and Levin, 2015). Disabled people's experiences seem persistently to be considered in a fragmentary way (Faye Waxman, 1991). In the early years of the disability movement in Britain, ground-breaking academic work, mainly by Abberley (1987a, 1987b), was undertaken on social oppression of disabled people. Influenced by earlier work on Black people's oppression and racism, it gave way in time to the Social Model of Disability which has its basis in an oppression-based conceptualization of disability. The Social Model, however, focuses more on the liberation of disabled people from oppressive barriers than on a consistent developed analysis of ableism and disablism and its manifestations at all levels which holds these barriers in place (Watermeyer, 2013).

Disablism features in just a small body of literature (Abberley, 1987a, 1987b, 1999; Miller et al, 2004; Kumari Campbell, 2008; Koppelman and Lee, 2010; Goodley and Runswick-Cole, 2011; Watermeyer, 2013); ableism even less so (Kumari Campbell, 2009; Goodley, 2014; Nario-Redmond, 2019; Thorneycroft, 2020). Some definitions place the emphasis on ableism, some emphasize disablism, while others recognize the significance of 'the background cultures' of both disablism and ableism (Iganski and Levin, 2015, p 26). There are varying views as to whether the emphasis should be placed on ableism, which values and elevates ability and views it as being 'fully human', whereas disability is viewed as less fully human (Campbell, 2008, p 153; Nario-Redmond, 2019) or whether the emphasis should be placed on disablism. Disablism highlights disabling attitudes and practices, which diminish and negate impairment, and lead to undervaluing and discrimination experienced by disabled people (Goodley and Runswick Cole, 2011). For this book, I find it helpful as set out in Chapter 1 to conceive of ableism as a prejudicial set of ideas, an ideology that has existed over time and that privileges abledness and inferiorizes disabled people and provides a rationale for ongoing prejudicial attitudes, and mistreatment at various levels. In this regard, ableism is perceived as akin to racism and heterosexism. It provides the ideological backdrop to the societal oppression of disabled people, which may manifest itself in various ways including through violent discrimination – hate crime. As Thorneycroft points out engaging with disablism and ableism involves recognizing how the very word dis/ability is itself 'a split term' and this split in the term dis/ability 'denotes the ways in which ability and disability, ableism and disablism are constituted in simultaneous relation to one another' (Thorneycroft, 2020, p 5).

Watermeyer (2013) has provided one of the more recent comprehensive accounts of disablism and its effects on disabled people's lives. He acknowledges social model adherents while being somewhat critical of them. Indeed, he is somewhat critical of all theoretical perspectives on the experiences of disabled people: 'no single theoretical narrative is able to mirror disability adequately' (Watermeyer, 2013, p 2). On Disability Hate Crimes specifically, Watermeyer wonders if they may depict a 'high water mark' of disablism, reflecting our 'ongoing, unconscious aggressive impulses towards the disabled minority, existing on a continuum with both everyday prejudice and eugenic fantasies' (Watermeyer, 2013, p 103). He links Disability Hate Crime to disablism, as do Goodley and Runswick-Cole (2011) who identify the manifestations of the violence of disablism as real, psycho-emotional, cultural and systemic. They conclude that the violence experienced by disabled people is more reflective of a dominant culture of disablism than of the 'acts of a few irrational, unreasonable, mean or violent individuals' (Goodley and Runswick-Cole, 2011, p 602). This has echoes in Joanna Perry's application of Galtung's concepts of structural and cultural violence to the experience of disabled people (Perry, J., 2013). However, such writings are still relatively rare in the literature on disability and disablism in Britain.

In 2004, a think tank report on disablism endeavoured to set an agenda on what it termed as the 'need to tackle the last prejudice' (Miller et al, 2004, p 1). However, its influence on policy debate remains unclear. More recently, literature from within the disability community has begun to reference and highlight disablism (Scope, 2007). Mason-Bish points to a tendency not to connect Disability Hate Crime to the linked prejudices of disablism or ableism in the way that we link racist crime to racism or homophobic crime to homophobia. This raises a question as to whether this may lead to a failure to identify the issue as hate crime at all (Mason-Bish, 2012).

In the context of this book, it is striking that, until 2017, there were no criminal justice publications that mentioned disablism or ableism, are entitled or cover the subjects of Disablist Crime or indeed Ableist Crime. There are publications on Disability Hate Crime (ACPO, 2005, 2014; CPS, 2007b, 2010a, 2010b) and references to Disability Crimes (CPS, 2006) and publications on Disability Hate Crime and other crimes against disabled people (CPS, 2017). However, there have been criminal justice publications on racist crime and homophobic and transphobic crime (ACPO, 2005; CPS, 2002, 2004). Thus, I was interested in exploring in this book the recognition and potential non-recognition of disablism and ableism among criminal justice agencies and whether a failure to recognize institutional disablism and ableism as potential challenges for the public sector, akin to institutional racism, have acted as a barrier to recognizing Disability Hate Crime, leading to conceptual, policy, and practice ambiguity and confusion on this issue. I was furthermore interested in exploring how in racist hate crime, there is a tendency to link the hate crime to the wider prejudice, racism, and we talk of racist crime and have racist crimes policies. In lesbian, gay, bisexual (LGB) hate crime, there is a tendency to link the hate crime to the wider prejudice, homophobia and to speak of homophobic crime. In Disability Hate Crime, there does not appear to be this tendency to link to a wider prejudice of ableism or disablism. Why might this be, and is it significant?

How public policy (including criminal justice policy) constructs disability and disabled people

Consideration of the writings on equality issues in Britain and the US indicates contributory factors to equality policy development and varied development pathways for different equality strands (Bagihole, 2009; Thane,

2010). Activist, policy, political and research–academic developments, together with focusing events separately and in interaction, appear to have paved the way for domestic civil law protections in the areas of race and gender equality initially (Fredman, 2000; Bagihole, 2009; Thane, 2010), which extended, albeit more slowly, into the area of disability (Bagihole, 2009; Millar, 2010). The literature indicates that, in time, these civil law protections were followed by legal protections in the form of criminal law provisions to address hate crime, namely racist crime, religious crime and, latterly, homophobic and transphobic crime and Disability Hate Crime (Grattet and Jenness, 2001a, 2001b; Jenness and Broad, 2005; Mason-Bish, 2009).

Scholars indicate that while disability is provided for in equality based legal protections, there is usually a time lag in relation to other protected statuses (Mason-Bish, 2009, 2013); it is 'last on the list' (Roulstone and Prideaux, 2012, p 25) and, as Healy aptly posits, is positioned 'on the margins' of the Hate Crime domain (Healy, 2018). The literature indicates that, in the US, the Americans with Disabilities Act came later than the civil rights legislation and the sex discrimination legislation. Equally, in criminal law, disability was included in US hate crime monitoring sometime after race, religion and sexuality (Faye Waxman, 1991). In Britain, the Race Relations Act and the Sex Discrimination Act preceded the Disability Discrimination Act by almost two decades. Again, in criminal law, disability hostility was included as an aggravating factor in crime sometime after race and religion and at the same time as sexual orientation. Why has a non-discrimination and rights focus for disabled people lagged behind other protected grounds? Why is this so given a history that points to disability discrimination, including violent discrimination?

Competing ideologies and problematizations of disability in public policy – care versus rights

While a rights-based problematization of identity inequalities influenced by equality movements and a linked discourse gained a gradual foothold in social policy after World War II and extended through the group-based inequalities over time (Thane, 2010), it did not emerge in the area of disability until later (Driedger, 1989; Bagihole, 2009; Millar, 2010). Scholars point out it was not the only problem representation, discourse and ideology in a competing battleground of ideas, problematizations and responses impacting disabled people's lives (McDonnell, 2007; Bacchi, 2009).

Scholars indicate that the Medical Model of disability continued to prevail after World War II, with its emphasis on disability as a functional impairment in the individual best managed by medical and associated professionals responding to personal and often tragic situations. It was reinforced with the rise of ideologies and problem representations of care and normalization in the area of disability (Barnes and Mercier, 2003; McDonnell, 2007; Bacchi, 2009; Oliver and Barnes, 2012). Authors also indicate that, since World War II, there remained a prioritization of addressing poverty and securing an adequate income for disabled people. This focus on basic survival supports for disabled people dominated the British welfare state's early decades. It was a quantity of life focus, rather than a quality of life focus on recognition and respect (Borsay, 2005; Millar, 2010; Roulstone and Prideaux, 2012).

The literature indicates that the developing ideologies and problem representations of care and normalization were posited as progressive policy perspectives that accepted that social attitudes posed a challenge in addressing the experience of disabled people. However, the answer was seen to lie in 'normalizing' disabled people's experiences, through seeking to make their experiences comparable to 'normal' people. This led to programmes of significant deinstitutionalization from special schools and residential homes, in a number of which violent abuse had been identified (Collins, 1993; Mason-Bish, 2013; Roulstone, 2013; Giannasi, 2015a). It led to the growth of community care and mainstreaming in wider schools (McDonnell, 2007; Oliver and Barnes, 2012; Roulstone and Prideaux, 2012). In this context, key policy representations and themes are care, community, independence, independent living, protection, vulnerability, mainstreaming and citizenship (McDonnell, 2007; Roulstone, 2019). These policy representations and themes are not always compatible with tensions between a focus on care and independence, and between independence and vulnerability. This caring and normalization ideology, and its close alliance with the Medical Model, continues to influence policy responses to disabled people. Even in the context of a policy of supporting people through enabling independent living (Beresford et al, 2011), a rights-based representation of disability still competes with the powerful ideological influences of care, normalization and medicalization in various policy contexts including that of violence against disabled people (Faye Waxman, 1991; EHRC, 2011a).

Constructing disabled people as vulnerable

Faye Waxman (1991) argued that disabled people's position at the margins of the hate crime policy domain is the result of two competing paradigms or problem representations: a Medical Model and a Socio-Political model. In her analysis of the ideas underpinning social policy in relation to disabled people in the US, she argued that the ascendant Medical Model largely constructed disabled people as vulnerable and powerless. She argued that, viewed through a lens of care and vulnerability, abuse can be the resulting experience, with dependent-adult legislation and adult care the ensuing social policy responses. Further, viewed through a lens of social rights, discrimination and hate crime can be the resulting experience, with hate crime laws, policies and practices then part of the social policy response. She was concerned at this construction of disabled people as vulnerable in public policy, including criminal justice policy. She pointed to a climate in the US where disabled people were viewed as inherently vulnerable and where the law protected disabled people but mainly when 'construed as vulnerable' (1991, p 190). She argued that an over-emphasis on vulnerability in seeking to account for disability related violence was 'too superficial' – 'people who are respected and considered equal are not generally abused' (1991, p 191).

Faye Waxman's perspective found an echo 20 years later in the findings of the first-ever statutory formal inquiry into disability related harassment (EHRC, 2011a) in Britain in 2010–11. The EHRC report, 'Hidden in Plain Sight', noted the existence of two problem representations and policy approaches to the experience of violence in the lives of disabled people in Britain: first, the safeguarding–vulnerable adult approach, and, second, the justice approach focused on Disability Hate Crime. The EHRC noted the prevalence of the safeguarding approach and recommended that this be counterbalanced with a Social Model of Disability in order to deliver justice for disabled people: 'the focus on help and protection within the adult safeguarding system can be at the expense of ensuring justice and redress' (EHRC, 2011a, p 135).

The focus on vulnerability in public policy in relation to disability and, in particular, criminal justice policy has been raised in a British context by a number of authors (Scope, 2007; Sherry, 2010; Quarmby, 2011; Roulstone et al, 2011; Roulstone and Sadique, 2013; Roulstone, 2019). Roulstone and others (2011) argue that the construction of disabled people as vulnerable has worked against disabled people getting the full protection of the law, particularly hate crime law, and that there may be something inherently paternalistic in designating other people as vulnerable. It has been highlighted by Roulstone and others (Quarmby, 2011) that this entrenched focus on vulnerability may have influenced the handling of a number of murders of disabled people as problems appropriate for a safeguarding review rather than for a criminal prosecution.

As mentioned earlier in this chapter, there has been a call for the reconceptualization of hate crime victimization in recent academic literature. This calls for a shift away from a focus on victimization based on identity alone to encompass perceived vulnerability and difference (Chakraborti and Garland, 2012). This is significant, particularly in the area of Disability Hate Crime where vulnerability is a highly problematic construct. Chakraborti and Garland (2012) argue that the 'vulnerable' concept encapsulates how many hate crime perpetrators view their target. The vulnerable concept does not, however, encapsulate how the majority of Disability Hate Crime victims and the wider disability movement view their victimization. In fact, it runs contrary to how disabled victims and the disability movement view their victimization. Chakraborti and Garland argue that a conceptual focus on perceived vulnerability should not be read as indicating there is an inevitability of inherent passivity in hate crime victims. While recognizing the significance of this contribution, and its constructive aims, there is a question – can such a focus appropriately address the specificities of vulnerability in the context of disability which this study considered? Taken as a whole, the evidence in this book does not support such a focus in terms of Disability Hate Crime.

Scholarly and disability movement debates on disability and vulnerability raise questions for the consideration of policy developments in relation to Disability Hate Crime. The original Crown Prosecution Service Disability Hate Crimes public policy statement (CPS, 2007b), which guided prosecution practice for ten years, placed a significant emphasis on vulnerability and referred to some crimes based on vulnerability rather than hostility. This focus was seen to have contributed to ambiguity and confusion in prosecution practice. The CPS sought to address ensuant community criticisms through issuing guidance distinguishing between a vulnerability focus and a hostility focus on crime (CPS, 2010b). Though welcomed by disability activists, challenges continued, and the CPS later embarked on an overall review and update of its Disability Hate Crime policy (2015–16). A revised Disability Hate Crime policy published in 2017 sought to outline a more nuanced understanding of vulnerability.

However, I noted that I was able to identify far fewer publications from the police, the CPS, the Sentencing Guidelines Council and government more widely on Disability Hate Crime than publications on and references to disabled people and vulnerability. In fact, the core policy and practice document within the CPS, 'The Code for Crown Prosecutors', historically conceived of disability in terms of vulnerability (CPS, 2013 and earlier editions) as indeed does the Sentencing Guidelines Council's overreaching principles (SGC, 2004) and the recent editions of the Judicial Studies Board's Equal Treatment Bench Book (JSB, 2008; 2018), which as recently as 2018 is flooded with a conception of disabled people as inherently vulnerable. Some of these are reflective of legislative definitions such as those of vulnerable persons in the Youth Justice and Criminal Evidence Act 1999. Given these potential pointers to a prevalent vulnerability perspective on disability in the criminal justice system, I explore in this book whether the naming of aspects of the problem of hate crime begin to shift the criminal justice focus to issues of rights and justice.? I also explore whether a focus on disabled people's perceived 'intrinsic' vulnerability contributes to masking issues of hostility. Might this have contributed to the non-recognition of what is now recognized as Disability Hate Crime and whether targeted hostility and hatred towards disabled people identified and responded to by criminal justice agencies, until recently, in a range of ways including occasional non-recognition and, at times, as crimes aggravated by vulnerability?

Policy making and developments on hate crime and on equality including Disability Hate Crime

While there are growing bodies of academic literature on hate crime and on disability, and a growing body of literature on the construction of disability in public policy debates, there is much less on the specifics of policy making on equality issues and on hate crime, including Disability Hate Crime. However, there has been a surge in governmental publications and literature from the independent statutory and NGO sectors on Disability Hate Crime.

One of the exceptions to this overall absence of an academic literature on policy making on hate crime is Best (2009). He traces the rise of issues as social problems, including key stages in the social construction of hate crimes in the US, in particular (2009, p 215). This may have some resonance in the recent construction of Disability Hate Crime as a social problem in Britain. Best talks about how the social construction of hate crime brings 'new' public policy attention to 'old' violence, and in this he echoes in part the much earlier work of Quinney (1970). 'Watchdog organisations' (Best, 2009, p 126) secure this attention through documenting cases, identifying and publicizing the significant harm associated with such violence, making policy reform proposals and calling on the law to intervene. These organizations engage in activism that both 'discovers' hate crime and promotes the interest of specific groups by 'demanding changes in public policy' (Best, 2009, p 217).

Best traces how hate crime first became identified as a social problem, second as a policy problem, and third as a problem requiring a legal response. This arose, he suggests, because hate crime was increasingly debated by activists, bureaucrats, politicians and academics with significant material produced on the causes, manifestations and consequences of hate crime, and the need for a legal response. He highlights how the recognition of the first hate crime categories – race, religion and ethnicity – meant that 'the stage was effectively set for discussions' (Best, 2009, p 222) on the recognition of other categories including sexual orientation and disability. He argues that the 'law has played a major role in defining hate crimes as a social problem' (2009, p 124) and that hate crime became a 'meaningful term' only with the adoption of legislation, which led to the victimization associated with it becoming properly apparent and officially and 'clearly defined' (2009, p 224). He identifies the law as that 'highly visible form of public policy' (2009, p 225) which significantly 'demarcates specific forms of bias – motivated intimidation and assault as hate crimes, thereby creating new policy categories of violent crime and new categories of crime victims' (2009, p 224). In doing this, he argues, the law has articulated 'what will and what will not "count" as hate crime and by extension who does and also does not qualify as a victim of hate crime' (2009, p 225).

Grattet and Jenness (2001b) emphasize the contribution of social movements to policy making in a US context and argue that hate crime is best viewed as a policy domain, a broad area of policy activity. They draw on ideas from Burstein (1991) in applying the concept of a policy domain to hate crime and use the linked concepts of domain establishment, expansion and exploration to explain the differential development of hate crime policies in the US. Similar to Best, Grattet and Jenness analyse the establishment of the first hate crime categories in the US (race, religion and ethnicity) and their expansion to include sexuality and disability. They present the process of domain expansion as relatively unproblematic. We will return to Grattet and Jenness' insights on hate crime policy making in subsequent chapters in this book.

When Mason-Bish (2009) applied the Grattet and Jenness policy domain template in a British context, she produced the first academic study to address hate crime policy development strand by strand including its expansion to include Disability Hate Crime. She highlighted the role of social movement actors and criminal justice policymakers in shaping hate crime policy at a macro level in Britain. She concluded that it is a policy domain marked by a relatively small number of contributors. She also highlighted how, in contrast to the US and Grattet and Jenness' insights, hate crime policy domain expansion in Britain to include disability has taken greater effort and time to establish. She pointed out that, although the legal provision recognizing disability aggravation in crime was introduced apparently relatively unproblematically in 2003, Disability Hate Crime policy as an active policy agenda did not emerge until four years later in 2007. This book explores these issues further.

In this context, I was interested in understanding how this legal provision emerged in 2003 and how it apparently took another four years for Disability Hate Crime to emerge as an active policy and practice agenda. Thus, I explore in subsequent chapters:

- What contributed to the emergence of a disability aggravation provision in the Criminal Justice Act 2003, known as Section 146?
- Did the introduction of a disability aggravation provision in the Criminal Justice Act 2003 (enacted in 2005) provide an impetus for criminal justice agencies to prioritize Disability Hate Crime?
- Why was it that, although a disability aggravation provision was enacted in 2005, it was not until 2006–07 that criminal justice policy and practice emerged on the issue of Disability Hate Crime?
- Was the disability aggravation provision, when legislated for in 2003, a provision before its time?
- By 2006–07, was the disability aggravation provision a provision whose time had come?

Policy making on equality in England and Wales and issues raised for hate crime

The catalytic influence of the Lawrence Inquiry

The Stephen Lawrence Inquiry, investigating institutional racism, had a catalytic influence on policy making on equality in Britain (Mason-Bish, 2009; Rollock, 2010; Hall, 2013; Shah and Giannasi, 2015). Numerous authors emphasize how the government response to the Lawrence Inquiry marked a step change in how public institutions were to consider and respond to issues of race equality in the first instance and other equality strands in due course. Some identify how the Lawrence Inquiry led to the emergence of the mainstreaming of the equality agenda in British public-sector policy making – with public-sector bodies required to proactively consider and promote equality in their daily functions. As mentioned in the Introductory chapter, this found legal expression in, first, the public sector duty to promote race equality, then extended to gender equality and disability equality, and was latterly refined into a general equality duty across a range of protected strands (Giannasi, 2015a).

The equality duties approach to advancing equality

The Lawrence Inquiry and the subsequent equality duties have been identified with a significant agenda-setting impact on public authorities, including impact on criminal justice agencies, in terms of advancing equality. The Race Equality Duty in 2002 was unprecedented in equality legislation in Britain. It required criminal justice agencies as public authorities to establish the race equality priorities of communities and to take these into account in the mainstream policy making, planning and delivery work of the authority. It was based on recognition of the challenge of institutional discrimination facing public authorities. It was an attempt using the law as a lever to institutionalize anti-discrimination into the daily work of public authorities (Ollereanshaw et al, 2003; Nathwani et al, 2007; Fredman, 2000, 2008). Criminal justice agencies were in effect required to 'discover' the 'problems' impacting on minority communities through consultation and to work to address these in mainstream policy making and daily service delivery.

When the Disability Equality Duty was introduced (2005), criminal justice agencies were further required to become proactive in promoting disability equality. It required the 'involvement' of disabled people in furthering disability equality and that steps be taken to eliminate harassment of disabled people. However, some disability scholars question the Disability Equality Duty (Pearson et al, 2011; Oliver and Barnes, 2012) in the incorporation of disability critique in the public sector and the bureaucratization of disability equality. Some scholars question the capacity of 'positive' equality duties to deliver substantive equality, given their focus on process more than content of equality decision making, their perceived superficial consultation with those social groups affected, their thin approach to compliance (McLaughlin, 2007). Some are critical of the response in the criminal justice system where a systemic challenge in addressing institutional discrimination was originally identified but changed over time to a more individual focus on individual victims of hate crime (McVeigh, 2017). Scholarly opinions vary on this issue. Other authors point to the significance of the public sector equality duties in leading to increased actions to advance equality (Nathwani et al, 2007; Hall, 2013; Giannasi, 2015). Fredman (2000) identifies the equality duties approach as heralding a new generation of discrimination law.

A number of governmental publications situate their actions on disability equality, including Disability Hate Crime, within a context of their work to implement the Disability Equality Duty. This includes the first Government Hate Crime Action Plan (2010), the CPS Single Equality Scheme (CPS, 2006) and the recent police work on hate crime (Giannasi, 2015). There is, nonetheless, a gap in our understanding of the significance of the Disability Equality Duty in criminal justice agencies deciding to prioritize Disability Hate Crime. Indeed, Mason-Bish identified this as a gap in her study in 2009. In this context, I explore in this book the government's response to the Stephen Lawrence Inquiry, including the official acceptance of institutional discrimination, and the subsequent introduction of a public duty to promote race equality set a far-reaching agenda for institutional actions on equality. I further explore whether these responses created the policy space within which other equality agendas, including disability equality, could be advocated and advanced. And whether disability community organizations and individuals availed of this opportunity and space? This book specifically goes on to explore if the introduction of a wider legal duty on public bodies in England and Wales to promote disability equality in their daily work provided an impetus for criminal justice agencies to 'discover 'and prioritize Disability Hate Crime and whether the subsequent emergence of a focus on Disability Hate Crime allowed criminal justice agencies to state and display their commitment to disability issues, and to be seen to do so in their mainstream service?

Hate crime, street-level bureaucracy and the exercise of discretion

Much of the hate crime literature, as noted, focuses on defining and conceptualizing the phenomenon. Less of the literature with notable exceptions focuses on hate crime policy making (Mason-Bish 2009; Hall, 2013). Even less still focuses on hate crime policy implementation in routine criminal justice practice (Bowling, 1999; Hall, 2013). Informed by the ground breaking work of Lipsky on street-level bureaucracy and the exercise of discretion by street-level workers, such as individual police officers, Hall critically applies this concept to the policing of hate crime and explores how this may help to better understand challenges in securing an appropriate response to hate crime across the police (Lipsky, 2010). In doing so, Hall helps build an understanding in particular of policing responses to hate crime that go beyond the individual or the institutional accounts to a fuller account of both in practice. In a book focused primarily on the emergence and development of Disability Hate Crime policy and practice I have some interest in exploring insights on street-level bureaucracy and the exercise of discretion in Disability Hate Crime cases. To what extent have police and prosecutors implemented agency policy clearly, without ambiguity and consistently? Are there significant gaps between agency policy on Disability Hate Crime and agency practice as evidenced in individual cases? Is there any evidence of routinized practices among police and prosecutors in the handling of Disability Hate Crime cases in practice? I raise these issues here in the context of the wider literature and provide a deeper discussion of these in Chapters 7 and 8 in light of an analysis of prosecutions, relating them specifically to vulnerability and ableism in turn.

Policy contributions by independent bodies, the community sector and others to the Disability Hate Crime agenda

A small body of literature that touches on or is directly focused on the theme of Disability Hate Crime has been produced by the independent statutory sector, the community sector and by individual authors. Between 2005 and 2007, the former Disability Rights Commission (DRC) produced documents on the themes of The Disability Debate and The Disability Agenda. The focus was on stimulating a debate regarding the main concerns of disabled people in Britain regarding the realization of disability equality and to set out an agenda of top priorities for disability equality to be handed over to the then newly emerging EHRC in 2007. There are three documents in this policy agenda setting series, namely 'Shaping the future of equality' (DRC, 2005), 'Creating an alternative future' (DRC, 2007a) and 'Changing Britain for good-putting disability at the heart of public policy' (DRC, 2007b). These documents were informed in turn partly by earlier research (DRC Scotland and Capability Scotland, 2004).

'Shaping the future of equality' positively acknowledges the recognition of hate crime against disabled people through the provision of Section 146 of the CJA 2003 (DRC, 2005). 'Creating an alternative future' referred to the 'significant numbers of disabled people who feel the sharp end of discrimination in the form of abuse or harassment, either in the community or in institutional settings' (DRC, 2007a, p 11). Referring to Section 146 of the CJA 2003, it states that, 'despite laws to tackle such abuse, there is little proactive work by criminal justice agencies to prevent it and ensure fair redress' (p 11). Clearly, this DRC publication sought to link the issue of abuse and harassment of disabled people with the criminal justice system's performance on the agenda.

Later that same year, in its document, 'Changing Britain for good – putting disability at the heart of public policy' (DRC, 2007b), the DRC identified ten priorities for future action by the then emerging EHRC. One of the priorities was 'Creating safe communities – tackling hate crime, harassment, bullying and negative stereotyping' (DRC, 2007b, p 18). This document flagged targeted harassment and disproportionate violence as one of the top ten priorities to deliver equality for disabled people in Britain. These appeared significant and informed the issues explored in this book.

In the mid-2000s, a number of publications emerged from disability community sector organizations on harassment, targeted abuse, and violence and hate crime themes. These included magazine publication 'The Hate Crime Dossier' (Disability Now, 2007) and 'Getting Away with Murder' (Scope, 2008). The publications highlighted serious cases including targeted murders of disabled people where the issue of disability aggravation was not recognized or considered. Some were considered for serious case reviews in terms of adult safeguarding. These reports were designed to spotlight policy-practice gaps even after formal policies on hate crime were adopted with the aim of galvanizing action to address perceived serious underperformance on Disability Hate Crime cases by criminal justice agencies. Both publications fit within the tradition of social movement research identified earlier (Best, 2009). They seemed concerned with activating the policy agenda and embedding the issue (Kingdon, 2011) and their significance was noted, in particular 'Getting Away with Murder' (Sherry, 2010).

An additional report, 'Another Assault' (Mind, 2007) outlined the results of a survey distributed to 5,100 people with mental health problems and another 1,100 to mental health workers. Surveys were completed by 304 people with mental health problems and 86 mental health support workers. Notwithstanding the low level of response, the surveys did portray 'a prevalence of abuse' (Giannasi, 2015). And, in the absence of 'official data', the report echoed what the disability community sector as saying. Interestingly, it was referenced in official publications on hate crime, including the Government's Hate Crime Action Plan (UK, HM Government HO, 2010).

The EHRC research report conducted by the Office for Public Management (OPM) on 'Disabled people's experiences of targeted violence and hostility' (EHRC, 2009) and the IPCC report (2011) into the contact between Fiona Pilkington and Leicestershire Constabulary 2004–07 appeared to be significant publications related to Disability Hate Crime.

The EHRC–OPM report was among the first substantial research studies on the issue of disability harassment and hate crime in Britain. Evidenced rigorously and nuanced, it highlights issues such as the 'clash of paradigms' in public policy and criminal justice responses to disability between protection and rights/justice. It queried the term 'hate crime' given the terms disabled people used in their research. Nonetheless, it highlighted a significant issue of targeted harassment and hostility and delineated the issue.

The 2011 IPCC report arose due to Fiona Pilkington's actions to kill her daughter, Frankie Hardwick, and to die by suicide herself due to the stress and anxiety regarding her daughter's future and ongoing anti-social behaviour and lack of agency response. The IPCC report does identify, acknowledge and profile the issue of Disability Hate Crime and how there was a failure to recognize the disability-based hostility in this family's experiences over a number of years. Giannasi (2015) points out that this case happened before disability had been included in the criminal justice system's common monitoring definition of hate crime. The police were less alert to a disability dimension than they should be now. The case was referred to as potentially a Stephen Lawrence moment for Disability Hate Crime. There was one stark difference: the report made no reference to institutional discrimination impacting disabled people. It did, however, highlight and emphasize vulnerability while also highlighting Disability Hate Crime. Thus it merited analysis whether this report, combined with the independent reports reviewed, could, cumulatively, have had a Lawrence-type effect.

Following the earlier OPM research and the deaths of Fiona Pilkington and Francesca Hardwick, the Equality and Human Rights Commission (EHRC) launched a formal inquiry into disability related harassment in 2009. The EHRC inquiry drew upon evidence from public sector agencies, community sector organizations, linked research and profiling of serious cases of targeted violence involving disabled people. It was the first time that such a formal statutory inquiry into disability related harassment including hate crime had been undertaken in any jurisdiction. This ensuing report, Hidden in Plain Sight: Inquiry into Disability Related Harassment (EHRC, 2011b), was hailed as a landmark report and again as a 'Stephen Lawrence moment' for Disability Hate Crime.

Conclusion

The remainder of this book explores the overall questions and the lines of exploration identified in this chapter through an in-depth case study approach involving key informant interviews, documentary analysis and analysis of individual cases. Mason-Bish (2009), as indicated in the Introduction, identified a clear gap in understanding the specifics for each hate crime strand in terms of hate crime policy development. This book aims to close that gap in respect of Disability Hate Crime. Indeed, more recently, Roulstone and Mason-Bish indicate that, notwithstanding the recent flurry of activity on Disability Hate Crime, 'it remains under-researched and an understanding is only in its infancy' (Roulstone and Mason-Bish, 2013, p 4). Having considered the range of publications in this area in depth, I explore in this book:

- How did the publication of a number of research reports, debates, inquiry reports and agenda-setting documents on disabled people's experiences contribute to the emergence and development of the Disability Hate Crime agenda?
- How (if at all) did disability community sector organizations and individuals avail of the opportunities created, first, by the legal duty on public bodies to promote equality and, second, by the disability aggravation legal provisions to campaign for policies and practices that focused on Disability Hate Crime?
- Did the criminal justice agencies prioritize Disability Hate Crime policy as a policy and practice concern in response to the Disability Equality Duty, the CJA 2003, and the activities of disabled people's organizations and individuals supported by available evidence?
- Did these activities merge (and how), leading to the criminal justice agencies opening a policy window and enabling an agenda to be set on Disability Hate Crime?
- How did the disability community sector and individuals then avail of the opening of this policy window, identify cases that fitted the 'new' crime category of Disability Hate Crime, identify criminal justice system shortcomings and secure an increased policy focus on this crime area?

4

Agenda Triggering

Key points

In the late 1990s and early 2000s, there was very little debate about the need to address Disability Hate Crime in England and Wales. Significant problematization and activism occurred to socially construct disability hostility as a problem worthy of political–policy attention. The introduction of new legislation addressing disability hostility is explored, noting the range of contributions to the securing of Section 146 of the Criminal Justice Act 2003, and particularly the critical political interventions by ministers and other politicians behind it. A strategic coupling occurred between activism and the political arenas enabled by policy entrepreneurs, who identified a policy window of opportunity in the form of the development of the 2003 Act, and successfully created a hate crime policy domain for Disability Hate Crime. In doing so, they homogenized Disability Hate Crime as simply another strand in the hate crime domain. Without significant problematization efforts by activists and critical interventions by some political actors, expansion of the hate crime policy domain to include disability hostility would not have occurred.

Introduction

An established view in hate crime studies is that this subject area is marked by the early influence of social movements and identity politics in policy making, particularly in the US context (Jacobs and Potter, 1998; Grattet and Jenness, 2001b). Grattet and Jenness argue that hate crime is best viewed as a policy domain that has been established, expanded and explored over time. Drawing on Burstein (1991), they used those concepts to explain the differential development of hate crime policies in the US. Grattet and Jenness (2001b) analyse the establishment of the first hate crime categories in the US (race, religion and ethnicity) and their expansion to include sexuality and disability, the latter process presented as relatively unproblematic.

In this chapter, I analyse the range of contributions in England and Wales to securing Section 146 of the Criminal Justice Act 2003, which addresses hostility in crime on the basis of disability or sexual orientation as an aggravating feature of the crime. I analyse these contributions through a consideration of the parts played by problematization, activism, politics and policy making in this earliest stage (Bacchi, 2009; Kingdon, 2011). While concurring with Mason-Bish (2009) that the expansion of the hate crime policy domain to include disability hostility appeared relatively unproblematic, this chapter shows that it was, in reality, quite problematic. Indeed, but for significant problematization efforts by activists and critical interventions by some political actors, expansion of the hate crime policy domain to include disability hostility would not have occurred. It was not simply a matter of a policy domain embracing and adding another to the list of protected characteristics (Grattet and Jenness, 2001a). This account significantly augments existing understanding on this issue.

Targeted harassment and hostility towards disabled people – some background

Available evidence points to targeted hostility and violence as one continuing thread in disabled people's experiences over time. The disproportionate experience of violence and targeted harassment has, however, been named and responded to (or not) in a wide variety of ways (Sobsey, 1994; Sherry, 2010; Quarmby, 2011). It has a varied genealogy as social problems and policy issues (Bacchi, 2009). It is only very recently that this targeted hostility, harassment and violence has begun to be problematized, constructed and considered as crime, and as hate crime in particular. Indeed, Disability Hate Crime is a peculiarly early 21st-century policy construct in response to centuries' old behaviour targeting disabled people.

Significant triggering role played by Values into Action NGO

Beginning in the mid-1990s, Values into Action (VIA), an NGO originally established to campaign for the closure of 'mental handicap' hospitals in England and Wales, highlighted the experience of what was then termed 'disability related bullying and harassment' faced by learning disabled people in transitioning from institutional to community living. In the words of an NGO expert involved at the time, VIA were concerned with "identifying the factors which make resettlement better for people and what were the factors holding it back" (R1).[1]

---

[1] R1 and so on is a notation to indicate a respondent number. See the Appendix for respondent profile information.

They observed that "the more we did that work, the more we started hearing stories, mainly from people with learning difficulties, about how they were frightened to do things because they got picked on and they got bullied. And the language we used … at the time was bullying" (R1). Furthermore, VIA found that criminal offences were being perpetrated against learning disabled people. However, they found a reluctance by criminal justice agencies to take such cases seriously or to even consider that such cases should be taken seriously. Such criminal acts were viewed as almost inevitable with limited expectation of any sanction. It was as if, with the increasing move from institutional to community living: "people with learning difficulties finally had been recognized as having the right to live in the community, but they still were not recognized as being equal before the law" (R1). This meant that in the move from institutional living to community living (increasing at that time), disabled people might be expected to add increased outdoor hostility to a known experience of indoor abuse, a phenomenon overlooked in academic and policy literature (Sunskiene, 2017). According to one disability activist: "Disability Hate Crime is now part of what disabled people experience as we struggle to inhabit the world" (R2).

This chapter considers how, as part of the disability movement's efforts in securing equality before the law for disabled people, hate crime emerged initially as a problem. It, however, emerged into a pre-existing hate crime domain with a pre-existing set of policy constructs, with the promise of criminal law protection.

Early activism and problematization

It is difficult to pinpoint a single moment when Disability Hate Crime first entered the policy domain in England and Wales. This study found that some policy related actors began to use the term and to construct the issue as hate crime at around the same time in 2001–02. I share Kingdon's view, that while specific origins may matter, ideas can come from anywhere and, indeed, numerous places. What matters in terms of policy emergence and change is that 'the key to understanding policy change is not where the idea comes from but what made it take hold and grow. It is critical that an idea starts somewhere, and that it becomes diffused in the community of people who deal with a given policy domain' (Kingdon, 2011, p 72). Based on analyses of numerous case studies, Kingdon argues that, in terms of policy emergence:

> a combination of sources is virtually always responsible … a combination of people is required to bring an idea to policy fruition and some policy actors bring to the process their political popularity,

others, their expertise. Some bring their pragmatic sense of the possible; others their ability to attract attention. (Kingdon, 2011, p 77)

The research underpinning this book indicated that a combination of sources has indeed contributed to the emergence of the Disability Hate Crime policy agenda. Of most significance is that it secured the sought-after problem representation as a legitimate policy agenda (Bacchi, 2009; Kingdon, 2011).

In the late 1990s and early 2000s, there was very little debate about the need to address Disability Hate Crime in England and Wales. In Mencap's 1999 study, 'Living in Fear', based on a survey of 900 learning disabled people, respondents revealed high levels of regular bullying, while making no reference to hate crime. The report did not elicit any significant response from criminal justice agencies or government more widely until four years later when an amendment to the Criminal Justice Act 2003, known as Section 146, was being considered. The Mencap study was then cited by activists, independent statutory bodies and politicians/ministers as evidence of the need to legislate to address Disability Hate Crime. In the intervening period, the issue of targeted harassment of disabled people had been, first, problematized as targeted crime based on disability hostility and, second, represented as a problem of Disability Hate Crime. To help secure policy agenda status, 'key indicators' of the problem were needed (Kingdon, 2011). The Mencap report was therefore drawn upon both by independent statutory bodies, such as the Disability Rights Commission in making the case for Disability Hate Crime, and by a Home Office minister for criminal justice tabling an amendment in the House of Lords providing for a form of recognition of Disability Hate Crime and LGB hate crime (Hansard HL, Deb 5 Nov 2003). Thus, a report that received limited attention on publication underwent a process of 'transformation' and legitimation that scholars indicate can occur in the policy making process. While data such as in the Mencap report does not speak for itself (Kingdon, 2011), its use and selected 'interpretations of the data transform them from statements of conditions to statements of policy problems' (Kingdon, 2011). Mencap's report secured a place in the 'evidence base' not because of depth of social science insight but because it 'chimed' with a wider trend around hate crime policy. This was to also occur with some other studies in subsequent years in the emergence and development of Disability Hate Crime policy and practice (Giannasi, 2015a).

A later report by the National Schizophrenia Fellowship in 2001, described significant harassment in the lives of 168 people experiencing mental health difficulties. Again, this report did not refer to hate crime and did not elicit any significant response from criminal justice agencies or government more widely upon publication. However, it was referenced in 2003 when the case was being made for the need to legislate for disability hostility. As with the Mencap report, it underwent a 'transformation' from a limited statement of conditions to an accepted and legitimized element in the evidence base for recognizing a policy problem (Bacchi, 2009; Kingdon, 2011). In this way, it was deployed to contribute to the problematization of targeted harassment of disabled people (Bacchi, 2009), and, in time, to the construction as Disability Hate Crime.

The problematization of targeted harassment and hostility experienced by disabled people as a crime problem and its representation as specifically a problem of hate crime, began to emerge in the late 1990s to early 2000s. It was articulated by a small number of activists, including some 'policy entrepreneurs' and NGOs. Parallel to this, there was a gradual coalescing around a shared focus problematizing targeted harassment and hostility towards disabled people as hate crime akin to other forms of hate crime. It is as if a form of concept diffusion was occurring and beginning to influence disability activism but was not named as such (Jones and Newburn, 2007; Bacchi, 2009). We now turn to looking at some of those actors driving this coalescence.

Values into Action NGO – first to use the language of Disability Hate Crime

Building on its earlier identification of targeted harassment and crimes as an issue in community transition, VIA produced policy research reports focused on equal access for disabled people to the criminal justice system. These included 'Just Gateways' (VIA, 2001) and 'Opening the Gateways' (VIA, 2002). The former considered the role of the police as a gateway (rather than gatekeepers) to justice for learning disabled people; the latter looked at violence targeted against learning disabled people. 'Opening the Gateways' (2002) is the first publication in England and Wales that this study identifies as using the term 'Disability Hate Crime'. A respondent involved with producing this report was clear about the rationale for framing disabled people's experiences as hate crime:

> 'The more we talked to people with learning difficulties and the more research we did on how this type of targeted violence was being dealt with in other areas such as racist crime, homophobic crime, it just became so obvious that the type of hostility and targeted violence disabled people were experiencing was the same as other types of hate crime. And, so, it became a natural thing to argue for and to advocate for. It was also connected to our general advocacy position which was dismantling the barriers to an ordinary life for people with learning difficulties specifically. And a key barrier to an ordinary life was this

constant daily harassment that they were experiencing and that could often escalate to violence and what was clearly hate crime ... it was saying, "If we have these types of laws to address and recognise racist crime, homophobic crime, religious crime, why not have a parity for disabled people?"' (R3)

This response illustrates well recognized arguments for the expansion of the hate crime domain, with the emphasis placed on the similarities between the experiences of disabled people and other hate crime victims, the call for parity of protection, and references to the daily occurrence of targeted harassment and how it constitutes a barrier to an ordinary life (Grattet and Jenness, 2001a). These were to become arguments marshalled by others in seeking a legal–policy response to Disability Hate Crime, including the newly established Disability Rights Commission. This was to the neglect somewhat of a focus on the differences in disabled people's experiences of hate crime. Emphasizing commonality with established hate crime strands was considered much more important to activists than acknowledging differences in this early phase when the overriding focus was on securing a home in the hate crime domain for Disability Hate Crime.

While 'Opening the Gateways' used the language of and called for hate crime legislation to address disabled people's experiences, there are no indications of a response to this report from government. It appears to have been used mainly at local level in seeking to have disability issues addressed in a then-developing agenda on Community Safety and Crime and Disorder Reduction (Nacro, 2002). It was also shared among an NGO alliance making the case for Disability Hate Crime recognition. When parliament was lobbied around Section 146 of the Criminal Justice Act 2003, this report too underwent a certain 'transformation'. Its messages 'chimed' with the direction of policy development and it formed part of the evidence base for legal change. It contributed both to the problematization of targeted harassment and hostility experienced by disabled people, and to its problem representation as hate crime (Bacchi, 2009).

Early role of South London NGO and activists

Other notable policy activists also framed disabled people's experiences as hate crime in the early 2000s. From 2001–02 onwards, in south London, a local disability action group began to articulate the experiences of disabled people in terms of harassment, hostility and hate crime. This occurred mainly through the campaigning activity of a key staff member. Both the action group and staff member were based close to the home borough of Stephen Lawrence and were acutely attuned to the agenda emerging from the Lawrence Inquiry, both in terms of hate crime and institutional discrimination. The staff member indicated that she borrowed from the Lawrence Inquiry agenda to read across to the disability experience because it resonated so much and it acted as her bedrock source to have disabled people's experience of harassment recognized (R37). This resonates with wider literature on later hate crime strands borrowing from more established strands and seeking to articulate similarities in experience (Grattet and Jenness, 2001a; Jenness and Broad, 2005). It also supports the finding of this study and earlier studies on the catalytic impact of the Lawrence Inquiry on all hate crime strands (Tyson, Giannasi and Hall, 2014; Giannasi, 2015; Tyson and Hall, 2015).

Policy entrepreneurialism

Another key activist driving the coalescence around Disability Hate Crime was a Campaigns Officer working with one of the national disability charities. He had previous experience working in the campaigns teams of several other national charities. He was also a Labour Party activist on disability equality and, latterly, a Labour councillor. He featured in interviews for the research underpinning this book as one of the first people to articulate disabled people's experience in terms of hate crime. As early as 2001–02, he was articulating, through his organization and with partner organizations, disabled people's experience of harassment within and the need for this to be addressed through hate crime legislation.

Numerous respondents spontaneously identified this Campaigns Officer as a 'policy entrepreneur' in enabling the emergence of Disability Hate Crime into the policy domain. Policy entrepreneurs are identified as occasionally playing a significant role in the emergence and development of policy agendas. They can do this by enabling coalitions of interests to form around a problem, to help identify policy solutions (that often already exist and which they know) and to occasionally enable a coupling to take place between activist and political-policy interests, facilitating a policy window to open and a new policy to emerge (Kingdon, 2011).

Indeed, this Campaigns Officer – and policy entrepreneur – carefully constructed the narrative of a case he 'discovered' in 2001 involving an attack on a disabled woman and her guide dog on a train. The woman with a visual impairment and her guide dog were confronted by a group of young people sitting opposite her. They set off firelighters in front of her dog and seriously disturbed both her and the dog. The young people sprayed the dog and the woman with the contents of a fire extinguisher, which appeared to escalate the dog's and the woman's distress.

The Campaigns Officer turned this 'signal case' (Kingdon, 2011) into an early compelling argument for the need for Disability Hate Crime legislation and the case was widely cited by many other activists. It was also recalled by other key research informants, including a senior cabinet minister of that time (R4; R5).

I consider this Campaigns Officer's contribution to securing legal provision to address Disability Hate Crime later in this chapter. Here, the focus is on acknowledging his very early problematization of targeted harassment of disabled people and his increasingly successful representation of the issue as a problem of hate crime (Bacchi, 2009). In this problematization and problem representation, he trod a well-established path in social movement policy activism, through his use of a particularly emotive signal case, his building of a coalition with LGB and other groups, and his strategic identification of a legislative 'window of opportunity' through the Criminal Justice Act 2003 to push for hate crime protection (Jenness and Broad, 1997; Best, 1999; Grattet and Jenness, 2001a; Bacchi, 2009; Kingdon, 2011).

Significant role of the new Disability Rights Commission

At broadly the same time, the recently established independent statutory Disability Rights Commission was embarking on its first legislative review. It had a power to undertake a review of the legislative landscape to identify issues of relevance to advancing disability equality. In its first legislative review, the Disability Rights Commission asked whether consultees felt the Disability Rights Commission should seek legislative provision to address disability hostility. Given its statutory role, the Commission's naming of aspects of disabled people's experience in terms of hostility was significant. In addition, given its responsibility for advancing disability equality, its action moved the issue of Disability Hate Crime closer to the legal-policy domain. Entering the legal-policy domain is a key moment in the construction of hate crime. The moment it becomes law is, in some respects, the moment it becomes real (Best, 1999; Grattet and Jenness, 2001a). The research underpinning this book found that the Disability Rights Commission's interventions from 2000 to 2007 were very influential in moving the Disability Hate Crime agenda forward. Its role has been under-recognized – and unacknowledged – to date in the academic literature. This influential role was recalled by key informant interviews and further evidenced through parliamentary references and other documentary evidence.

One then senior NGO disability charity manager highlighted the significance of the Disability Rights Commission including consultation on disability harassment and hostility in its first legislative review and how charities, such as that where the Campaigns Officer–policy entrepreneur worked, availed of the opportunity to articulate the need for Disability Hate Crime provision. Indeed, former Home Secretary of the time David Blunkett MP stated, when interviewed for the research underpinning this book, that the creation of the Disability Rights Commission brought a "focus which had not been there before to Disability Hate Crime for the first time". This study has found that the Disability Rights Commission brought a successful straddling of insider–outsider status to advancing the agenda of Disability Hate Crime. It was staffed by a mix of peoples, with backgrounds in senior roles in NGOs in the disability movement, other social movements and within government. It was as if a form of institutionalized expert activism and advocacy entered the statutory sector. The Disability Rights Commission was to play effective dual roles of activist and policy adviser, less hermetically sealed into separate streams than Kingdon's model might suggest. This study found that the role played by such insider–outsider actors in advancing equality agendas is not to be underestimated. It echoes findings of others such as Outshoorn's (2004) analysis of the contribution of the femocracy to advancing aspects of gender equality in The Netherlands. This book acknowledges the Disability Rights Commission's significant role in these early stages of issue emergence and later in agenda development.

Building momentum

Between 2002 and late 2003, the issue of the problematization of harassment and hostility experienced by disabled people began to gather pace. A series of activities and interventions developed mainly in the activism, the independent statutory and political domains. Some overlapped, some were discrete but, considered together, impacted the securing of Section 146 of the Criminal Justice Act 2003. Activity on this issue was still, at this relatively early stage, confined to the activist and political domains, with the policy domain largely dormant on the issue.

A loose coalition helps trigger the agenda

In 2002, a loose coalition of groups emerged. It included the Royal National Institute of Blind People (RNIB), Guide Dogs for the Blind, Mencap, Nacro, VIA, Disability Rights Commission and, at times, the lesbian, gay and bisexual (LGB, only much later LGBT) rights charity Stonewall. It met with the support of the social justice charity, National Association for the Care and Resettlement of Offenders (Nacro) and began to develop and articulate the case and lobby for extensions to hate crime legislation. As the literature indicates that hate crime social movements in other contexts have tended to do, this coalition focused on collating elements of an evidence base, particularly compelling cases of disability hostility (Jenness and Broad, 1997; Best, 1999; Grattet and Jenness, 2001a). The group also submitted briefings to parliament and met with parliamentarians (R3). Respondents in this study identified the Campaigns Officer identified earlier as the key person coordinating this loose coalition (R4).

This Campaigns Officer was also simultaneously working closely with the Disability Rights Commission and Stonewall in forging a time-limited strategic alliance that proved significant in securing Section 146 of the Criminal Justice Act 2003. As a policy entrepreneur, he was enabling and forging coalitions of interests, identifying a strategic parliamentary opportunity in the form of the Act. Over a period of 18 months, he was to advance the coupling of politicians' and activists' agendas through seeking an amendment to the Act, which became known as Section 146 (Kingdon, 2011).

Having identified disability hostility and harassment as a potential priority in its first legislative review, by mid-2002, the Disability Rights Commission had confirmed it. Mindful of the legislative 'window of opportunity' (Kingdon, 2011) offered by the Criminal Justice Bill, and encouraged and aided by the Campaigns Officer–policy entrepreneur, the Disability Rights Commission prepared for the Labour Party conference in early autumn 2002. They had identified an open forum question-and-answer session with the relevant Cabinet Minister and ministerial team, which was to focus on criminal justice reform and the developing Criminal Justice Act 2003. Based on a joint NGO–Disability Rights Commission briefing, a Disability Rights Commission officer asked the Home Secretary about the issue of disabled people being targeted on the basis of hostility as victims of crime. The example cited was the signal case of the attack on the visually impaired woman on the train with her guide dog. The questioner asked if the Home Office and Justice Ministers were aware of this form of crime and what were they going to do about it in the context of their reforming criminal justice legislation. A former senior Disability Rights Commission official stated:

> 'All the ministerial team were there. The question was kind of directed at the Home Secretary and he was the one who picked it up first. He sort of looked a bit perplexed really and said, "You know, what you have told me is a bit shocking and I wasn't aware of the scale of this but now that I am, obviously, it is an issue that I want to look at."' (R6)

The Disability Rights Commission and RNIB regarded this as an important first stage in prising open the policy window to get Disability Hate Crime through and onto the legislative agenda. This was to become a first window of opportunity for the Disability Hate Crime agenda (Kingdon, 2011). Following the Labour Party Conference, within a few days, the RNIB and Disability Rights Commission reminded the Home Secretary of what they had raised in relation to disability hostility and hate crime and provided further contextual information. They pointed to the opportunity offered through the reforming Criminal Justice Act 2003 and requested that the issue be addressed in the developing legislation (R6). The coupling of activist interests and politicians' priorities emphasized in the policy studies literature was beginning to occur. However, unlike some case studies analysed in the policy literature, the policy window in this case did not swing open for just a short time. Here, the policy window had to be prised open, and it remained ajar as opposed to fully open for a considerable time before the Disability Hate Crime policy fully emerged (Kingdon, 2011). It is as if the Disability Hate Crime agenda emerged in stages, rather than in the form of a single breakthrough window of opportunity as highlighted by Kingdon (2011).

David Blunkett MP and agenda triggering

The Home Secretary considered the Criminal Justice Act 2003 one of his own "proudest achievements" (R5). The context for him was one of criminal justice modernization and reform, and this was New Labour's "flagship criminal justice system reform legislation". He described why:

> 'It was becoming clear that hate crime in relation to disability was more identifiable and visible, perhaps on the back of the creation and expansion of the Disability Discrimination Act and the creation of the Disability Rights Commission. So there actually was a focus which had not been there before, and I think the creation of the Disability Rights Commission obviously was fundamental to that construction. But, also, because I think there had been a real, as opposed to perceived, increase in hate crime on people with, what is now called, learning difficulties.' (R5)

The range of contextual factors identified here are informative and instructive in understanding the emergence of Disability Hate Crime policy. There was not only a coupling of activism and political initiatives through possible inclusion of Disability Hate Crime in the reforming Criminal Justice Act 2003, but there was a particular coupling that was a good 'fit' with New Labour's blend of policy approaches. New Labour in the early 2000s was keen to be seen as 'tough on crime' and 'new' forms of crime, but it was also keen to be reforming on identity inequalities, including disability equality. Enacting Disability Hate Crime legal provision enabled New Labour to offer criminal law protection in this new civil rights era for disabled people. It was a coupling strategically played to by disability activists in the early 2000s. Indeed, it reflects an approach to policy advocacy on hate crime whereby 'advocates for hate crime laws were able to achieve considerable traction by framing their calls for law reform within popular "tough on crime" discourses of crime control' (Mason, 2015, p 59).

Referring to the specific raising of the issue of disability hostility – including the signal case of the woman and the guide dog attack – at the Labour Party Conference in 2002, David Blunkett MP, Home Secretary in 2003, stated:

> 'That is how politics should work. Politicians are neither full of all wisdom, nor should we expect them to be. What we should expect them to be is amenable and responsive to the genuine concerns of people who are closer to it, who are campaigning on behalf of or with or have experienced themselves a particular problem, in this case, an obvious one. And I was not aware of the scale of the issue and they did have it because you always need examples and they had.' (R5)

This comment is instructive in considering the respective roles played by activists and politicians in the earliest emergence of the Disability Hate Crime agenda. Even though it was the activists alongside the Disability Rights Commission that posed the initial question, without David Blunkett MP's willingness as Home Secretary to allow a coupling of activists' demands (for hate crime provisions) and his own political initiative (Criminal Justice Act 2003), Disability Hate Crime would not have emerged as and when it did in 2003.

The former Home Secretary recalls that coalescing factors were influential in his support for legislation to address Disability Hate Crime and also Homophobic Crime. These included issues related to parity across hate crime strands given that Section 145 of the Criminal Justice Act 2003 existed to enhance sentencing in areas of racial or religious aggravation.

> 'To begin with, people rightly said, "If we're going to deal with hate crime in respect of race or ethnicity or faith, then we ought to be having a comprehensive approach". And, quite rightly, organizations, whether they were Stonewall and others in relation to sexual orientation or organizations with, of and for people with disabilities said, "And what about this?"' (R5)

For him, legislating for Disability Hate Crime and Homophobic Crime was about: "Making sure [that] where there are inequalities, they're dealt with fairly and on the same basis ... you can see that this has a synergy, it fits in. A parity of protection and an overall approach which is fair" (R5).

His comments reflected the calls of the activists also interviewed. There was an emerging congruence of rationales for legislating on this issue, framed around parity of protection with other hate crime strands. These claims for parity of protection are identified in the hate crime literature as among the most common arguments articulated by equality movements making the case for hate crime domain expansion (Jenness and Broad, 1997; Mason-Bish, 2009; Grattet and Jenness, 2001a). Indeed, a theme in some hate crime literature is that once an equality issue has been legislated for as a protected characteristic in civil law on equality, it makes the pathway to hate crime criminal law protection easier though not inevitable (Grattet and Jenness, 2001a). In this context, disability equality had been prioritized by the New Labour government: one former senior manager at the Disability Rights Commission talked about New Labour's initiatives on disability equality heralding the start of "the civil rights era for disabled people in Britain" (R7).

Linked to this is the significant emphasis placed by the former Home Secretary on how Disability Hate Crime had a synergy with established hate crime strands. This book considers the issue of the nature, extent and challenges posed by the 'fit' of Disability Hate Crime in Chapters 6 and 7. Kingdon and others identify an issue as much more likely to be taken on as a policy issue by government if it can be shown to have a synergy, a feasibility and a values 'fit' with an already established policy approach (Kingdon, 2011). The then Home Secretary's emphasis on the perceived and accepted 'fit' echoes this significant theme in the public policy literature. In a sense, a solution already existed on the policy shelf called 'hate crime', and Disability Hate Crime was presented as fitting that existing policy solution. The extent to which this one-size-fits-all approach to hate crime was appropriate was to be challenged later with the further development of Disability Hate Crime policy. That fit and the early emphasis on commonality with existing hate crime strands is what the early activists argued successfully in relation to Disability Hate Crime and what politicians accepted. It can be argued that it led to an early neglect of legitimate differences between the strands of hate crime. This was to prove problematic in practice, as I describe in later chapters.

The then Home Secretary also identified challenges raised in defining as Disability Hate Crime, cases such as attacks on guide dogs or a disabled person's other aids, which were effectively hostile attacks on disabled people, and cases like the enslavement of disabled people, which he clearly viewed as fuelled by a disability hostility. He reflected that these varied and perhaps more complex manifestations of disability hostility highlighted the need to get the definition right. He reflected that having a legal test of hostility that reflected motivation and or demonstration of hostility was important in this context.

> 'The only thing that was in doubt was the definition. How do you get this right so that in practice, the prosecution can deal with it, the judiciary have a basis on which to deal with it, and the signals you send, which is why the enhanced penalty was so important at this point of sentencing.' (R5)

This senior cabinet minister held a broad view of what disability hostility is and the range of offending behaviour that should be covered by this legislative provision. As is evident in Chapter 5, it is questionable whether, over 20 years later, day-to-day institutionalization of the concept matches the broad ministerial vision of disability hostility held at its inception.

Activism gathers further pace

While some time was to elapse between the lobbying of the then Home Secretary by the Disability Rights Commission, RNIB, and Guide Dogs for the Blind and the introduction of a government amendment introducing Section 146, the loose coalition of activists and independent statutory sector did not lose time in the intervening period. The Disability Rights Commission, RNIB, Stonewall, VIA and others continued to build the evidence base and to lobby for Section 146. This focus on securing 'key indicators' of the problem is significant in many case studies in the literature on securing policy agenda status. Kingdon (2011) points out that what matters more is that the 'key indicators' are accepted by all as valid, and crucially by politicians and policy officials deciding on the issue, rather than on the evidential rigour of the key indicators. Senior politicians referenced in this book stated that they needed evidence to act; in their view, the evidence was provided by the loose coalition of activists and independent statutory sector (R5; R9).

A former senior Disability Rights Commission official who was also involved in preparing parliamentary briefings on the evidence base concluded that, to secure Section 146:

> 'There had to be evidence, so there was some pretty good evidence, and not just from one organization. There was enough strong evidence of the problem and that something needed to be done and without that, obviously, forget it. ... But there was a kind of base, an evidence base obviously.' (R6)

It is clear that both the Disability Rights Commission and NGOs involved, including Stonewall, were aware that the available evidence was limited and that they were, in a sense, playing an 'evidence game' as part of constructing the policy problems of Disability Hate Crime and Homophobic Hate Crime. Reflecting recognized themes in the policy making literature, they were alert to two issues. They were acutely aware that one of the rules of the policy game was having acceptable evidence to move this policy agenda forward, so they played their limited evidence base to best effect. They were also acutely aware that robustness and rigour mattered less than resonance and acceptability of evidence to politicians–policymakers (Kingdon, 2011). In the absence of sufficiently robust data, they occasionally resorted to profiling shocking–emotive cases, a well-established social movement tactic to gain a response. This was a tactic deployed many times by the Disability Hate Crime movement over the coming years (R14). Later in this chapter, we see how activists' playing of the evidence game and construction of the evidence base was largely accepted by politicians when it suited politicians own policy priorities (Kingdon, 2011).

A time-limited strategic alliance

Another key element in the efforts to secure Section 146, as evidenced in this study, was a time-limited strategic parliamentary alliance forged between disability groups, the Disability Rights Commission and Stonewall. This was a strategic alliance formed within the wider coalition seeking change. Central to forging this alliance was another coupling strategy deployed by the Campaigns Officer mentioned earlier (Kingdon, 2011). Disability groups, the Disability Rights Commission and LGB groups were campaigning to secure hate crime legal provisions on the respective grounds of disability and sexual orientation. The Campaigns Officer queried whether they should continue to campaign separately or seek to 'travel together' through parliament (R4). It was decided, with the active encouragement of the Campaigns Officer, that they should seek to 'travel together', particularly through the House of Lords. A former senior staff member at an LGB NGO said:

> 'Stonewall was a very opportunistic organization in trying to sort of do legislative change. This opportunity came up and, from Stonewall's perspective, making sure that disability and sexual orientation travelled together was a way of trying to get that through because, in disability terms, the Conservatives were actually quite pro-disability. I think, before this parliament, the only piece of equalities legislation that the Tories had ever introduced was a Disability Discrimination Act, which I think was in 1995. So, all the race stuff and everything else had always been done under Labour. So, from Stonewall's perspective, the strategy of "let's get sexual orientation and disability together so they can't be separated, they've got to travel together" was a way of trying to ensure that the sexual orientation bits went through. ... It was opportunistic travelling together.' (R4)

However, there were also advantages, attractions and affinities for the disability organizations involved to 'travelling together' with the LGB lobby for Section 146. There was recognition that Stonewall were adept at parliamentary lobbying but, in the early 2000s, getting legislation through the House of Lords on LGB equality was 'tricky'. On the contrary, disability issues found a more favourable airing in the House of Lords and across political parties, including the Conservative Party. A former senior official at the Disability Rights Commission reflected: "Once a bill was in the Lords that was easier for us because that's where all our great people are. We have got fantastic people there. We have advocates in the Commons as well but the House of Lords was just playtime central, it was fantastic" (R6). The same former senior staff member at an LGB NGO summed this up as: "So that's the quid pro quo then, isn't it? We'll join together so sexual orientation won't get dumped out, but actually we'll make sure that Stonewall does the kind of parliamentary lobbying. That made a lot of sense. And I think that was successful" (R4). This strategic alliance was not solely opportunistic. There was also a shared sense of affinity evident in interviews with activists from both disability and LGB sectors. This seemed to spring in part from both being 'newer' equality strands (R4; R6).

The time-limited strategic and opportunistic nature of this alliance was brought home in this study through the dissolution of the alliance once Section 146 was secured.

Increasing focus on the political stream

During its existence, this strategic alliance between disability and LGB organizations increasingly turned its attention to parliament and to developments in the political stream, in particular, the development of and opportunities offered by the Criminal Justice Act 2003. The interaction between the various sets of actors and activities, not least the direct intervention of politicians themselves, also contributed to this legislative activity.

Policies vary in the extent to which they involve significant political intervention and the extent to which policy activity takes place at official levels. The research underpinning this book found, and a key respondent noted, that the hate crime policy domain in Britain is marked by a relatively low level of political intervention and significant involvement at the level of policy officials within criminal justice agencies (R8). This study has found that there are limited but critical interventions by politicians at key policy-defining moments in the hate crime domain, particularly in the framing of overall policy direction. The development of policy detail and ongoing policy development and institutionalization is overwhelmingly driven by policy officials in interaction with activists. Without strategic interventions by politicians at cabinet, other ministers and members of the House of Lords, Disability Hate Crime would not have entered the policy domain when and as it did.

All the campaigning-related activities described were designed to influence an amendment to the Criminal Justice Act 2003 as it went through its later stages in parliament. The outcomes of these activities were reflected in briefings to and meetings between campaigning interests and parliamentarians. As well as linking directly with government ministers, the campaigning groups also linked with a range of peers (members of the House of Lords) across political parties. Two particularly active peers in support of such an amendment were Lord Navnit Dholakia (Liberal Democrat) and Lord Waheed Alli (Labour). Lord Dholakia was already associated with social liberal causes and was a former senior staff member at the then Commission for Racial Equality from 1976. He had been instrumental in the first consideration of racial harassment and violence nationally. Lord Dholakia was supportive of the Disability Rights Commission's work and regularly raised disability issues in the House of Lords, including on issues of policing, anti-social behaviour, and citizenship and highlighting the issue of 'vulnerability'. Lord Alli was strongly identified with the LGB equality agenda, having become the first openly gay member of the House of Lords in 1998, and was close to Stonewall. Both peers, although from different parties, were close and, more pertinently, were close to Minister Baroness Scotland QC, who led on the Criminal Justice Act 2003 in the House of Lords (R9; R4).

In the second half of 2003, while the Act was going through the Lords, Lord Dholakia, supported by Liberal Democrat colleagues, indicated his intention to propose an amendment to the Act, which would introduce sentencing enhancement for crimes aggravated by hostility on the basis of disability or sexual orientation. It would also, interestingly, provide for mandatory monitoring of the implementation of these provisions by the police and the reporting of same. In a House of Lords address, he drew upon and expressly commended the briefing and evidence base provided by the Disability Rights Commission (Hansard HL, Deb 5 Nov 2003). During that same debate, Baroness Scotland introduced a government amendment known as Section 146 providing for sentencing enhancement in cases where hostility on the grounds of disability or sexual orientation was a factor in crime. In introducing Section 146, she indicated the government was 'guided by the evidence' in relation to targeted crimes experienced by disabled people and gay people, and referred to some of the evidence collated and placed in the policy arena by Disability Rights Commission, Stonewall and other groups (Hansard HL, Deb 5 Nov 2003). However, she rejected Lord Dholakia's specific calls for statutory monitoring and reporting on the implementation of such legal provisions. Instead, she indicated that the government would ask the then ACPO to address the issue of implementation monitoring through its guidance to and links with local police forces. In subsequent years, this monitoring activity was to develop into the first and subsequent ACPO Hate Crime Manuals (ACPO, 2005, 2010) and ultimately was reflected in the criminal justice system's adoption of a common definition of monitored hate crime in 2007.

What were the political factors and interventions influencing the government's introduction of the Section 146 amendment? Alongside and partly overlapping with the strategic alliance lobbying activity of the Disability Rights Commission and Stonewall and the wider coalition, VIA undertook specific work with parliamentarians based on their research. Following the publication of 'Opening the Gateways' in 2002, VIA staff contacted a Liberal Democrat MP and met with a Liberal Democrat Party adviser to discuss the issues raised by their recent report and, in particular, their recommendation that Disability Hate Crime be legislated for. The adviser undertook to review the report and suggested that the Liberal Democrats would consider this in terms of their House of Lords' contribution. Subsequently, Lord Colville spoke in the Lords in favour of Section 146 to say that, as all these other grounds were included, it made no sense not to include disability (Hansard [HL], 5 Nov 2003).

Clearly, there was some time gap between the raising of the issue by the Disability Rights Commission and RNIB with Home Secretary David Blunkett MP and ministerial colleagues at the Labour Party Conference in 2002 and the introduction of the government's amendment in November 2003. This did not surprise a former senior official at the Disability Rights Commission:

'There would have been a bit of a gap because there would have been a bit of toing and froing … and it would have been during the passage of the bill, when the bill had already been going through because that's when there's a sort of onus to act, you know.' (R6)

The former senior Disability Rights Commission official recalls being contacted by the Ministerial Bill Team who requested a meeting to discuss a potential amendment to the Criminal Justice Act 2003. It was under instruction from the Home Secretary:

'They said very specifically to me, very very clearly, "The Minister, he said this comes from Secretary of State, this has to be done, go off and do it", and you know, so they were under marching orders … it was basically very clear in the meeting. They said, "Secretary of State has told us to do something about this and the Bill is going through so we're going to do it. We're going to do something." And I was like, "Ok." So, we just talked through what it is we wanted. So, I just relayed the party line as it were, talked around it a bit so they kind of understood it a bit.' (R6)

However, the drafting of Section 146 was not to prove so simple. In the weeks after this meeting, there was interaction between the Ministerial Bill Team and the Disability Rights Commission on possible draft wording for an amendment to address disability hostility. Not without significance, the initial draft produced by the Bill Team focused on targeting disabled people on the basis of vulnerability rather than hostility. This was of serious concern to the Disability Rights Commission. The former senior official at the Disability Rights Commission involved recalled:

> 'I remember receiving their draft wording and thinking, "You've got the wrong end of the stick" … It was obvious to me that they were going down the sort of route of people being targeted because they were vulnerable … so I remember typing back saying, "No specifically, this should be about somebody being targeted because of their disability. It's because of hatred, prejudice, all the rest of it, hostility." So, I remember that, thinking, "Thank God they didn't just stick that down because otherwise we'd have had to brief against it" and I told them that. I said, "If you put that down, that's not what we're having."' (R6)

A focus on vulnerability targeting in seeking to frame Disability Hate Crime would have undermined the entire policy agenda at the outset. The activists and Disability Rights Commission wanted the law to recognize that disabled people were targeted based on hostility towards disabled people, not based on vulnerability. To frame the Disability Hate Crime provision as based on vulnerability would have situated disability at odds with other hate crime strands. It would have prevented parity of consideration and parity of protection.

She went on to say that this potential focus on vulnerability posed the single biggest risk to securing Disability Hate Crime legal provision. And for the Disability Rights Commission:

> 'for any proper disability activist, the whole vulnerability sort of strand of argument … that would not have been helpful, that was a risk. Actually, that was the biggest risk, that they got the wrong end of the stick and refused to let go of the sodding stick and then we ended up having to brief against something. So that would have been a big risk, but it was averted and that didn't happen. The wording averted it, otherwise that would have been a horrible mess to sort out.' (R6)

It is as if a policy conception of disability as equating with vulnerability was already prevalent in 2003, if not embedded as a default policy position, at least for policy officials. The competing problem representations of disability targeting as an issue of vulnerability targeting rather than hostility targeting was present for policy officials from the outset. However, the activist stream was momentarily in the ascendancy alongside the political stream. In this context, the activists and Disability Rights Commission successfully secured a policy silence of the issue of vulnerability. A sufficient albeit temporary problematization as hate crime prevailed to get Section 146 on the statute books. This was to prove a passing policy silence. Vulnerability loomed large if silent in the construction of Disability Hate Crime from the outset and was to prove problematic in achieving institutionalization in the years that followed (Bacchi, 1999, 2009). In fact, a focus on vulnerability was to constitute a unique challenge to effective settlement of the Disability Hate Crime agenda, given that it reflected a competing problematization of the issue of targeted hostility and was linked to a different set of policy and service responses.

It is very interesting that, notwithstanding the clear focus on hostility in what emerged as Section 146 with no mention of vulnerability, in the years since its enactment, the issue of vulnerability continued to feature and a persistent pull towards vulnerability continued to 'cloud the issue of disability hostility' (Macdonald, 2008). This book considers this unique challenge in Chapter 8.

Reviewing the securing of Section 146, the former senior official at the Disability Rights Commission felt that the political intervention by the Home Secretary was key:

> 'He cared a lot about the work we were doing because obviously he got it ... we were obviously incredibly lucky that we had him in government. I don't remember another time where he'd used his position in that way. ... I think he thought, "Oh hang on, I can make this happen, there's an issue here". And he did.' (R6)

And the activists and key organizations also made it happen, with their evidence base, time-limited strategic alliance and parliamentary lobbying. It seems that at this early stage in the emergence of Disability Hate Crime policy, the key contributions were made by activists and politicians. Policy officials did play a role, complying with instructions from politicians informed by activists' concerns. This contrasts with subsequent stages of this policy agenda's development when policy officials assumed a more significant role and politicians less of a role. This is not unexpected (Kingdon, 2011). It is also striking that, following the securing of Section 146 in late 2003, the loose coalition that played a role in securing the provision seemed to dissipate. There followed a time lapse between securing legal provision and the policy domain becoming active. Other policy actors were to emerge in the intervening years, with some of the same contributors as the earlier phase but many different policy actors also involved. Notably, the Disability Rights Commission continued to play a significant role in subsequent stages of policy development and implementation.

Conclusion

In this earliest stage of the emergence of Disability Hate Crime policy into the criminal justice system in England and Wales in 2003, significant problematization and activism occurred that helped to construct disability hostility as a problem worthy of political and policy attention from the late 1990s to early 2000s onwards. It is also clear that critical political interventions by ministers and other politicians occurred without which no legal provision to address Disability Hate Crime would have been enacted as and when it was in the early 2000s. It is furthermore clear that a strategic coupling occurred between activism and the political arenas enabled by policy entrepreneurs. These policy entrepreneurs identified a policy window of opportunity in the form of the development of the Criminal Justice Act 2003 and successfully pushed on that window to secure entry into the hate crime policy domain for Disability Hate Crime. In doing so, they homogenized Disability Hate Crime as simply another strand in the hate crime domain. They successfully problematized the issue, identified an existing solution, and politicians bought its 'fit' with the established hate crime domain. In doing so, they emphasized its commonalities (to the neglect of its specificities) with existing hate crime strands. They also argued for parity of protection. It can be argued that activists may have overstated the commonalities and understated the specific features of Disability Hate Crime. They did this to secure their overarching aim of a home in hate crime for disability hostility. Politicians took their arguments on board and the Act had the appeal of a ready-made solution with the minimum of policy disruption for politicians and policy officials, a recognized feature in the literature on securing policy adoption (Kingdon, 2011).

In successfully securing the emergence of Disability Hate Crime via an amendment to the Criminal Justice Act 2003, activists and the Disability Rights Commission engaged in a series of understandable policy compromises and policy silences that were to prove challenging in subsequent stages of policy development and implementation. A former criminal justice system leader interviewed in this study reflected that, in a sense, when taking Disability Hate Crime into the hate crime legal provisions, no one stood back and questioned whether the same approach as existed for established hate crime strands should apply, and whether there were differences in disabled victims' experiences of targeted hostility that may require a differentiated legal approach to best respond to disability hostility (R19).

Linked to this, activists and politicians settled for a sentencing uplift provision in a domain previously marked by specific aggravated offences in the areas of racist and religious crimes. In doing so, it can be argued that, contrary to the rhetoric of parity of protection, a disparity in protections became institutionalized in the criminal justice system in 2003. This too has proven problematic in subsequent years (see Chapter 5). Key activists together with Disability Rights Commission staff involved were fully aware of this compromise. They were also aware that they pursued what was feasible and what they thought would work.

A former senior official at the Disability Rights Commission recollected: "We went for what we could get then, to get it on the map in a meaningful way ... you know you can do all the kind of hard work later, because obviously the legislative thing, you got it there" (R6).

It is interesting that these enacted legal protections for the Disability Hate Crime strand were to prove challenging in the years that followed and led to an initial Law Commission review in 2013 on potential extension of aggravated offences on hate crime, and form part of a further comprehensive Law Commission Review of Hate Crime Law underway in 2020–21 and still ongoing at the time of writing (Law Commission 2013; 2021).

Policy silences (as mentioned earlier) were also evident in this earliest stage of Disability Hate Crime policy emergence. As evidenced in subsequent chapters, this was to prove a very temporary policy silence and the competing problematization and problem representation of disabled people's experience as one of vulnerable people was lurking just around the corner (Bacchi, 1999, 2009).

Through a blend of successful problematization, activism and successful coupling with political–policy priorities, Disability Hate Crime emerged into the legal policy domain in late 2003. However, the Criminal Justice Act 2003 was not to be enacted for another two years, until 2005, and the policy domain was not to become more fully active until 2006–07. Reflecting on this emergence of Disability Hate Crime into the policy domain in 2003, I draw on Kingdon (2011) who talks of such a key moment as 'agenda setting', that critical moment when an issue secures its substantive place on the government's policy agenda. However, considering what occurred for Disability Hate Crime in 2003 and the silence that followed, I hesitate to describe it as agenda setting. I tend to view the enactment of Section 146 as about agenda triggering rather than agenda setting, a view shared by key informants interviewed as part of the research for this book.

The agenda was triggered in that Disability Hate Crime was formally on the statute book. It was now a legal fact. A policy agenda was not yet set in terms of how it would be defined, recognized and responded to within the criminal justice system for policing and prosecution purposes. Agenda setting for Disability Hate Crime was to take further significant activation over the next four years in the policy and activist streams. In conclusion, I present this first phase in the emergence of Disability Hate Crime policy diagrammatically as follows (see Figure 4.1). This is an adaptation of Kingdon and Bacchi's analytical frameworks, constituting

AGENDA TRIGGERING

Figure 4.1: Diagram of Phase 1 developments

Phase 1: Agenda triggering

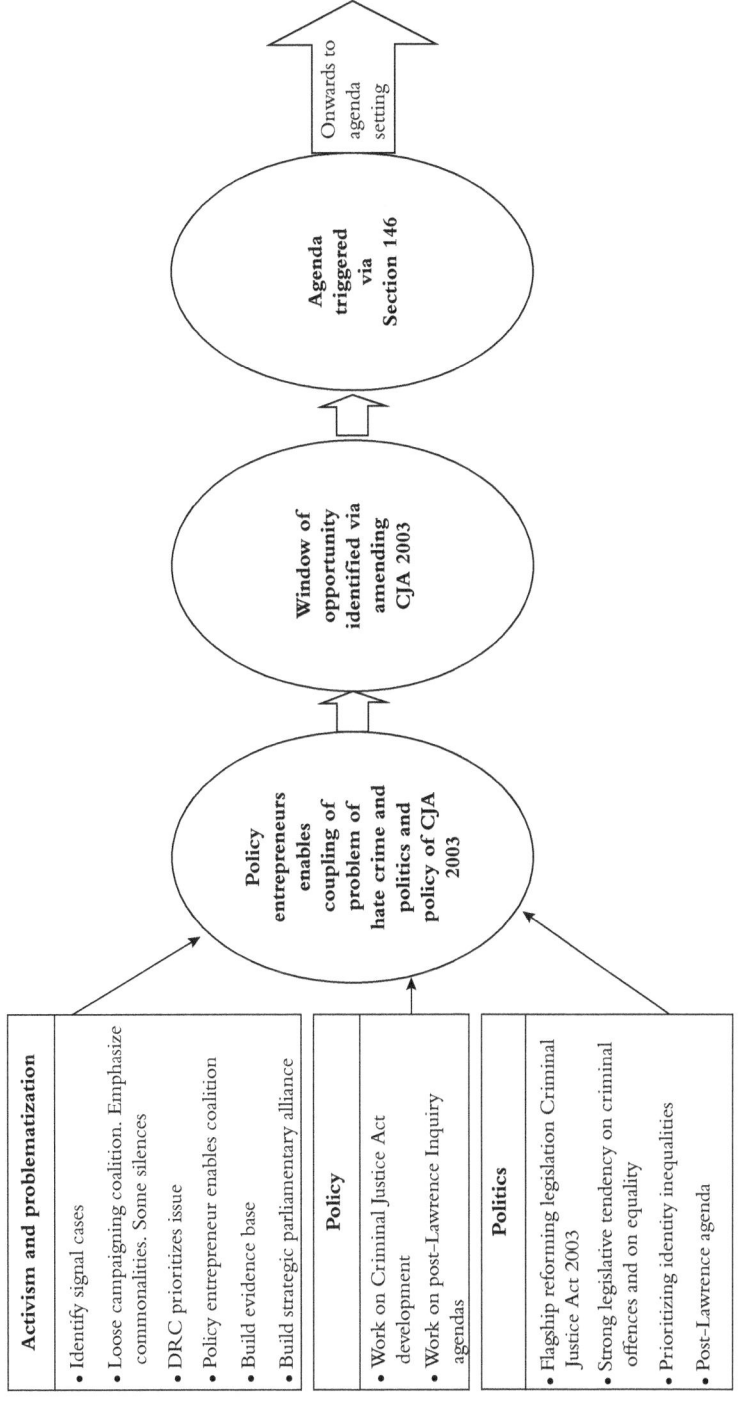

agenda triggering rather than full-scale agenda setting, which was yet to follow. Furthermore, this was a policy issue where the first set of activists who secured the legal provision largely dissolved post-2003, and a second wave of activists and policy officials with some continuity were to become active later in 2005–06 onwards. Given the time lapse between legislating on the issue and fuller activation of the policy domain, it raised a question as to whether Disability Hate Crime was an issue before its time in 2003 and, then four years later, in 2007 an issue whose time had come. The next chapter addresses this question and, in particular, the development of Disability Hate Crime policy in the years post-2003 through the activation of the policy domain beyond legal enactment.

5

Agenda Development

Key points

This chapter analyses the policy journey of Disability Hate Crime from agenda triggering to substantive agenda setting. The arrival of Section 146 on the statute books by the end of 2003 has been regarded as the birth of the Disability Hate Crime policy agenda. Section 146 was not enacted until 2005, however, and in the meantime, Disability Hate Crime came to be a way of conceiving of targeted victimization of disabled people that was in advance of the prevalent view of hate crime in 2003. Sharply awake to equality agendas after the Lawrence Inquiry, the criminal justice system was receptive to the new policy agenda. The arrival of the Disability Equality Duty applying to the public sector from 2004 shaped the 'discovery' of Disability Hate Crime by the criminal justice system. The Pilkington case opened a policy window of opportunity. In contrast to the agenda triggering phase where politicians determined the direction of travel, in Phase 2, policy officials take the lead and the policy agenda became set.

Introduction

While a Disability Hate Crime agenda was triggered with the inclusion of Section 146 of the Criminal Justice Act 2003 to address hostility aggravation, it took significant further policy activity, activism and problematization to move from agenda triggering to agenda setting. This chapter aims to analyse the development of Disability Hate Crime policy and practice beyond the issue's first emergence. The focus is on analysing the policy journey from agenda triggering to substantive agenda setting. The chapter aims to do this by tracing and analysing the contributory factors and challenges in the setting of a policy agenda on Disability Hate Crime.

The arrival of Section 146 on the statute books by the end of 2003 has been regarded as the birth of the Disability Hate Crime policy agenda (Mason-Bish, 2009). Although an essential moment, it was simply a milestone on the journey to a Disability Hate Crime policy agenda. Although legislated for in 2003, Section 146 was not enacted until 2005, and a substantive policy agenda, this chapter evidences, only began to develop from 2004–08 and beyond. Chapter 4 concluded with a query as to the significance of this time lapse. Was Disability Hate Crime an issue before its time in policy terms in 2003? Had its policy time come in 2007, when significant evidence of policy development was available? The evidence indicates that Disability Hate Crime was a way of conceiving of targeted victimization of disabled people that was in advance of the prevalent view of hate crime in 2003 and an issue whose embrace into the policy domain was to come in 2007.

This chapter critically traces the increasing social construction of Disability Hate Crime policy and practice in 2003–10 and beyond. The issue began to be constructed as a problem requiring a legislative response in the period 2000 to 2003. It required significant further construction to secure substantive policy agenda status, which was to occur some years later (Best, 1999; Bacchi, 2009). Revisiting Kingdon's policy streams approach (2011), the evidence in this book now indicates how Disability Hate Crime shifted to the policy stream while also remaining in the activist–problematization stream. In contrast to phase 1 on agenda triggering, less activity occurs in Phase 2 in the politics stream, albeit not absent at strategic moments.

Working in the glow and shadow of the Lawrence Inquiry

The report of the Stephen Lawrence Inquiry (1999), with its findings of institutional racism, had a catalytic impact on the development of wider equality policy and practices in the public sector, as well as a specific impact on the development of the hate crime agenda in the criminal justice system. This study's findings are consistent with others in this area (Hall, 2013; Giannasi, 2015; Tyson and Hall, 2015). In 2003, public sector organizations in the criminal justice system responded to the then recent Race Equality Duty and started to put race equality schemes in place. Alongside this, the criminal justice system had developed policy on racist and religious crimes (CPS, 2002). There were now tangible criminal justice system policy products and minority community offerings demonstrating what was possible at least in respect of one protected characteristic, race. This did not go unnoticed by activists and policy officials involved, and as one national disability activist commented: "The Stephen Lawrence Inquiry … gave a framework which we could overlay across other equality strands" (R10). And disability activists were able: "to turn themes from the Lawrence Inquiry from institutional racism into institutional discrimination; from racist crime into hate crime, and in time into Disability Hate Crime" (R10). This resonates with existing literature on the influence of the earliest equality strands on those that come later (Grattet and Jenness, 2001a) and on policy transfer and diffusion (Jones and Newburn, 2007). Senior criminal justice system officials, both in policing and the prosecution services, shared these views of the catalytic impact of the Lawrence Inquiry, although expressed differently. A senior manager at the London Metropolitan Police said:

> 'I don't recall, prior to the Stephen Lawrence Inquiry, much interest at all in this area (equality and hate crime). ... The Stephen Lawrence Inquiry report utterly changed how we act in the police force, so it was a pivotal moment. And obviously, it started off with the recommendations. ... Initially it was on the basis of race ... and introducing processes and procedures to make sure that we would not mess up, for want of a better expression, as badly again. ... Then it started to move into wider areas and ... there was a recognition ... that there are other people who are underrepresented and who may be vulnerable. I remember it very quickly moved into LGBT policies and then it started to migrate into, "We need this approach for other groups, including disability".' (R11)

This is a recognized theme in the literature on the impact of the Lawrence Inquiry on equality and hate crime policy making (Hall, 2013; Giannasi, 2015).

A striking feature in analysing the language used by respondents when referring to the Lawrence Inquiry impact on equality and hate crime policy making was the use of phrases such as 'opening up space', 'opening doors', 'seizing opportunities'. This resonated with Kingdon's emphasis on opening windows of opportunity through which new policies may emerge (Kingdon, 2011). Some respondents linked the catalytic impact of the Lawrence Inquiry to wider societal developments at the time, enabling a coalescing of issues such as the Lawrence equality agenda and other equality agendas together with the 'tough on crime' agenda.

> 'You had a pretty strong disability rights movement (in the late Nineties) which was well established and pushing on all fronts, in fact, you had a flowering of a kind of new civil rights movement ... from the late Nineties. I think because you had New Labour and you had a kind of relatively progressive regime on civil rights, except on terrorism ... you had this space for things to happen, which meant that ... there were reforms happening in lots of areas. So, you had relatively reformist Home Secretaries who were willing to do things, at the same time as control other things.' (R12)

A top tier civil servant with responsibilities on hate crime policy said of the Lawrence Inquiry's influence on the equality and hate crime agendas:

> 'We had the seminal moment in the criminal justice system which was about Lawrence … about race for obvious reasons. … What then took place is that a number of other strands of equalities, and the people who champion their causes, came forward and said, "You know, we experience those very same things and we need to be heard too …". That seminal moment brought about a step change for race, and then other people were saying, "But we mustn't be forgotten".' (R13)

He added that the Lawrence inquiry and its aftermath: "created the language … this idea of rights, which was not a language we'd used before" (R13). However, he cautioned that this language and framework of equality did not deliver for all equality strands, in particular disability, what might have been expected:

> 'This was the view … you send one equality and right (race) through the door and the rest get pulled along on the coattails, and that wasn't true. It did it for religion, I think, and belatedly it started to do it for LGBT equality. It hasn't done it yet for disability, and that's what we need to do.' (R13)

This vividly articulates Grattet and Jenness' identification of a journey from core protected statuses in hate crime to a second tier of protected statuses (Grattet and Jenness, 2001a). The analysis now turns to this issue of disability journeying through the hate crime policy window.

How the policy stream further activates the development of Disability Hate Crime policy

A central issue highlighted by the Lawrence Inquiry was the challenge of institutional racism potentially facing Britain's public sector. In accepting the inquiry recommendations, the government undertook to legislate to place a duty on public bodies to promote race equality and plan racism out of these institutions. This Race Equality Duty took effect across 42,000 public bodies in Britain in 2002. Notwithstanding critiques of the equality duties approach (McLaughlin, 2007; McVeigh, 2017), in particular how a systemic challenge became redefined as a bureaucratized response in terms of equality schemes, the research underpinning this book has found that these duties marked a seminal moment in policy development on equality and hate crime. As a senior independent research respondent commented:

'The Stephen Lawrence Inquiry led to the first public sector equality duty, the Race Equality Duty, and then the Disability Equality Duty came after that, shortly followed by the Gender Equality Duty and now, of course, we have the Single Equality Duty. So, in a sense, the Stephen Lawrence Inquiry was a scene setter and complete watershed moment. … The state now had a role in terms of moving away from that passive reactive model of just trying to manage and deal with an event after it has happened, to moving to a more proactive approach of promoting and raising equality and requiring public bodies, including the criminal justice organizations, to start adopting that more proactive approach.' (R14)

Discovering the solution and problem

Scholars have noted the significance of the enactment of legal provisions to address equality and hate crime as a key stage in the development of the equality agenda (McLaughlin, 2007) and the hate crime agenda (Best, 1999). Legislation marks a key stage in the 'institutionalisation' of hate crime with 'laws on the books and bureaucrats keeping records' and these issues transition to become 'the objects of social policy' (Best, 1999, p 63). Mason-Bish (2009) notes that the specific impact of equality anti-discrimination legal provisions on the establishment of hate crime policy and practice in Britain was a research gap that merited consideration. This book addresses this gap and considers these equality law impacts in this first academic analysis of the influence of the Disability Equality Duty on Disability Hate Crime policy.

Considering the influence of the Disability Equality Duty

The Disability Equality Duty came into effect in 2004 and required public sector bodies to advance disability equality. Public organizations had to involve disabled people in identifying the priority areas that their organization should focus on. They were also required to proactively work to eliminate disability harassment as it related to their functions. Public organizations were required to set out their planned response in a Disability Equality Scheme or a Single Equality Scheme – a plan for advancing equality over a three-year period.

The context in which the duty emerged into the criminal justice system is significant. The criminal justice system had been subject to significant criticism in the Lawrence Inquiry, with the Race Equality Duty and racist crime initiatives following in its aftermath. Issues of equality and diversity rose significantly up the policy agendas of criminal justice system agencies in the early 2000s (Giannasi, 2015; R11).

A strategic focus on issues of equality and diversity emerged in the criminal justice system. Thus, the organizational climate was amenable to responding to equality and diversity issues (McLaughlin, 2007; Ollearanshaw, Schneider, Jackson and Iqbal, 2003). Respondents in the research underpinning this book were often critical of the wider public-sector response to the Disability Equality Duty but singled out the positive response of parts of the police and the prosecution service. A former senior manager at the DRC commented: "I think the Disability Equality Duty played a positive role in organizations like the Crown Prosecution Service and the police and others in their thinking about equality and hate crime" (R7). However, he was less positive about its impact in the wider public sectors: "The big opportunity that was there with the duty to address disability related harassment more widely in the public sector … is one that was never really taken up" (R7).

The influence of the Disability Equality Duty

The Disability Equality Duty's requirement for criminal justice system agencies to involve disabled people in identifying their priorities for disability equality led to unprecedented levels of engagement between the criminal justice system and disabled people. This led to the 'discovery' of Disability Hate Crime as a shared priority between disability activists and policy officials charged with framing organizational responses to the Disability Equality Duty.

Criminal justice system respondents highlighted the Disability Equality Duty as the single most significant contributory factor to the development of the Disability Hate Crime agenda in the hate crime domain. They identified the Disability Equality Duty as moving the Disability Hate Crime agenda from inactive statute book provision to an active policy agenda.

A policy official involved on Disability Hate Crime policy recalled paying attention in a meaningful way for the first time:

> 'When the duty (Disability Equality Duty) came into force, that gave the system some levers to actually develop and then implement a policy around Disability Hate Crime. My sense is that Disability Hate Crime wasn't really recognized as a hate crime before the Disability Equality duty came into force.' (R16)

One criminal justice system policy official with recent involvement on hate crime policy felt that the Disability Equality Duty was central to criminal justice system agencies prioritizing Disability Hate Crime as a policy agenda:

> 'There's the establishment of the Disability Equality Duty and the DRC because, as you'll appreciate, public sector institutions will take that

statutory framework very seriously … it was not an item that could be ducked once it was on that statutory agenda, once that framework had been set. That was a key contributory factor … because that sort of set the thing in motion. It gave the framework.' (R17)

Respondents emphasized that with the Disability Equality Duty a space had to be created where criminal justice officials met disabled people face-to-face, explained what their organizations do and asked disabled people what their priorities were for the future from this organization. Criminal justice agencies indicated they were 'in the business', so to speak, of preventing, detecting, responding to and prosecuting crime, reassuring communities and, within all this, they had a focus on hate crime. In this context, not surprisingly, disabled people identified Disability Hate Crime as a priority.

This was a classic policy coupling with ingredients co-existing in the policy domain – a policy solution existing coterminous with, if not in advance of, a policy problem. This hate crime solution available in the criminal justice system could be provided almost as an off-the-shelf solution to the Disability Hate Crime problem that disability activists were articulating. Kingdon (2011) describes this as a scenario where the solution precedes the problem, and the solution seeks the problem. Indeed, a hate crime policy official commented that when Disability Hate Crime emerged in the hate crime domain, some chief constables queried, somewhat sceptically, whether this was not a solution in search of a problem (R8).

This context of a coupling of disabled people's priorities and criminal justice system organizations' new duty to respond led to the 'discovery' of Disability Hate Crime in a serious policy focused way. Disability Hate Crime moved closer to securing policy agenda status (Kingdon, 2011). To meet their new statutory duty, policy officials allowed Disability Hate Crime to move up the hate crime policy agenda, allowing increasing coupling to occur. They enabled the three streams of activism (where the Disability Hate Crime problem existed), politics (which had recently legislated for equality duties and hate crime) and policy activity (which now had to respond to the equality duty with a policy response informed by disabled people's priorities) to flow closer together, moving Disability Hate Crime up the hate crime policy agenda

These processes of discovering Disability Hate Crime did not occur in one fell swoop or in unproblematic ways. They involved, yet again, rearticulating and enhancement of the evidence base, and the move up the policy agenda came in stages. Criminal justice agencies gave policy commitments in their Equality Schemes to such initiatives as 'Putting in place a Disability Crimes Policy' (CPS, 2006) and committed to establishing a monitoring of Disability Hate Crimes (CPS, 2006; MPS, 2006). These acts of framing Disability Hate Crime policy commitments in statutory equality documents are significant policy moments. Thus, Disability Hate Crime began to move from inactive legal construct to active policy construction. Its social construction was increasingly underway.

This consideration of the influence of the Disability Equality Duty on the development of the Disability Hate Crime agenda highlights other themes in the policy studies literature. It points to the value of considering the political and policy environment impacting disabled people from the late-1990s to the mid-2000s, referred to as the beginnings of the 'civil rights era' for disabled people in Britain by respondents (R7; R12). Both civil law protections, such as the Disability Equality Duty, and criminal law provisions, such as Section 146, can be seen as part of a wider disability policy approach informed by themes of equality, rights and justice (Roulstone and Prideaux, 2012). Kingdon (2011) points to the significance of the political–policy climate to understand the progress on any one-policy initiative. The developing civil rights agenda went beyond Disability Hate Crime while enabling further progress to be made. Without the wider 'pro-disability' climate engendered by the Disability Equality Duty, Disability Hate Crime would not have developed as it did in the mid-2000s.

The research underpinning this book also shows that the Disability Equality Duty was uniquely influential for a time in the police and the prosecution service. There is not the same evidence that the duty was as influential in the wider public sector. In fact, there is critique of the limited contribution of the equality duties approach to advancing substantive equality, including scholarly articles calling on disabled people not to get involved with this largely processual response to challenges of systemic inequality (McLaughlin, 2007; Pearson et al, 2011). The most trenchant criticisms highlight how the equalities duties approach can fail to address systemic challenges, despite their origins as a response to institutional discrimination. Over time, it is argued the institutional discrimination challenge has slipped from view while a hate crime agenda has been promoted as a criminal justice system domain that is largely individual victim focused. What were originally both institutional and individual-level challenges have been repackaged to focus almost exclusively on the individual level, namely hate crime. In the process, institutional discrimination easily goes unchecked, in an era where criminal justice system agencies have successfully positioned themselves as on the side of hate crime victims. In this increasing slip from the institutional to the individual, which has occurred over 15 or more years, critics have argued the risk is an over-individuated focus on inequality, while institutional inequalities go unquestioned (Piggott, 2011; Conrad, 2014; McVeigh, 2017).

However, it is clear that, at a specific moment in the mid-2000s in the criminal justice system in England and Wales, a significant flowing together of streams of policy activity on disability equality arising from the

Disability Equality Duty, together with activist demands for prioritization of Disability Hate Crime, met in policy terrain predisposed to progress, and the Disability Hate Crime agenda was able to further develop.

Significantly, the emphasis was on parity of protection and equivalence in experience across hate crime strands. This is understandable for the Disability Hate Crime agenda still seeking to secure a firm policy and practice home in the hate crime domain. Explicit recognition of the differences in the Disability Hate Crime experience were still unidentified; policy silence on differentiated experiences remained and was to do so for a while (Bacchi, 2009).

The differing benefits of a policy stream and activist stream

Public policy statement developed on Disability Hate Crime

The criminal justice system policy stream, particularly in the prosecution service, the police nationally and the then Office for Criminal Justice Reform (OCJR), began to engage seriously with the Disability Hate Crime agenda on the back of the Disability Equality Duty. This led to the CPS and the police prioritizing Disability Hate Crime in their first Disability Equality Schemes or Single Equality Schemes (CPS, 2006; MPS, 2006) and with the CPS publishing a Disability Hate Crimes Policy in 2007 (CPS, 2007b).

The research underpinning this book indicated that the CPS set about producing this Disability Hate Crimes policy based on an established policy production formula from the existing hate crime strands of racist and religious crimes and homophobic crime. Its Disability Crimes Policy Working Group comprised CPS lawyers and officials, a senior ACPO representative and a range of disability NGOs.

Indeed, the structure of the first CPS Disability Hate Crimes Policy closely reflects the previous CPS Racist and Religious Crimes Policy and the previous CPS Homophobic Crime Policy. There is limited issue-specific content. The CPS Disability Hate Crimes Policy was drafted to fit within an existing hate crime policy template – "a hate crime family", according to one senior prosecution respondent (R29). A CPS policy official involved said: "This policy architecture was there, the system could be adopted or tweaked for another hate crime policy, there was a reason to introduce it. … We followed the template (for hate crime policies) really in producing the policy guidance. It was quite easy to put together" (R16). The working group chair reflected that this use of an existing hate crime template "might have strait-jacketed us as, I suppose, if you know something works, you tend to use that" (R18).

This resonated with existing analyses of policy making and the importance of 'fit' with an established policy approach, emphasized by Kingdon (2011), and the issue of hate crime domain expansion following an established path identified by Grattet and Jenness (2001a). However, two elements distinguish the CPS policy statement on Disability Hate Crime from earlier hate crime policies.

Firstly, the CPS' hate crime policy to address hostility based on disability was entitled 'Disability Hate Crimes Policy' (CPS, 2007). Although this title explicitly located the policy within the hate crime domain, it set the Disability Hate Crime Policy apart from other strands. While there was no mention of 'hate' in the title of the established hate crimes policies – the Racist and Religious Crimes Policy and the Homophobic Crime Policy (CPS, 2002, 2004) – the existence of hostility and hate was probably more accepted in these areas. Meanwhile, the emphasis on 'hate' in the title of the Disability Hate Crimes Policy set a high linguistic and conceptual threshold for disability hostility (Roulstone et al, 2011). For the established hate crime strands, there was an immediate location of the policy statements within wider prejudicial ideologies of racism and homophobia. However, there was no mention of a Disablist or Ableist Crimes Policy or a location within disablism or ableism. Reflecting on this difference, a former criminal justice system senior manager recalls considering – but not using – the term Disablist Crime: "I remember us discussing that, as to how we termed it but, of course, disablist doesn't seem to exist as a sort of established term of prejudice in the same way as racist or homophobic" (R18).

Reflecting on this issue of title of the policy statement as Disability Hate Crime, in contrast to the other hate crime policies, one former criminal justice system leader wondered if:

'It may mean that, subconsciously, the threshold for Disability Hate Crime is higher than it is for other strands of hate crime, because prosecutors might ask themselves, "Is this a racist crime?" And they might identify something as racism without asking themselves, and is it hatred? They are more likely to conflate and merge hostility and hatred together whilst, in the disability field, if you are sticking with Disability Hate Crime, means that you are arguably not approaching it in the same way.' (R19)

In constructing it in this way, while very well-intentioned to explicitly locate it within the hate crime domain, the criminal justice system may have inadvertently set higher thresholds for Disability Hate Crime than exists for other hate crimes strands, linguistically, conceptually and even legally for some practitioners.

This failure to locate disability hostility within wider disability prejudice is considered in the penultimate chapter on the relationship between Disability Hate Crime and ableism. Here, it has been identified as an element in the further social construction of the policy in its policy development phase. Foregrounding hate in the title of this policy statement may well have contributed to future institutionalization challenges. Roulstone et al have questioned whether its consequences for practice are that it 'proves too high a legal and linguistic threshold to afford disabled people an equitable and responsive criminal justice system' (2011, p 362).

The second issue that marks the CPS Disability Hate Crimes Policy Statement out from other hate crime policy statements is the attempted distinction between crimes based on vulnerability and crimes based on hostility. The issue of vulnerability as a challenge in respect of Disability Hate Crime is considered in Chapter 7. Here, I focus on how the issue of vulnerability entered into and featured in the policy development phase.

Chapter 4 showed how vulnerability attempted to surface in the first phase of agenda triggering but was subject to policy silence by the activists and DRC, helped by the ascendance of the activist stream. However, now the policy stream was in the lead on framing the CPS Disability Hate Crimes Policy and the issue emerged again. This time it secured a distinct focus in the Disability Hate Crimes Policy Statement. This marked a significant development in the social construction of Disability Hate Crime, when competing problem representations of vulnerability targeting and hostility targeting became problematically intertwined in a policy statement on Disability Hate Crime (Bacchi, 2009). Dealing with the consequences of this has posed one of the biggest challenges in addressing Disability Hate Crime.

Those involved in drafting the first CPS policy statement on Disability Hate Crime, while perceiving a distinction between crimes based on vulnerability and crimes based on hostility, identified this issue as the most challenging aspect of the policy development on Disability Hate Crime. It was challenging because distinguishing between crimes based on vulnerability and crimes based on hostility was, in their view, a tricky, subtle difference. Their view was also influenced by the engagement with NGO members of the working group involved in framing the Disability Hate Crime Policy. Difficulties in the working group revolved around how the issue of vulnerability was to be addressed in the policy. A former NGO staff member and criminal justice system official who felt the vulnerability focus was inappropriate reflected:

'I remember having some back and forth … I felt there was a set way that the CPS was doing it and it was not so responsive … to some of the points that I was putting in … I remember there being some resistance really … I was being quite strong about the need to strengthen the language to get rid of the word "vulnerable" … When the force fit was being challenged, there was in part a lack of creativity about it. …

It felt like we had to either force ourselves into this racist hate crime model or fall back on the thing of a vulnerable adult.' (R3)

Notwithstanding different views, the views of criminal justice system agencies prevailed. The policy stream was in the ascendant, and vulnerability was constructed as central to the issue in the CPS' first policy statement on Disability Hate Crime in 2007. The statement was framing the targeting of disabled people as either hate crime or vulnerability targeting. It did not allow for targeting based on vulnerability to be driven by hate or hostility. In a trenchant critique of the CPS construction of Disability Hate Crime, Roulstone et al (2011) comment:

It is perhaps odd that having established the powers that attach to disablist hate crime responses, that blanket exceptions come into play where crimes are seen to be motivated not by hatred but by the perceived 'vulnerability' of a disabled person … it is concerning that vulnerability should weaken disabled people's right to legal redress, especially where institutional practices have helped cement notions of difference and where their categorical status is seen to weaken rather than strengthen such rights. … The notion of vulnerability, although not unique to disability, can be seen as categorically more pernicious when used in certain criminal justice debates. … It seems unjust to blame the individual. (p. 357)

Nonetheless, the 2007 CPS policy statement on Disability Hate Crime was seen as central to activating the policy domain on Disability Hate Crime by policymakers, practitioners and activists involved. There now existed a policy statement that enlivened the 2003 Criminal Justice Act for operational purposes.

On reflection, key officials wondered if they could have framed the policy statement to focus more clearly on disability hostility:

'I think we definitely recognized it was an issue (i.e. issues of vulnerability focus and hostility focus), but I'm not sure we took all the steps we could to address it.' (R16)

The subsequent years highlighted challenges still to be addressed on this topic with the CPS having to issue further guidance to clarify the distinction between issues of hostility and vulnerability in Disability Hate Crime cases in 2010 and instigating a full review of the Disability Hate Crime policy in 2015–16 and agreeing a revised Disability Hate Crimes and other crimes experienced by disabled people policy in 2017.

A common definition of monitored hate crime

Simultaneously, another criminal justice system strand of work was underway in the policy stream. The then ACPO led a cross-government work programme on hate crime based in the OCJR-Ministry of Justice (MOJ), including development of a common definition of monitored hate crime in the criminal justice system. The policy stream was very active, not only in defining Disability Hate Crime and codifying this in a Policy Statement but also in including Disability Hate Crime in what was to be criminal justice system-wide hate crime monitoring. The further social construction of Disability Hate Crime was gathering pace. Disability Hate Crime was progressing towards 'institutionalization', a crucial step in its policy development journey (Best, 1999).

To understand the policy activity on securing a common definition of monitored hate crime in 2006–07, it is important to revisit the Lawrence Inquiry and related developments within the CPS. The Lawrence Inquiry contained a simple, yet far-reaching, recommendation in relation to defining and recording racist incidents. It recommended that an incident and/or a crime should be recorded as a racist incident or crime if the victim or any other person perceived it to be motivated by racism. This recommendation was accepted by the government. This definition remains at the heart of criminal justice system definitions of hate crime. It is sometimes referred to as a victim-centred definition or a perception-based definition (Hall, 2013). The rationale was to enable reporting of hate crime and to minimize the risk of institutional blindness to hate crime exposed in the Lawrence Inquiry. Indeed, the continued use of the victim-centred definition when defining Disability Hate Crime for criminal justice system policy and operational purposes confirms, yet again, the foundational influence of the Lawrence Inquiry agenda on the hate crime domain (Hall, 2013; Tyson and Hall, 2015).

In 2000, one year after the Lawrence Inquiry, the CPS launched the Denman Inquiry into potential racial discrimination in the prosecution service. The Denman Inquiry had its origins in racial discrimination in employment tribunal findings against the CPS in the late-1990s. The focus was largely on equality in employment, although it raised questions and made recommendations regarding prosecution practices and potential racial bias in charging decisions (CPS, 2001). The then DPP, Sir David Calvert Smith, accepted the challenge of institutional racism in line with the Lawrence Inquiry definition. A programme of work was launched to plan the potential for institutional bias out of the CPS and to promote equality (Taylor, 2009). One aspect was a project by Professor Gus John to analyse CPS charging decisions, to identify any potential racial bias within prosecutors' decision making. Among the recommendations in the ensuing report, 'Race for

Justice' (CPS, 2003), was a recommendation that the Attorney General should take a lead across the criminal justice system in moving forward issues raised in this project, 'not least in respect of the handling of race crimes by the police, the CPS and the Courts' (CPS, 2003).

It was 2005 before the then Attorney General, Lord Goldsmith, appointed Mr Justice Fulford to chair a task force to address the issue. In its report in mid-2006, the Race for Justice Taskforce highlighted patchy and poor monitoring of racist crimes across the criminal justice system and recommended that: 'All the agencies track cases from receipt of an allegation to the end of the court process using some core, common terminology' (AGO Race for Justice Taskforce, 2006).

The Taskforce's recommendations regarding the need for common definitions, training, monitoring and service delivery were accepted by the Attorney General and the criminal justice system. Although the Fulford Taskforce report has had limited profile, I propose that it set the scene for the emergence of a common definition of monitored hate crime (R8; R3). It also set the scene for the development of a cross-government programme of work on hate crime for the first time and for the institutionalization of Disability Hate Crime in the hate crime domain (Giannasi, 2015). It also stands as the sole significant positive engagement by the judiciary with the development of the hate crime policy agenda.

A Race for Justice Programme of work was put in place in early 2007 across government to address the Taskforce recommendations in relation to common definitions, training, monitoring and services to victims. Coordinated by an ACPO lead based in the then OCJR, it developed into the Cross-Government Hate Crime Programme and is located to this day in the MOJ, supported by an independent advisory group. It has provided key elements of the overarching national framework within which the hate crime agenda, including Disability Hate Crime, continues to develop. The Programme's approach – reading across from racist crime to apply the recommendations equally to other hate crime strands, including disability – was to prove very significant.

Following a period of assessment, ACPO produced a common definition of monitored hate crime, with the categories set out as race, religion, sexuality, disability and gender identity. The inclusion of Disability Hate Crime in this common definition of monitored hate crime was, according to respondents in the research underpinning this book, a significant moment in the construction of Disability Hate Crime policy and practice in the hate crime domain:

'It brought disability into the hate crime canon, into the fray in the UK and it meant that every year ... there was a scrutiny on disability along with all the rest. ... It was bringing together disparate agendas on hate crime ... so racist crime, homophobic crime, disability crime now came into this overall hate crime policy agenda. ... It made hate crime policy definitions coherent. It made a cohesive whole, if you like, with these recognized specific strands.' (R3)

Another respondent emphasized how this definition: "placed disability on an equal footing in terms of other hate crime strands and conveyed government policy that this is one of the issues we will look at" (R20).

Other respondents emphasized the symbolic and substantive recognition conveyed through such inclusion, reflecting the importance of the 'politics of recognition' for minority identities such as disability:

'It meant that Disability Hate Crime was interpreted on the same footing as other equality strands where previously there's been a difference, which was symbolically important. I think that was important because it was in a sense linking disability to areas where it is already framed in terms of justice and equality.' (R21)

Such recognition, akin to the cultural recognition analysed by theorists of multiculturalism such as Charles Taylor, goes some way to understanding the symbolic and substantive importance for the disability movement of the inclusion of Disability Hate Crime in this common definition. A group who expressed a sense of social injustice based on misrecognition now felt affirmed, felt an injustice was in part righted and felt included, echoing the significance of the thrill of recognition for victim groups (Taylor, 1994).

While activists tended to emphasize the importance of symbolic recognition per se, policy officials tended to emphasize the pragmatic benefits of having a common definition of monitored hate crime. A HMIC respondent reflected:

'I think it was very significant. I think institutions with large numbers of people working in them need definitions in order to trigger a service ... if you don't have a definition, you don't know what you're doing and whether even the basics are being covered properly. And then in dialogue between agencies, particularly in the criminal justice system, you have to be talking more or less about the same thing along that chain, otherwise you don't trigger the right services at the right time.' (R23)

Those more centrally involved in the policy activity to secure a common definition were cognizant of the significance of this stream of activity. Lead officials commented on it as of "massive significance" (R8), as a step in developing hate crime policy that "helps massively" (R36).

For activists, the politics of recognition, conveyed through an inclusive definition, mattered most (Taylor, 1994) – for some, it was as if recognition was the substance. For policy officials, recognition mattered, but having what they regarded as an operable definition against which crimes could be recorded mattered more. However, the move towards a common definition of monitored hate crime was not universally welcomed by activists; some argued that the focus should remain on racist crime until there was greater progress towards eradicating it (Scotland, 2007; Giannasi, 2015a). This view was resisted by the criminal justice system agencies that were concerned with a cross-strand approach in this era of multi-strand equality duties. Policy officials enlisted politicians in demarcating the policy terrain for the future. In late 2007, Baroness Scotland QC, then Attorney General, in a keynote speech to a European Hate Crime Conference in London endorsed a cross-strand approach without countenancing any dilution of efforts to combat racism.

In this moment, the policy and politics streams flowed closer together, enabling the further construction of the Disability Hate Crime policy agenda. By now in 2007, there was a legal provision to address Disability Hate Crime on the statute books, enactment of that legal provision and a prosecution Policy Statement that sought to enliven and make the statute operable. There was an agreed definition of what was to constitute monitored hate crime which included disability. All of this was underwritten by the relevant politician delineating the hate crime domain with disability at its centre. The policy domain was, in a sense, opening for business on Disability Hate Crime. Now it remained to test the policy in practice and to populate the category with cases. Activists were not slow to do so.

Activists challenge Disability Hate Crime policy in practice

Alert to the policy developments that had occurred, the gains made in problematizing disability hostility, and securing increased problem representation as a problem of Disability Hate Crime, activists were keen to further activate the domain to secure increased agenda status and appropriate criminal justice system responses.

It is interesting that the activist stream members pursuing the Disability Hate Crime policy agenda changed somewhat from 2005 onwards. Of those involved pre-2003, Mencap, VIA, the DRC, and activists in south and east London involved in police Independent Advisory Groups (IAGs) remained involved. They were joined, from 2005 onwards at different times, by a new Disability Hate Crime Network, Voice UK, *Disability Now* magazine, Disability Rights UK, and charities Scope and Mind. Post-2005, the DRC's involvement moved firmly into the policy stream, reflecting its organizational evolution. It made influential interventions to move the agenda forward, including strategic documents that foregrounded the issue of disability hostility (DRC, 2005, 2007a). Strikingly, the evolving Disability

Hate Crime movement was somewhat separate from the wider disability NGO sector. The wider disability movement engaged with the Disability Hate Crime agenda in bouts of action rather than sustained ways. In the decade from 2010 inwards, with many disability organizations focused on mitigating welfare benefit changes due to austerity measures, issues such as Disability Hate Crime decreased as a priority (R21).

Nonetheless, the activist stream, largely through the Disability Hate Crime Network, continued to contribute significantly to the further construction of the policy agenda on Disability Hate Crime. Key activist-driven developments occurred in 2006–07 when *Disability Now* magazine linked up with disability activists to focus on the issue. The magazine had come to the issue through profiling of high-profile cases, beginning with the case of Kevin Davies, a disabled man who was tortured and kept in a shed in the Forest of Dean (R12).

At the same time, other activists engaged with the CPS, the then ACPO, the Metropolitan Police and the Metropolitan Policy Authority in pushing forward the Disability Hate Crime policy agenda. They were securing an essential foothold in the hate crime domain as the elements of a policy and practice architecture were beginning to be put in place. However, activists were concerned at how Disability Hate Crimes were still not being recognized and responded to appropriately by the criminal justice system (Sin, 2014).

In 2007, *Disability Now* magazine published a hate crimes dossier of 50 cases, produced by activists, which they argued should have been investigated as hate crimes. *Disability Now*, with a reputation for exposing previous abuse against disabled people in institutional settings, was now lending its weight to this exposé of Disability Hate Crime. A cabinet minister in interview noted the significant contribution that *Disability Now* made to setting a policy agenda on Disability Hate Crime (R5).

The *Disability Now* hate crimes dossier was informed by the close collaboration between the campaigning journalist involved and activists engaged with the police and CPS, including the Disability Hate Crime Network. One criminal justice system policy official commented: "They are quite a powerful journalistic lobby. They are effective from an organizational reputation point of view … particularly in high-profile cases … they know which strings to pull and how to have issues highlighted when there are shortcomings" (R17).

The activists' approach lay in part in media exposé and campaigning journalism, not surprising given the backgrounds of some key activists. One disability activist reflected that his background enabled him to 'almost sell the concept' of Disability Hate Crime to the criminal justice system through exposing 'the good' – the criminal justice system's willingness to set a policy agenda on Disability Hate Crime – and 'the bad' – the criminal justice system's failure to respond appropriately to the issues (R24).

The activists' approach was also informed by their involvement with various criminal justice system groups involved in addressing the Disability Hate Crime agenda. They sat on CPS working groups, on Police Independent Advisory Groups (IAGs) and on Hate Crime Scrutiny Panels. They began to shift their modus operandi, from active campaigners for Disability Hate Crime policy development to active critics of gaps in performance. They quickly and adeptly shifted from problematizing disability hostility to problematizing criminal justice system failures to address it through cases. They engaged in critique of a neglected form of hate crime often dealt with inappropriately by criminal justice system agencies. Their criticisms revolved around the following narrative to the criminal justice system: 'This form of hate crime is widespread, you just don't recognize it; your response is inadequate, and you are failing on very serious cases. How can you expect us to have confidence to report if you do not recognize and respond appropriately?' As one disability activist commented:

> 'People like myself and X and Y also were involved in various police advisory groups. So, being on IAGs, we suddenly were then able to say, "Hang on, let's look at what we're talking about here and relate it back to what we're doing on the policy bodies (on Disability Hate Crime) and find the gaps". Suddenly we find that there was not just a gap but a great black hole. The police ... weren't being negligent in not charging hate crime, they just didn't know of Disability Hate Crime. So that was an issue, and therefore the Crown Prosecution Service hadn't got anything to go on. ... And all of us activists were in advisory positions anyway and we were able to bring these things to agencies' attention.' (R24)

Activists did not rely on working as outsiders on the inside, raising issues with the criminal justice system agencies through various working groups. They also worked in collaboration with others and used their well-established tactic of campaigning journalism and research drawing on their insider knowledge to expose policy implementation gaps in seeking to further progress the Disability Hate Crime agenda. These led to the publication in 2008 of the activists' report, 'Getting Away with Murder', published by Scope. The report sought to expose, through a series of case profiles that perpetrators were getting away without a murder charge, and sometimes without any charge at all, in cases involving targeted crimes against disabled people (Scope, 2008). 'Getting Away with Murder' fitted into classic social movement activism on hate crime where shocking cases are used to highlight the seriousness of hate crime and serious gaps in criminal justice agencies' response. It suggested a near epidemic of serious cases resonant of earlier social movement activism (Best, 1999; Grattet and Jenness, 2001a). It served an agenda-grabbing function to move beyond agenda triggering to firm agenda setting (Kingdon, 2011).

The response to the report was significant with supporting statements issued from a Home Office Minister, the DPP and a Metropolitan Police Assistant Commissioner. Policy stream respondents were privately critical of the report's methodology, while acknowledging its agenda-setting impacts. They indicated, however, that it was the first report from the disability movement highlighting Disability Hate Crime shortcomings that elicited a whole-of-government response.

One senior EHRC official commented:

> 'The landmark moment really was the "Getting Away with Murder" report because that was so shocking in its evidence. Of course, its evidence was ripped to shreds in terms of ability to create research that was robust and effective, but the evidence was there nonetheless. … That was the first thing that came out of the disability rights movement that put the test to the criminal justice system to think differently about it.' (R20)

As with other reports on this agenda, 'Getting Away with Murder' underwent a transformation, a sort of evidence-cleansing exercise and, as a result, both chimed with and propelled forward the direction of travel underway in the policy stream (Kingdon, 2011).

In the research underpinning this book, one disability activist wondered if the report's focus on very serious cases set up future challenges to identifying Disability Hate Crimes:

> 'This is something we were partly responsible for. The "Getting Away with Murder" report set the bar too high because the cases reported in there were very serious. They were murders and they were serious injuries. What we wanted to do was make people recognize that crimes against disabled people should be reported but we almost got to the point of, we turned people off by saying, "Well, I haven't been injured" or "I'm alive, so therefore I've got nothing to report", and the big battle remained.' (R24)

Notwithstanding the potential shortcomings of this 'shock and awe' strategy, it did, on balance, impact in progressing the agenda. It partly influenced the CPS in including a keynote contribution from an NGO Director at its Senior Management Conference in 2008 which was also attended by senior police colleagues. This NGO Director spoke about the criminal justice system response to disabled victims and witnesses, a theme wider than hate crime, and addressed the issue of Disability Hate

Crime. She highlighted some of the cases profiled in the 'Getting Away with Murder' report and the shortcomings in the criminal justice system response. She asked whether the criminal justice system had to await a Lawrence-type case for Disability Hate Crime to be taken seriously. A former criminal justice system leader responded that, in his view, the 'Lawrence Cases' had already occurred in Disability Hate Crime, they just had not been acknowledged, and he pledged that this issue would be taken seriously (R30).

After this conference, the policy stream, via the CPS and the police, were further propelled into developing the Disability Hate Crime policy agenda. A few months later in October 2008, in a keynote address on Prosecuting Disability Hate Crime at a joint Bar Council–Equality and Diversity Forum-hosted seminar, the DPP stated that, in his view, Disability Hate Crime was widespread. He said that cases, including very serious cases, were not being prosecuted as they should be. He went on to say: 'This is a scar on the conscience of criminal justice. And all bodies and all institutions involved in the delivery of justice, including my own, share the responsibility' (Macdonald, 2008). That speech not only accepted disability activists' criticisms of criminal justice system failures but also challenged the criminal justice system to recognize its failings. It was a leadership call to prioritize a focus on Disability Hate Crime. Activists said they felt their core arguments regarding non-recognition, poor response and vulnerability 'clouding the issue' were, for the first time, accepted by a criminal justice system leader.

Activists and policy stream respondents spontaneously mentioned this speech as a significant contributory factor in the development of the Disability Hate Crime agenda. One disability activist said:

> 'There was one Ken Macdonald who made that wonderful speech, disabled people are being let down. ... Suddenly, the circle was squared. ... That speech resonated through the whole criminal justice system. I think that was very important. We all did our work, but he was in a position to be public, and that was what was needed. I'd say that speech did more to get the police, the criminal justice system, and therefore ourselves ... the support we needed to go up into the next gear. It was a very powerfully received speech.' (R24)

Policy stream officials involved were also aware of the speech's significance. They saw it as reflecting a developing policy agenda underway since 2006 and which gathered pace in 2007–08. A hate crime policy official involved reflected: "Ken Macdonald's talk about a scar on the country's criminal justice system was a massive influential point and something I've quoted endlessly since" (R8).

Agenda setting propelled by Pilkington case

During 2006–08, there was increased coupling activity from the policy stream, namely the impact of the Disability Equality Duty; the impact of the adoption of a common definition of monitored hate crime, together with ongoing activism and policy acceptance of shortcomings, and political endorsement of a way forward based on an espousal of parity of protection across hate crime strands. This was accompanied by what may be termed a focusing event in bringing the policy, activist and political streams closer together at this time (Kingdon, 2011). This focusing event was the Pilkington case or the deaths of Fiona Pilkington and Francecca Hardwick. The aftermath of this event and the publication of the coroner's inquest report and an IPCC report into the deaths created a window of opportunity, through which the Disability Hate Crime agenda emerged (again) and a policy agenda status was secured.

Fiona Pilkington (38) and her daughter, Francecca Hardwick (18), died in October 2007. The coroner's report was issued in September 2009, followed by an IPCC investigation report into their deaths in 2011. When she died, Fiona was a mother of two learning-disabled children, Francecca and her brother. Fiona lived on a mixed tenure housing estate in Barwell, Leicestershire with her two children and her mother.

Fiona and her two disabled children experienced sustained anti-social behaviour, targeted harassment and Disability Hate Crime over a ten-year period (Quarmby, 2011). Fiona contacted the police on over 30 occasions to report incidents of harassment and disablist abuse of her and her children and targeting of her property. She also had contact with her local council. Fiona reported incidents of her children being called 'mong', 'spastic', 'freaks', 'Frankenstein', 'perv', 'nutcase', 'spazzo' and 'lunatic'. Both children were also subject to what was termed 'bullying' and targeted harassment at school. This verbal abuse often took place in the context of other harassment, which included frequent window breaking, damage to the family's car, damage to the family's garden and, on one occasion, taking the boy captive, locking him in a shed and holding him at knife point.

Fiona reported all these incidents to the police and was frequently able to name the youths involved. A number of diary entries express Fiona's deep sense of frustration with the lack of official responses to the harassment. In a letter to her MP in 2004, she wrote, 'I really am getting to the stage where I am at a loss as to what to do about most things.' Then, three years later, with little progress she wrote to her son: 'The street kids are still being intolerable ... well, I have just given up ... I am just not cut out to take this much harassment' (IPCC, 2011).

The bodies of Fiona and her daughter, Francecca, were found in a burnt-out car in a lay-by near Earl Shilton in Leicestershire in October 2007. An inquest concluded that Fiona unlawfully killed her daughter and died by suicide herself. The inquest found that the responses of the police and the local council to reports made to them by the family about the sustained disability harassment and hostility they had experienced contributed to Fiona's decision to act as she did (Inquest, 2008).

There are two sets of pertinent responses to the Pilkington case. There are the police and other agencies' responses over the 11-year period of the targeted harassment. Then, latterly, there are the responses by a range of bodies in the aftermath of Fiona's and Francecca's deaths. Over the period of ongoing targeted harassment, incidents were dealt with in isolation and in an unstructured approach. There was little attempt to link incidents and appraise the extent and nature of the targeted harassment that the family were experiencing. The vast majority of incidents were closed soon after reporting and noted as incidents of 'anti-social behaviour' (Bacchi, 2009; IPCC, 2011). There was no identification by the police or other agencies of the incidents as hate incidents or hate crime, despite the police having a hate crime policy since 2004. However, the area did not incorporate national guidance on hate crime until late 2007.

The anti-social behaviour categorization became the problem representation for what happened to Fiona and her family. Police did not distinguish between the level of seriousness of general anti-social behaviour and targeted harassment of this particular family. Beyond problematizing each incident as anti-social behaviour, there was a lack of strategic appraisal of the range of incidents and lack of awareness of disabled people's experience of hate crime. They failed to respond to Fiona's repeated reports that this harassment was 'ongoing' and that it was her disabled family that was particularly targeted. Consequently, the police failed to consider the family's treatment as Disability Hate Crime (IPCC, 2011). These failures to recognize the targeted nature of the harassment and to respond appropriately linked to the tragic events of October 2007.

Latterly, the Pilkington case led to the critical inquest mentioned earlier, which linked the lack of appropriate response by local agencies to the deaths of Fiona and Francecca. It also led to an IPCC inquiry into the police handling of the family's contact with the force over 11 years. In the next chapter, this study will consider the institutionalization of the Disability Hate Crime Policy agenda and the influence of the Pilkington case on the EHRC's decision to proceed with a formal inquiry into disability related harassment.

Kingdon (2011) defines a focusing event in policy making as a final 'push' that a problem may require 'to get the attention of people in and around government' (pp 94–5). Kingdon proposes that a focusing event may be 'a crisis or a disaster that comes along to call attention to the problem, a powerful symbol that catches on' (pp 94–5). He acknowledges that focusing events are not all of the same nature and impact – in some areas, focusing events may be a determining factor in setting the future policy agenda, while in other policy areas, they may take on an 'influence to make an item in a less visible arena move up a government agenda' (p. 95). The evidence points to the Pilkington case as a focusing event, but a second-order focusing event. The case moved Disability Hate Crime, a less visible area of hate crime policy, up the government agenda. It opened a window of opportunity through which Disability Hate Crime emerged yet again, this time to secure policy agenda status.

Most respondents in the research underpinning this book identified the Pilkington case as a focusing event. However, many qualified their view, saying that the Pilkington case, albeit a focusing event, was not a focusing event in the way they viewed the Lawrence case. Here, as in so many aspects of the development of this policy agenda, the long shadow of the Stephen Lawrence case is present. It is as if that case had, for some respondents, become synonymous with a hate crime focusing event. One hate crime champion working in the criminal justice system said: "Clearly, there have been some focusing cases in Disability Hate Crime … we've Fiona Pilkington. There have also been some horrendous cases involving homicides and, while they had a high profile, they've not been as enduring as Stephen Lawrence" (R25). For many respondents, I suggest, the Lawrence case was a first-order focusing event, with a far-reaching policy agenda that has been sustained for over 20 years. The Pilkington case was a second-order focusing event, which moved Disability Hate Crime significantly up the government agenda, such that it secured policy agenda status, but with less far-reaching impacts.

The Pilkington case was, in a sense, simultaneously familiar and different. At one level, it fitted the dominant narrative in the sense of an ordinary deprived neighbourhood and the corrosive effect of so-called 'low-level' hate incidents over time. This confirmed its continuities and fit with established hate crime strands important for securing agenda status (Kingdon, 2011). It was also different in that this was a mother killing her disabled daughter and herself in response to this sustained disability harassment. In one sense, it was not a Disability Hate Crime but a reaction to Disability Hate Crimes. That said, it demonstrated how devastating the impact of hate crime can be and when faced with inaction by responsible agencies.

Some respondents reflected that the Pilkington case is better understood alongside a number of other serious cases of Disability Hate Crime. One former director in a disability NGO commented:

> 'There have been a number of events but they're more fragmented than one particular thing … the deaths in Leicestershire of the two women, the death of Stephen Hoskins … the deaths of other folk all around the same time. … Instead of these being one event, there were quite

a number of more fragmented tragedies that drew people's attention to it. ... A lot of people had to lose their lives before this (Disability Hate Crime) was taken seriously.' (R26)

This view on a number of second and lower-order focusing events is congruent with Kingdon's analytical framework in which he identifies that, for some policy issues, sustained 'awareness of a problem comes only with the second crisis, not the first, because the second cannot be dismissed as an isolated fluke, as the first could' (Kingdon, 2001, p 98). In a sense, the Pilkington case was such a stark case in the aftermath of previous serious cases. Likewise, the Stephen Lawrence case was not the first racist murder in Britain (Bowling, 1999). Rather, these cases succeeded in a coalescing of politics, activism, events and policy making such that the policy issues moved up the government agenda in significant ways (Thorneycroft and Asquith, 2017).

The Pilkington case and subsequent coroner's and IPCC investigation reports constituted the opening of a policy window of opportunity through which Disability Hate Crime secured agenda status in the hate crime domain. The case impacted the increased focus on recording, monitoring and responding to disability hate incidents (Giannasi, 2015). It acted as the trigger for the announcement of the EHRC's formal statutory inquiry into disability related harassment (R14; R7); it enhanced the receptive responses to an OPM study on disabled people's experiences of harassment and targeted violence (R14; R7). It gave Disability Hate Crime a higher profile in both policing and prosecution policy and practice activity (R36; R8; R3). It formed a backdrop to political party manifesto pledges in 2010 to improve monitoring of Disability Hate Crime and to its subsequent inclusion in the programme for government in 2010 (Liberal Democrats, 2010).

However, while achieving all of this, challenges, competing representations, silences and ambivalences lurked within all this policy agenda-setting activity. These challenges were to emerge in a very short time as the agenda moved towards institutionalization as discussed in the next chapter of this book.

Conclusion

In this second phase of the development of Disability Hate Crime policy and practice in the criminal justice system in England and Wales from 2004 onwards, it was then that the policy stream became actively engaged with this agenda and the activist stream fully engaged where it could with these policy stream developments. In contrast to Phase 1 on agenda triggering where politicians determined the direction of travel and policy officials did what they were told, here, in Phase 2, policy officials were in the lead, steering developments and only occasionally asked politicians to intervene in support, which they did.

The arrival of the Disability Equality Duty applying to the public sector from 2004 shaped the 'discovery' of Disability Hate Crime by the criminal justice system. Stung by past criticisms and alert to equality agendas after the Lawrence Inquiry, the criminal justice system was keen to be proactive on equality issues. Thus, Disability Hate Crime entered a receptive criminal justice environment. The Disability Equality Duty led to a tweaking of a pre-existing solution to hate crime by the criminal justice system that offered it to the disability movement to address disability hostility. The policy stream allowed this coupling of a hate crime policy solution and the disability hostility problem because it fitted their new statutory requirements to advance disability equality. In doing so, a largely off-the-shelf hate crime template was placed around Disability Hate Crime with limited attention paid to its differences. In fact, in an otherwise chequered history, the development of the Disability Hate Crime agenda is one of the relatively few examples of the Disability Equality Duty contributing to positive policy development.

Policy stream activity to implement a common definition of 'monitored hate crime' constituted another significant moment in the development of the Disability Hate Crime agenda. The significance lay in the recognition conveyed by the inclusion of disability within the monitored strands. This was hailed by activists for its symbolic recognition value and by policy officials for its pragmatic value. For many activists, recognition was the substantive issue while, for policy officials, having an operable definition was the substance. In the context of this study, this marked a key moment in the construction of the Disability Hate Crime agenda. Furthermore, policy stream activity to develop a CPS public policy statement on Disability Hate Crime constituted an equally significant moment in the construction and development of a Disability Hate Crime policy agenda.

Taking Section 146 of the CJA 2003 as its launch pad, it enlivened and codified what it would mean for prosecution purposes. It made Disability Hate Crime real for lawyers and police having to investigate and prosecute it and for communities in raising awareness and appraising performance. It reflected established realities in that it largely replicated a model of hate crime devised some years earlier to fit racial hostility. It also broke the policy silence on vulnerability targeting and hostility targeting in Disability Hate Crime cases and constructed them as if they were wholly different forms of disability targeting in crime – in so doing this surfaced a challenge in the Disability Hate Crime domain (see Chapter 7).

Alongside these policy developments, activists contributed to both the development of a common definition and the development of a public policy statement on this policy agenda. Having done so, they were alert to the need to test the policy in practice and to populate the category with cases. In a short timeframe, activists switched from being friendly critical contributors to policy development to becoming stringent critics of criminal justice system failings. Activists used insights gained from policy involvement to highlight failure to prosecute particular cases as Disability Hate Crimes. They majored on exposing the policy–practice gap, partly through media exposé and campaigning reports. They gained traction with a narrative of lack of recognition and response and failure to deliver justice.

During 2006–08, there was increased coupling activity from the policy stream, with the impacts of the Disability Equality Duty, the development of a common definition, inputs from the activist stream highlighting stark policy–practice gaps, together with political and policy endorsement of a way forward based on espoused parity of protection across hate crime strands. This increased coupling of the policy, activist and political streams was significantly enabled by the influence of a second-order focusing event, namely the Pilkington case. Its aftermath and the related reports created a window of opportunity through which the Disability Hate Crime agenda emerged (again) and policy agenda status was secured (see diagram).

While the Pilkington case moved Disability Hate Crime significantly up the policy agenda, it did not launch a wholesale policy agenda for the years ahead. Various challenges, competing problem representations, breaking silences and the dilemmas of disability difference lurked within this policy agenda-setting activity (for a summary see Figure 5.1). These became an issue in a very short time as the policy agenda journeyed on from agenda setting towards agenda institutionalization, as we will see in Chapter 6.

AGENDA DEVELOPMENT

Figure 5.1: Diagram of Phase 2 developments

Phase 2: Agenda development

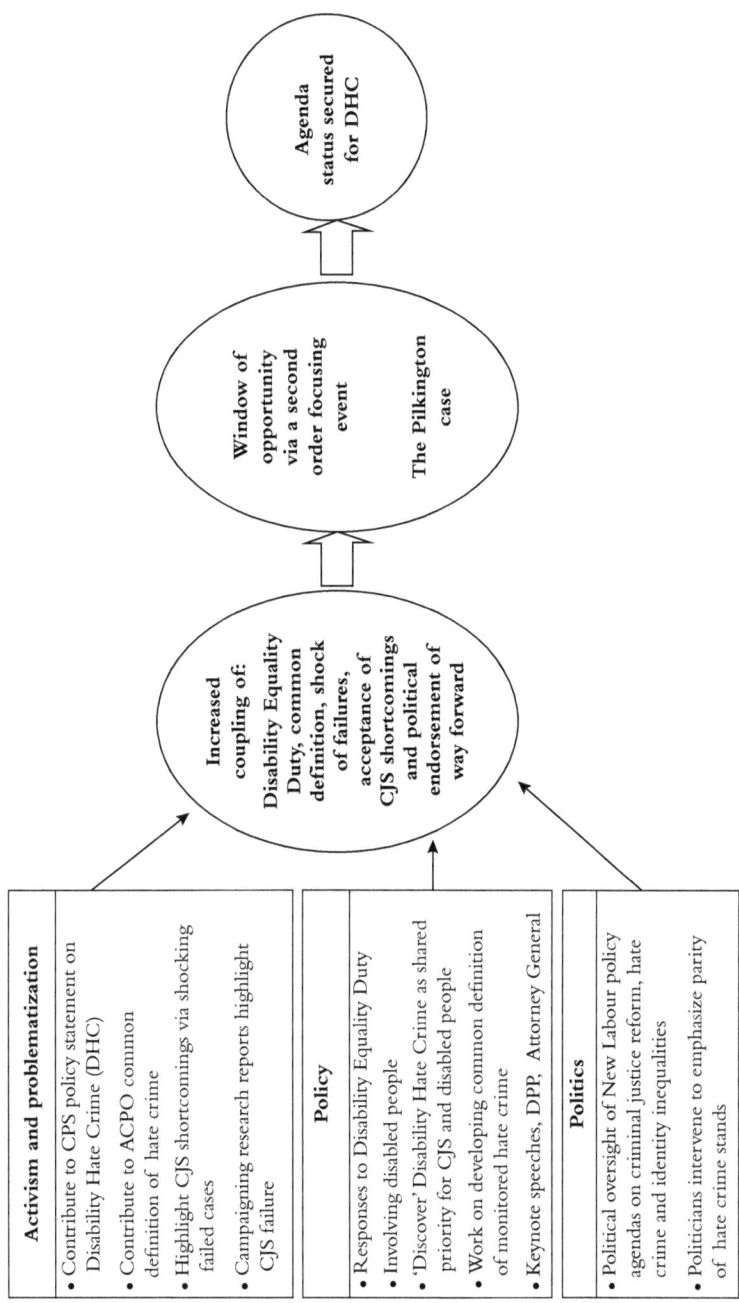

6

Towards Agenda Institutionalization?

Key points

This chapter analyses the policy journey which embeds and institutionalizes Disability Hate Crime within the hate crime domain in terms of law, policy and daily practice. The development of this agenda is explored in the three streams of 'activism', 'politics' and 'policy' (Kingdon, 2011). The evidence in this chapter points to policy development, policy institutionalization and evaluation on Disability Hate Crime taking place simultaneously at times. These do not take place in discrete, sequential stages. The evidence presented here illuminates the ways in which policy becomes, or fails to become, embedded within criminal justice system business. It points to the importance of criminal justice actors, namely police, prosecutors and judiciary sharing a common understanding of and focus on Disability Hate Crime.

Introduction

The introduction of Section 146 of the Criminal Justice Act 2003 triggered a Disability Hate Crime agenda for the first time in England and Wales. The Pilkington case of murder–suicide in 2007, and the responses to it, secured its policy agenda status. From 2009 onwards, the Disability Hate Crime agenda continued to develop and move towards institutionalization. This chapter analyses the policy journey that seeks to embed and institutionalize Disability Hate Crime within the hate crime domain. Institutionalization here refers to efforts to embed Disability Hate Crime in the criminal justice system in terms of law, policy and daily practice (Powell and DiMaggio, 1991; Best, 1999).

There are three streams in which the development of this agenda has been explored, applying Kingdon's model of policy change (2011). In this study, these are termed 'activism', 'politics' and 'policy'. Kingdon's model shows that although the three streams may operate independently of one another, all three need to come together in order for a policy to emerge. Each has its own forces acting upon it and ultimately influencing it. Timing and flow of policy actions is central to this model. Coalescence comes from consistent and sustained action by advocates.

Up to this point, activity on Disability Hate Crime was mostly focused in the activism and policy streams. Some strategic interventions, but less activity, have been evident in the political stream. Although the primary focus in Kingdon's analytical perspective is on issue emergence and agenda setting on policy issues, his policy streams' perspective offers some insights into the institutionalization phase of policy making. The evidence in this chapter points to policy development, policy institutionalization and evaluation of Disability Hate Crime taking place simultaneously at times. The insight that can be drawn from this evidence is that that policy development, policy institutionalization and policy evaluation do not take place or lend themselves to analysis in discrete, sequential stages.

This chapter goes beyond Kingdon's analysis of how an issue gets onto a policy agenda to explore how it becomes embedded in practice. The evidence presented here illuminates the ways in which policy becomes embedded within criminal justice system business.

Institutionalizing the Disability Hate Crime agenda

While institutionalization of the Disability Hate Crime agenda gathered pace in the aftermath of the Pilkington case, its origins lay in the legal recognition conferred by the introduction of Section 146 into the Criminal Justice Act 2003. Policymakers and practitioners must 'operationalise the category' (Best, 1999, p 60), and in respect of Disability Hate Crime, this meant that criminal justice agencies responsible for enforcing the new law had to define Disability Hate Crime for law enforcement purposes, record this 'new' form of crime, respond to, investigate and prosecute this crime. In doing so, they had to engage in significant ongoing social construction of Disability Hate Crime for day-to-day law enforcement purposes. In this process also, they were beginning to place boundaries around this new crime, in terms of deciding what it was and what it was not (Best, 1999).

The concept of institutionalization referred to here is informed by the insights of scholars on policy institutionalization analysis such as Powell and DiMaggio (1991) and adapted by Grattet and Jenness (2001a) in their analysis of policy making on hate crime and the insights of Best (1999) on institutionalization. Key elements in this perspective include the emphasis placed on policy formation as influenced by the importance of endorsement of a particular policy model by powerful state organizations giving rise to a policy domain; that policy domains are characterized by adopting similar ways of responding over time – 'temporal homogenization': how the 'taken for grantedness' of a policy approach becomes reflected in how a policy topic is discussed and approached. It can take time for 'debate and discussion to diminish as actors converge around a set of policy practices and definitions'. In time also, the part played by 'collective action' should lessen as an established 'policy formula' takes hold and there is less need for constant 'active promotion by particular collective actors' (Grattet and Jenness, 2001a, p 12). Finally, at different times in the policy making process, definitions, conceptions and categories can be used differently and evolve.

In his analysis, of the social construction of a range of social problems (including the emergence of hate crimes) as a 'new crime problem in the 1980s' (1999, p 63), Best explored the institutionalization of hate crime as a criminal justice policy and practice in the US and the part played by legislation in achieving such institutionalization. He emphasized the importance of the part played by criminal justice officials in terms of how vigorously they choose to enforce new laws once a policy is agreed and 'how the courts rule on the new laws' in influencing whether hate crime becomes a fully institutionalized crime category, or whether it may fade from public attention. The institutionalization of hate crime in the criminal justice system was, he argued, a daily process of social construction of hate crime by criminal justice system officials (1999, p 71). I drew upon these theoretical insights together with those cited earlier in considering the continuing policy making journey of Disability Hate Crime and, in particular, in this phase of assembling the architecture and practices of institutionalization.

Institutionalization underway

Chapter 5 considered the inclusion of Disability Hate Crime in the common definition of hate crime by the criminal justice system, and how that constituted an important moment in the social construction of Disability Hate Crime. Following this, the police began to produce Annual Hate Crime data (starting in 2012) and the CPS began to produce Annual Hate Crime Reports. These provided information on numbers of cases reported or referred, prosecutions and prosecution outcomes. These data were located alongside data on established hate crime strands of racist crimes, religious crimes and homophobic crimes (refined in time to include transphobic crimes). This marked a very significant step in the institutionalization of Disability Hate Crime. It required from the criminal justice system institutions a parity of consideration in practice via the police and Crown

Prosecution Service Annual Reports, with boundaries being placed around the officially reported hate crime problem. From the outset, these annual reports and data emphasized that these official hate crime figures were evolving administrative data sets with significant limitations and likely to underrepresent the scale of hate crime in society.

This emphasis in this institutionalization period on under-representation of the scale of hate crime has been accompanied by an equal emphasis on encouraging hate crime victims to report their experiences of targeted crimes and an emphasis on how the criminal justice system takes such crimes seriously. Alongside this, to further institutionalize the agenda, the criminal justice system welcomed year-on-year increases in hate crime reporting as indicative of increased victim confidence to report rather than an increase in hate crime. It had confidence in this approach in part because the British Crime Survey (now the Crime Survey for England and Wales) had for some time indicated very significant under-reporting of racist crime victimization. The British Crime Survey introduced a measure of disability and victimization rates for the first time in 2009. The Crime Survey for England and Wales' inclusion of questions on disability targeted victimization in 2011–12 was a significant underwriting of the institutionalization of the policy agenda on Disability Hate Crime being pursued by the criminal justice system activists, policy officials and politicians. One top civil servant respondent in this study described the 2011 EHRC report analysing British Crime Survey data on targeted disability victimization (Iganski et al, 2011a) as an "invaluable wake-up call" (R13). He talked of using this wider prevalence data to frame a call to staff for institutional action. It was a sobering reminder to the criminal justice system of how, in the words of a former Director of Public Prosecutions, the criminal justice system 'was still "only in the foothills" of institutionalising this agenda' (Starmer, 2011).

The evidence assembled here demonstrates that elements in this process of institutionalization of Disability Hate Crime included, first, the adoption of a common definition, second, embedding that definition within the criminal justice system and third, the criminal justice system's emphasis on addressing the under-recognition and under-reporting of Disability Hate Crime, along with encouragement of further reporting and highlighting of the prevalence–reporting gap. These elements can be seen as institutional efforts in terms of both system management and system convergence. They attempted to make Disability Hate Crime 'real' in manageable terms for police and prosecution services, and to secure a convergence of definitions and practices across the criminal justice system (Powell and DiMaggio, 1991). Analysis of criminal justice system annual reports, press releases and policy statements/speeches on Disability Hate Crime figures from this institutionalization period convey an identifiable criminal justice system discourse in relation to Disability Hate Crime which emphasized the following themes:

- A significant and prevalent problem of Disability Hate Crime exists.
- There is significant under-reporting of Disability Hate Crime.
- There is a historical and understandable lack of confidence by victims' communities to report Disability Hate Crimes to the criminal justice system.
- The seriousness with which the criminal justice system now takes Disability Hate Crime reporting and its encouragement that victims report any hate crime experiences.
- That the criminal justice system can be trusted to take Disability Hate Crime seriously and respond robustly to reports.
- That increases in Disability Hate Crime reporting reflect increases in public confidence in the criminal justice system more than actual increase in hate crime.
- That the criminal justice system stands with victims of Disability Hate Crime and their communities in their commitment to tackle hate crime.

These are powerful discursive messages to minoritized communities that have had mixed and often negative experiences of the criminal justice system historically, including experiences of stereotyping, neglect, discrimination and police victimization (McVeigh, 2017). These messages, often packaged as 'public confidence measures' and/or 'victim-centred services', also served to legitimize a criminal justice system that has historically often faced a legitimation crisis in its contacts with minoritized communities.

The dilemma of disability difference

While this increased institutionalization of Disability Hate Crime was intended to 'normalize' it as part of the established hate crime domain through processes of shared definitions, reporting, recording and responses, it not only led to increased policy convergence, but also began to highlight differences in the manifestations of Disability Hate Crime. A dilemma for the criminal justice system was, and remains, whether the differences raised by Disability Hate Crime in terms of its manifestations in particular crimes can be responded to within the hate crime domain.

Over time, identifying the common features of Disability Hate Crime has been helped by internal monitoring and annual reports from the CPS (2007–18), the police and independent research by the Equality and Human Rights Commission (EHRC) (2009), and the evidence amassed through the EHRC Inquiry (2011) into disability related harassment. There was also developing international evidence (Fundamental Rights Agency, 2015a,

Table 6.1: Principal offence category by hate crime strand, 2018–19

Offence category	Hate crime strand		
	Disability	LGBT	Racist and religious
Homicide	0.0%	0.1%	0.0%
Offences against the Person	53.5%	60.0%	88.5%
Sexual Offences	3.4%	0.4%	0.2%
Burglary	3.9%	0.2%	0.2%
Robbery	6.9%	0.6%	0.3%
Theft and Handling	8.8%	1.7%	0.9%
Fraud and Forgery	5.4%	0.4%	0.1%
Criminal Damage	3.0%	3.4%	2.2%
Drug Offences	1.3%	2.2%	0.5%
Public Order	11.8%	29.7.7%	6.5%

Source: Crown Prosecution Service Annual Hate Crime Report 2018–19

2015b) pointing to commonalities between Disability Hate Crime and established hate crime strands. That international evidence also pointed to specific features of Disability Hate Crime which were not shared with established hate crime strands (although some of these were shared with violence against women). Table 6.1 adopted from the CPS' Annual Hate Crime Report 2018–19 highlights the shared and specific features of Disability Hate Crime.

The continuities between Disability Hate Crime and racist and religious and homophobic crime are indicated in the similarity in offending levels for homicides, offences against the person and offences of criminal damage. They serve to support the institutionalization of Disability Hate Crime within the hate crime domain. The specificities of Disability Hate Crime are indicated in the heightened levels of aggravated sexual offences, burglaries, robberies, theft and handling, fraud and forgery among Disability Hate Crimes, and in the lower levels of recorded public order offences.

These features of Disability Hate Crimes are also reflected in findings from CPS internal monitoring reflected in guidance to prosecutors (CPS, 2010b), in OPM research (EHRC, 2009) and in the EHRC statutory inquiry into disability related harassment (2011a). These findings include:

- The frequent presence of previous incidents.
- Perceived 'opportunistic' offending becomes systematic with regular targeting.
- Perpetrators are sometimes 'mates', carers, acquaintances or neighbours.

- The escalation of incidents in severity and frequency.
- The occasional involvement by multiple perpetrators in incidents condoning and encouraging the main offender(s) – often filmed on a mobile phone and images sent to friends/social networking sites.
- False accusations of the victim as being a paedophile or 'grass'.
- Sustained attacks, excessive violence.
- Cruelty, humiliation, degrading treatment, often related to the nature of the impairment.
- Negative experiences of reporting to criminal justice agencies.
- Disabled people's tendency to report incidents to a third party rather than to the police.

The EHRC Inquiry (2011a) also identified the most frequently mentioned types of harassment in their inquiry as:

- damage to property;
- exploitation, theft and fraud;
- cyber-bullying and cyber harassment;
- sexual violence and harassment;
- bullying;
- anti-social behaviour;
- domestic violence;
- physical violence; and
- institutional abuse.

In attempts to try and institutionalize Disability Hate Crime and its manifest differences within the hate crime domain, the criminal justice system broke the policy silence on the features of Disability Hate Crime. The CPS issued further guidance to criminal justice system practitioners designed to help them better recognize Disability Hate Crime and its different manifestations, while continuing to firmly locate it in the hate crime domain (CPS, 2010b). Having emphasized its commonality with other hate crimes for over seven years, in order to gain entry into the hate crime domain, the emphasis then shifted to the need to recognize its different manifestations without relocating it outside the hate crime domain.

However, the specificities of Disability Hate Crime appeared to pose challenges to its further institutionalization. These specificities challenged whether a homogenization of a policy and practice response is possible, whether the wider 'taken-for-granted' approach (Powell and DiMaggio, 1991) is appropriate in the Disability Hate Crime domain, whether a 'policy formula' for responding to Disability Hate Crime that fits within the hate crime domain can be settled, and whether there is still a need for ongoing discussion and collective action to settle the institutionalization of

Disability Hate Crime. The evidence in this study indicates that the efforts at institutionalizing Disability Hate Crime have and continue to pose challenges for the accommodation of the differences it brings to the wider hate crime domain, as noted by Thorneycroft and Asquith (2015). The wider hate crime domain although evolving and flexible, has well established if not homogenized policy and practice approaches.

The issues raised by the EHRC Inquiry

The institutionalization of the Disability Hate Crime agenda secured further impetus when the EHRC announced a formal statutory inquiry into disability related harassment in 2009. While some criminal justice system respondents in this study indicated their surprise with this further step in institutionalization, analysis indicates that it was some time in the making. It is another strand in the institutionalization of this agenda in which the contribution of the earlier Disability Rights Commission, its legacy agenda and the work of its former staff can be traced.

On its dissolution and merger into the EHRC in 2007 as mentioned in Chapter 2, the Disability Rights Commission had a clear recommendation that a top ten priority for advancing disability equality was a focus on disability harassment, safety and security (Disability Rights Commission, 2007b). The then new EHRC responded and published a developing strand of work on the safety and security of disabled people in 2009 (EHRC, 2009). This study on disabled people's experience of targeted harassment, hostility and violence (EHRC, 2009) was a nuanced, rigorous account of the available evidence on this issue. However, this did not in itself trigger a commission-level response to concerted action on Disability Hate Crime. Notwithstanding the evidence-based approach, as with other studies, this study had to undergo the required process of transformation, where it moved from being a mere statement of conditions to being hailed as compelling evidence of the need for further institutional action. This transformation occurred when the Pilkington case and the reports into its handling became a significant media issue in 2009 and beyond. Respondents working in and with the EHRC said that the Pilkington case played a pivotal role in 'crystallising action within the Commission' (Smith, 2015, p 38) (R14; R7).

However, there were significant aspects of the problem representation in relation to the EHRC's formal inquiry into disability related harassment. While the impetus lay in concerns about Disability Hate Crime, the problem was deliberately framed as disability related harassment to capture the continuum of disabled people's experience and because of a recognized difficulty with the language of hate (R7). Furthermore, the EHRC Inquiry was framed within the terms of the Disability Equality Duty responsibilities of public bodies to advance disability equality, work to eliminate disability harassment and address unlawful discrimination. Thus, the EHRC was firmly locating the issue on the continuum of disability discrimination including violent discrimination. This was significant in institutionalizing the issue as an issue of discrimination akin to other protected discriminations. It reinforced the case made in the previous chapter about the influence of the statutory equalities duty approach to hate crime developments. One national disability activist involved summarized the approach adopted by the EHRC inquiry:

> 'this approach was significant because it was thorough and inclusive and looked right across the field and was framed in such a way that could be understood by institutions and it did include activists, and it did it all within an equality duties framework. I think that made a huge difference.' (R10)

Over a two-year period, the EHRC undertook a broad range of evidence-gathering exercises. Respondents who worked on the EHRC Inquiry said the process was a catalyst for change and institutionalization in the public sector. One senior EHRC official reflected:

> 'The beauty of doing an inquiry is that it's a lengthy process ... it allows change to happen along the way ... because, during the investigation, when you're asking questions, when you're taking evidence, when you're talking to witnesses, you then find that people shift in the way they think, and it enables them to start doing things differently as a result.' (R20)

The EHRC Inquiry highlighted conceptual and problem representation issues that resonate with findings in this study and highlighted central challenges in recognizing and responding to Disability Hate Crime. It also implied a significant issue, which did not surface explicitly and was, in effect, silent. The first significant issue lies in the title of the EHRC Inquiry, Hidden in Plain Sight, an apt title proposed by the then Chair of the EHRC (R27). The Inquiry found that criminal justice agencies and wider public-sector organizations had often not recognized the hate crime dimension of cases, simply because they were not looking for it. Their perspectives were too often focused on anti-social behaviour and vulnerability. One EHRC Commissioner at the time wrote subsequently: 'If anyone had been looking, the issue of disability related harassment would be in plain sight, but it was hidden from the collective consciousness of these organisations that should be doing something about it' (Smith, 2015, p 46). This study has found a similar tendency by criminal justice system agencies, particularly in the identification, investigation and prosecution of cases in which a disabled person has been a targeted victim.

The second significant issue was the focus by state agencies on victims' perceived 'vulnerability' rather than dealing with the perpetrators' offending behaviour. Through a consideration of ten serious cases, the EHRC Inquiry highlighted how an undue focus on vulnerability led to some of these cases being dealt with as social care reviews and never entering the criminal justice system, resulting in justice being denied for disabled victims of targeted crimes. This goes to the heart of the unique challenge in Disability Hate Crime cases, the competing problem representations of vulnerability and hostility, which this study has also found, and which is the focus of Chapter 7.

The third significant issue relates to the Inquiry highlighting similarities in manifestations between Disability Hate Crime and crimes of violence against women in particular as they relate to abuse of power and exploitation. It might be argued that disabled people, because of their social positioning in society find themselves at heightened risk of experiencing an imbalance in power whether on the streets, in their homes or in care contexts. This again goes to the heart of challenges raised by Disability Hate Crime and whether the difference that violent disability discrimination brings to the hate crime domain can be responded to within that domain. I consider this in Chapters 7 and 8.

The final issue implied – but never named – by the EHRC Inquiry relates to the issue of institutional discrimination. The Inquiry talks about 'the systemic failure' by public authorities to recognize disability related harassment, to act to prevent it and to intervene effectively when it does occur. It emphasizes institutional and 'organisational failings' to address the issue and how attempts to address disability related harassment need to focus on 'organisational change' alongside the challenge of transforming how disabled people are treated and included in society (EHRC, 2011a). The focus is clearly on institutional discrimination without naming it as such, a policy silence that appears to have been consciously decided by the EHRC given a perceived negative legacy in relation to the challenge of institutional discrimination in the public sector in the aftermath of the Lawrence Inquiry. One EHRC commissioner reflected:

> 'We had to be careful of what we wrote and claimed in the report. It seemed lazy at the time to have just used the same language and said there was institutional disablism. Also, we did not feel that people had been able to focus and deal with the Lawrence Inquiry on institutional discrimination. This is why we said instead that there was systemic failure on the part of the relevant bodies. It was carefully chosen language to try to infer the same thing without using the same language.' (R28)

This section of the chapter questions whether the EHRC Inquiry constituted a call to action for public sector organizations or was it a challenge to institutional responses to date? The evidence in this study indicates that it had elements of both a call to action and a challenge to institutional responses. There is a level at which the EHRC Inquiry could be seen as an agenda-setting document but one that emerged during an institutionalization phase. It bore some features of a focusing event (like the Lawrence Inquiry or Pilkington case): it contained shocking cases highlighting institutional failure and conveyed starkly how disabled people were being let down by the criminal justice system.

The impact of the EHRC Inquiry attracted a variety of opinions, in part reflecting different expectations of the Inquiry. Some criminal justice system officials thought the EHRC Inquiry would constitute a road map to further institutionalize the agenda in the criminal justice system hate crime domain. They felt let down by another "shock report" (R15). One former senior criminal justice system manager said:

> 'The whole "Hidden in Plain Sight" report was a missed opportunity. It had the potential to do so much more than it did ... this is the programme for change, this is what you need to be doing within organizations ... this is what professionals were looking for. ... They were looking for the Inquiry to provide that piece of future policy guidance that would energise the agenda again.' (R15)

Other respondents felt that the very undertaking of the EHRC Inquiry was symbolically and substantively important, and its lengthy process and long-term reporting on progress helped institutionalize the agenda. A former criminal justice system leader reflected:

> 'It was important that the EHRC picked up the baton for a period. ... I think if you are going to change things and they are cultural things ... when you are talking about cultural change, you have to get the arrangements right. Then you have to constantly come back to them, monitor, change, monitor and develop a strategy for change, and so these reports are more important in that respect.' (R19)

The EHRC did put in place a monitoring framework for tracking public sector progress against the Inquiry's recommendations at yearly, three-yearly and five-yearly intervals. Reflecting on this challenge of achieving institutional progress in responding to Disability Hate Crime, one senior EHRC official involved said:

> 'It will be ten years before you see any significant change and it's really hard for an organization like ours, or any actually, to invest in

something that is going to happen in five years' time because we do not know where we'll be, what our business plans will be, what our strategic purpose will be.' (R20)

The research underpinning this book found that criminal justice agencies felt the impact of the EHRC Inquiry in the first years, 2011–14, following publication. However, agencies reported that, three years on, its impact as an impetus for further development and institutionalization of the agenda declined. Respondents felt that an opportunity to further institutionalize the agenda had not been sustained. An EHRC commissioner said:

'I do not know that the Commission has done an awful lot on the area publicly since, and I wonder if the relevant bodies just feel like they are not being watched as much. ... I would have liked to have seen more progress by now, and I think that is reflected in the national numbers [the low level of cases coming through to the criminal justice system].' (R28)

However, there is no doubt that the EHRC Inquiry contributed significantly to delineating the contours of the Disability Hate Crime agenda. It became a focal point for a lot of work and, because of its formal statutory basis, it commanded serious attention and is perceived to have influenced the criminal justice system inspectorates and the Law Commission in taking up the agenda.

One former senior manager at the Disability Rights Commission involved with the Inquiry summed up its impact and this reflection resonates with the findings of this research:

'Without doubt, the EHRC's Inquiry was significant more ... because of its formality and focus. ... It had a lot of buy-in and became a focus for a lot of work. I don't think it particularly took us forward in our knowledge necessarily, maybe it was not intended to, and I don't know what impact it subsequently had. I think, in terms of profile raising, it was key.' (R7)

Policy making on hate crime, and indeed public policy making more widely, does not lend itself to analysis in terms of discrete sequential stages. The EHRC Inquiry was indeed a profile-raising and agenda-setting Inquiry and report that occurred in the agenda institutionalization period for Disability Hate Crime. It was as much a call to institutional action as it was a challenge to institutional responses. That is not to detract from its contribution to further institutionalizing the Disability Hate Crime agenda through its architecture of formality and through this call to action, a call taken up by other institutionalizing contributions which we consider in the following.

When the EHRC published the formal inquiry into disability related harassment in 2011, the understanding was that they were launching a ten-year agenda of change, that they would sustain a focus on over the ten years up to 2021. This was conveyed in interviews to this author by then senior commission staff in interviews underpinning this book. However, in 2017, just six years after the launch of the formal inquiry into disability related harassment, the EHRC published its final progress report on this agenda. In the intervening years in 2012 and in 2013, the EHRC published two progress reports, which highlighted some limited progress, but with significant work still to be done by the criminal justice system to address disability related harassment. In the 2017 final report the EHRC concluded that while they could identify many positive steps taken by public bodies in Britain to address disability related harassment they ended with a call for an enhanced 'pace of change, particularly in areas of law and policy, and evaluation and victim support' (EHRC, 2017b, p 1). The EHRC called for a fundamental review of the hate crime law in respect of aggravated sentences and sentencing uplift provisions, and better recording of the application of sentencing uplift provisions in Disability Hate Crime cases.

In more recent times the Law Commission has embarked on such a fundamental review of Hate Crime Law (Law Commission, 2020) and the CPS has very significantly improved the monitoring of the application of the sentencing uplift provisions in hate crime cases. However, data indicates that the application of sentencing uplift provisions in Disability Hate Crime cases continued to lag significantly behind other hate crime strands (CPS, 2018–19). Given the formal status of the EHRC Inquiry and its statutory basis, it seems a lost opportunity for further progress that the EHRC did not sustain a ten-year focus on Disability Hate Crime as originally envisaged and conveyed.

While the EHRC Inquiry was under way, momentum gathered around a disparity in the tariff for murder charges involving disability hostility. This study found that this disparity had been picked up by criminal justice system officials in 2007–08. As officials engaged with activists, they appraised them that the calculation for the minimum tariff in hate crimes (excluding disability) was 30 years if hostility was proven. Activists latched onto this and linked with politicians to highlight another lack of parity in protection on the basis of disability. They were assisted by policy officials identifying a window of opportunity to address this anomaly through the Legal Aid, Sentencing and Punishment of Offenders Act 2012, which was successfully availed of. This was yet another agenda-setting initiative occurring far into the agenda institutionalization phase just as the EHRC Inquiry itself was.

Institutions failing to institutionalize Disability Hate Crime?

Throughout the mid- to late 2000s, the criminal justice system embarked on further initiatives aimed at institutionalizing Disability Hate Crime within the hate crime domain. Initially, these reflected elements of a 'top-down approach' to policy institutionalization reflected in government action plans to address hate crime which specifically set actions on hate crime including improving reporting, recording and responding. In the earlier period, similar approaches included the setting of Disability Hate Crime targets to reduce unsuccessful outcomes by the CPS. These early initiatives fit within classic 'top-down' policy implementation approaches identified in the institutionalization and implementation literature (Ramesh and Howlett, 1996; Hill, 2013). This broadly top-down target-driven performance management-based approach to institutionalizing the Disability Hate Crime agenda was sustained for five to six years. A move away from this approach appears to have been influenced by a change in government in 2010, the prioritization of a localism agenda and the attendant move away from centrally controlled performance agendas. It may also have been linked to the impacts of increasing austerity and the consequences of "Disability Hate Crime coming very late to the hate crime party" (R29). However, the criminal justice system emphasized continuing priority be afforded to implementing Disability Hate Crime in the hate crime domain. A new focus emerged with CPS local areas working to a hate crime assurance system. This was an attempt at a more blended top-down bottom-up approach to policy institutionalization reflecting a shift in the political emphasis (Sabatier and Weible, 2014) within a nationally defined framework where local criminal justice areas had autonomy to take action and demonstrate achievements.

Meanwhile, the criminal justice inspectorates – Her Majesty's Crown Prosecution Service Inspectorate (HMCPSI), Her Majesty's Inspectorate of Constabulary (HMIC) and Her Majesty's Inspectorate of Probation (HMIP) – embarked on a joint review of criminal justice system responses to Disability Hate Crime. Triggered by a concern about the handling of cases involving disabled victims and media reports of poor handling of Disability Hate Crime cases that had caused concern among disability groups, the criminal justice system inspectorates decided to undertake a joint thematic review. Inspection of public sector policy implementation fits within the 'top-down' policy making approach. It is significant that the criminal justice inspectorates, in subtle but significant messaging, went beyond a limited performance review focus. They stated that Disability Hate Crime required a specific focus because society's attitudes had not yet changed to the extent they had on other equality issues. Thus, in many ways, 'Disability Hate Crime ... is the hate crime that has been left behind' (HMCPSI, HMIC, HMIP, 2013, p 3; R54).

The first thematic inspection report published in 2013 revealed significant failures to institutionalize the Disability Hate Crime agenda within the criminal justice system. It highlighted fundamental failings of the criminal justice system in respect of lack of clarity and understanding of what constitutes Disability Hate Crime, failure to prioritize the issue of Disability Hate Crime, failure to record Disability Hate Crime appropriately, failure to fully consider Disability Hate Crime issues in daily policing and prosecution work and failure to use and record use of Section 146 in Disability Hate Crime court cases (R54; HMCPSI, HMIC, HMIP, 2013).

These findings indicated that the criminal justice system faced basic agenda-setting challenges in what should be a further advanced agenda-institutionalization period. Considering the gaps highlighted alongside the classic features of institutionalization identified by Powell and DiMaggio, one can see the extent of the institutionalization challenge which remained in 2013. Contrary to the classic features of adoption of a particular policy model (in this instance Disability Hate Crime) giving rise to a policy domain characterized by shared definitions, ways of responding, shared ways of approaching and considering the issue, and a shared policy formula, this inspection of Disability Hate Crime highlighted the need for ongoing debate and discussion, different definitions in operation and a lack of a settled conception and policy formula. These features of agenda setting remained unsettled and continued into the agenda institutionalization period for Disability Hate Crime (Powell and DiMaggio, 1991).

After this joint inspectorate report was published, the criminal justice system acknowledged that progress in implementing Disability Hate Crime policy had been slow and 'a new impetus is required' (HMCPSI, HMIC, HMIP, 2013, p 1). In classic institutionalization steps, further criminal justice system action plans followed. There were, however, some time lapses in getting these further improvement plans in place. A criminal justice system inspectorate follow-up inspection in 2014 highlighted limited progress in institutionalizing the Disability Hate Crime agenda in the criminal justice system. It stressed that the 'additional focus and attention' required to implement Disability Hate Crime policy 'at an operational level, has yet to gain sufficient traction' and concluded that 'performance has not improved sufficiently' (HMCPSI, HMIC, HMIP, 2015, p 1).

The Inspectorates reminded the criminal justice agencies of their statutory equality duty to address this agenda: 'This is a necessity and not an option as the criminal justice agencies have an obligation to tackle the underlying prejudice that drives all hate crime' (HMCPSI, HMIC, HMIP, 2015, p 1). They highlighted the need to keep the focus on institutionalization. The criminal justice system responded by assigning lead responsibility for the agenda to the most senior management, devising further action plans, reviewing policy statements and guidance, and committing to prioritizing

Disability Hate Crime yet again in a further cross-government Hate Crime Action Plan in late 2016. The effects of the institutionalizing improvements taken by the criminal justice system agencies were the focus of a third criminal justice system thematic inspection in 2018. This latest inspection found that there had been substantial progress in some aspects of addressing Disability Hate Crime. These included improvements in the handling of casework, use and recording of the uplift provision in sentencing, and some perceived improvements in CPS guidance. The 2018 Inspection also found significant areas of criminal justice system practice requiring further improvements including the application of a Disability Hate Crime definition in cases and improvements to the investigation stages of Disability Hate Crimes.

The 2018 Inspection report noted significant improvement in the application of the sentencing uplift provision in Disability Hate Crime cases. However, there is no room for complacency in overall outcomes for Disability Hate Crime cases. In 2018–19, Disability Hate Crime had a conviction rate of 72 per cent, which lags 12 per cent behind the overall Hate Crime conviction rate and at the time of writing this book sentencing uplift provisions were successfully applied in just 32 per cent of Disability Hate Crimes compared to 79.2 per cent application in Hate crime cases overall (Crown Prosecution Service, 2021). This is a clear reminder of the journey yet to be travelled to institutionalize Disability Hate Crime as another embedded, predictable and routinized area of hare crime performance.

All of this evidence points to the ongoing challenge in institutionalizing Disability Hate Crime in the criminal justice system and the persistent nature of agenda setting in this area, which overlaps with efforts to embed the agenda in practice. Fifteen years on from initial agenda triggering, Disability Hate Crime is yet to become a settled concept in the criminal justice system, working to a policy formula that is agreed, shared and implemented across the system. Indeed, the extent to which the legal construction of Disability Hate Crime has provided such a settled concept was itself to become the subject of a review, instigated by the Law Commission in 2013.

Further institutionalization?

In the drive towards institutionalization of hate crime, including Disability Hate Crime in the criminal justice system, the government and criminal justice system agencies issued various 'action plans' or 'work programmes' to improve the institutional responses to hate crime. In 2012, the then coalition government, building on its manifesto and programme for government commitments mentioned earlier, published a plan to tackle hate crime, 'Challenge it, Report it, and Stop it' (HM Government, 2012a). It contained a commitment to 'conduct a review of sentences for offences motivated by hostility on the grounds of disability, sexual orientation and gender identity to consider whether there is a need for new specific offences similar to racially and religiously aggravated offences' (HM Government MOJ, HO, 2012, p 21). In time, this was framed as a formal request from HM Government (MOJ) to the Law Commission to:

> look at (a) extending the aggravated offences in the Crime and Disorder Act 1998 to include where hostility is demonstrated towards people on the grounds of disability, sexual orientation or gender identity, and (b) the case for extending the stirring up of hatred offences under the Public Order Act 1986 to include stirring up of hatred on the grounds of disability or gender identity. (Law Commission, 2014, No. 348, p 1)

This first Law Commission Review (2014) raises significant points in relation to the development of institutionalization assessed in this study. Indeed, the Review reflected and unintentionally served to reproduce an institutionalized hierarchy of criminal law provisions for Disability Hate Crime. The Law Commission reflected that, while persuaded by the equality arguments made by consultees for parity of protection across hate crime strands, it was constrained by an established and embedded set of aggravated offences designed over 15 years earlier to address the specifics of racial hostility (Law Commission, 2014, No. 348, p 12): 'We had to assume (for this project) that if the aggravated offences were extended, they would take the form of the existing aggravated offences in the CDA. We were not asked to look at whether some other form of offence would be preferable' (Law Commission, 2014, No. 348, p 10).

The Law Commission also highlighted that consultees recognized this institutionalized constraint, when they questioned whether the Law Commission 'should simply graft onto three distinct characteristics (disability, sexual orientation and gender identity) a set of offences that were designed two decades ago to address racial hostility' (Law Commission, 2014, No. 348, p 10). Consultees understandably said the existing offences may not be appropriate given the offending now being committed due to hostility on two quite different grounds (Law Commission, 2014, No. 348, p 10). Consultees also said that targeted offending in respect of disability, sexual orientation and gender identity involved more sexual offences and financial crimes and aggravated offences may need to reflect these different offence patterns. The Law Commission accepted the principle of the equality of protection argument.

Notwithstanding this, because it was not commissioned to do so, it did not recommend moving beyond the current differentiated sentencing enhancement regime, pending its recommended wider review of all hate crimes offences. The net effect has been that nearly seven years on from this first Law Commission review, the hierarchy of criminal law provisions remains institutionalized within the criminal justice system. The symbolic messaging and substantive consequences of such differentiated criminal law provisions was not lost on the Law Commission and was acknowledged in their comments on the differences in maximum sentences that can be handed down for a racially or religiously aggravated offence and an offence based on disability, sexual orientation or gender identity (Law Commission, 2014, No. 348, p 7). The Law Commission Review summed up the situation well when it said that some consultees stated: 'Our terms of reference were too narrow. They suggested that a wider scope would have helped … to take proper account of differences between the types of hate crime affecting disabled, LGB and transgender people' (Law Commission, 2014, No. 348, p 12).

The Law Commission delivered a competent informed review within significant constraints. However, with the Ministry of Justice commissioning and structuring it as a refining review within an established institutionalized hate crime domain, rather than a fundamental review of the wider institutionalization of hate crime overall, the report could only reflect, refine and ultimately reproduce the institutionalized legal–policy hierarchy. This institutionalization of a hate crime domain that includes disability, but on terms not of its own choosing or suitability, was similarly reflected in the government's rejection of the EHRC's questioning of the language of hate crime in its Formal Inquiry into Disability Related Harassment. The EHRC recommended its preference for the language of hostility, harassment and abuse of power rather than the term 'hate'. However, the government rejected this recommendation, saying such a language change could not be done because it would 'not be in line with hate crime language for other protected strands' (Smith, 2015, p 51). This illustrates the price of the 'force fit' of acceptance into the hate crime domain, albeit on the basis of an 'accepted fit'.

These efforts to institutionalize Disability Hate Crime highlight how, simultaneously, there is a wider hate crime domain that is increasingly normatively embedded and institutionalized while Disability Hate Crime remains only partially institutionalized in that domain. When Disability Hate Crime raises issues of incremental refinement of the established hate crime approach, evolutionary change within the normatively embedded hate crime domain, these issues can be accommodated. However, issues of transformative change, such as adopting discriminatory selection of victims as well as or instead of animus-based selection, cannot be so easily accommodated. Disability Hate Crime points both to the flexibility in the expansion of the hate crime domain, while also illuminating the 'embeddedness' and 'constraints' of the field (Greenwood and Hinnings, 1996). These attempts at institutionalizing Disability Hate Crime increasingly led to situations where Disability Hate Crime pushes at the boundaries of possibility in terms of institutionalization in the hate crime domain. These attempts to institutionalize Disability Hate Crime increasingly pushed at the boundaries of what might be possible within the hate crime domain.

Seven years after the Law Commission's first review of hate crime law, the Law Commission was commissioned to undertake a new comprehensive review of Hate Crime law in England and Wales. This included a review of the Incitement to Hatred law, the complete aggravated offences provisions, the sentencing uplift provisions and significantly the legal test of proof to be used in hate crime cases, the latter including critical consideration of a motivation test of proof, a demonstration test of proof and/or a discriminatory selection test of proof. The Law Commission produced, in autumn 2020, a very comprehensive consultation document that stands as a work of considerable legal and policy scholarship. In this comprehensive consultation document, the Commission outlines and explores the challenges in addressing Disability Hate Crime. They identify the challenge of the vulnerability categorization often inappropriately applied in Disability Hate Crime cases. They undertook an extensive consultation across the breadth of the hate crime domain throughout 2020. At the time of writing this book we are awaiting both the Law Commission's response to their public consultation, their concluding proposals for hate crime law reform and the government's response if any. While confident that the Law Commission, based on their track record to date, will deliver comprehensive evidence-based proposals for reform, the same level of confidence cannot be applied to the current Conservative government's response – if any, given that they have demonstrated little appetite for progressive law reform on any aspect if identity inequality, let alone, hate crime.

Judicial engagement with Disability Hate Crime?

This study now turns to the key role of the judiciary in the institutionalization and legal construction of Disability Hate Crime, in their determination of the scope and meaning of Disability Hate Crime. The judiciary, through their decisions over time, deliberate and fix meaning for hate crime laws. As Grattet and Jenness (2001a) point out, while the politicians provide the basic legal templates through passing laws, it is judges in the courts who give 'authoritative meaning to these templates' (p. 103).

To date, there is limited evidence of active judicial engagement with the issue of Disability Hate Crime in England and Wales. Disability activists, police and prosecution officials, together with independent statutory actors, all identify limited judicial engagement with the Disability Hate Crime agenda as constituting a significant challenge to further institutionalization in the hate crime domain. This study also found judges at all levels of the judiciary expressing a view that Disability Hate Crime had a low profile, that it arose rarely in courts and that, perhaps, it did not have the profile it ought to have as a form of hate crime. The judges interviewed tended to say that police and prosecutors were not raising the issue of Section 146 of the Criminal Justice Act (2003) for consideration at sentencing stage. This view was echoed by the first criminal justice system joint inspection of Disability Hate Crime (HMCPSI, HMIC, HMIP, 2013).

What is striking from this study is that most activity and institutionalization effort in England and Wales appears to be concentrated in the activist, policing and prosecution sectors, with very limited evidence of institutionalization effort in the judicial system. This is in contrast to the US where Grattet and Jenness (2001b) found that, following activist and legislative activity, the next institutional arena where most early activity occurred was in judicial decision making and in the gradual construction of hate crime by the judiciary through their decisions on its meaning.

This research found, in the UK, the absence of an institutionalized understanding shared across police, prosecutors and judiciary to implement a sustained focus on Disability Hate Crime. Indeed, other senior criminal justice system actors were forthright in their views of the judiciary's limited efforts. A former senior manager in London Metropolitan Police commented:

> 'The Magistracy, the judiciary, I'm not sure that they get it, and they hate being told that they might not be doing something well. … I got a really un-warm feeling about their willingness to accept negative feedback … it doesn't look like there's a huge deal of recognition that this is an issue.' (R11)

A former criminal justice system leader said:

> 'I don't know what's going through the judge's mind when he or she is confronted with facts that seem so blatantly obviously to be motivated by hostility. … There may be a broader hostility to the whole concept of categorizing hate crime as any different from any other crime because there is some reluctance on the part of judges to do that. … Many judges would say, "Look, an assault is an assault". … They're just instinctively reluctant … there seems to be a complete failure to acknowledge the gravity of this area of offending.' (R30)

Reflecting on judicial engagement with Disability Hate Crime through their engagement with the EHRC Inquiry, a senior EHRC official involved at the time commented: "I think they (the judiciary) were not as engaged as public servants, as some other sectors have been" (R20).

One national disability activist involved with campaigning for criminal justice system progress on responding to Disability Hate Crime commented:

> 'I think police officers have come a long way since 2007 and do understand it. I think prosecutors have also come a long way and do understand it. I think the missing link now is the judiciary ... I think that's the real problem ... what happens in court. I think we've seen a lot of change in the other two bits of the criminal justice system.' (R12)

This was echoed by another leading disability activist:

> 'The challenge is to get the judiciary to take these things on board because we know that the Crown Prosecution Service can't drive it themselves. They have a very definite policy on Disability Hate Crime. The police now, through ACPO, have a very definite policy. We can't seem to get anywhere with the judiciary.' (R24)

Yet, this study found limited efforts by activists or other criminal justice system agencies to engage with the judiciary on this agenda. It found varied views among the judiciary interviewed, including some recognition of and receptiveness to the need for progress.

In this study, members of the judiciary at various levels were interviewed, including at levels of district judge, Crown Court judge, central criminal court judge and appeal court judge. A feature of judges' responses was the strength of view that Disability Hate Crime is, in their experience, a rare form of crime brought to their attention in court and that they are more used to dealing with disabled people targeted on the basis of vulnerability. A district judge commented: "Disability Hate Crime is very rare in my experience ... I'd be very surprised if it was 1 to 2 per cent of the cases that come before me, a tiny fraction" (R31). He said this rarity may pose challenges for police, prosecutors and judges alike:

> 'It is not everyday fare when it comes up. ... When Disability Hate Crime is so rare in the courts, which fact finder is going to build up the experience, or which prosecutor is going to build up the sophistication to say, "Actually, you can draw this conclusion, and it's a safe conclusion". ... So, it's a perennial challenge.' (R31)

At the same time, judges at all levels expressed increased awareness of and confidence in responding to issues of vulnerability in cases involving disabled victims. The same district judge commented that now:

'the criminal justice system is reasonably good at spotting vulnerability. ... Not only is vulnerability going to be regarded as an aggravating feature in its own right, but increasingly it leads to a different approach in terms of case management. ... The criminal justice system has intensified its desire to deal with vulnerability.' (R31)

While, in recent years, the profile of Disability Hate Crime has risen somewhat, this judge reflected: "It would be unsurprising if the situation were still not the same, if it's a focus on vulnerability rather than hostility" (R31).

Other judges echoed this institutional focus on vulnerability. One central criminal court judge commented: "Vulnerability, put broadly, is an issue. ... We are pretty used to having our antennae up" (R32). In the analysis of Disability Hate Crime cases for this book, there was evidence of judges' simultaneous embrace of vulnerability and non-recognition of hostility in court cases involving targeted crimes against disabled people (see Chapter 2 and Appendix). In one case, where a disabled man visiting a skate park was targeted, taunted and assaulted by young people, the case was prosecuted as a Disability Hate Crime by the CPS. However, in open court, the judge rejected the prosecutor's case that it was a crime aggravated by disability hostility. The judge stated this was an attack on a vulnerable person and "not your [prosecutor's] argument" about hostility (Case 5).

In another high-profile case involving targeted abuse of learning-disabled people in a residential care home, the judge left aside the prosecution case that it was a Disability Hate Crime. The judge focused on vulnerability and mistreatment of adults in care under the mental health legislation, notwithstanding that prosecuting counsel focused on disability hostility ('Sunset View care home').

One judge working at the Crown Court level initially said in interview that a focus on vulnerability rather than hostility was not unduly problematic if it led to an aggravated sentence. However, he also stressed the scope for improvements in the judicial response to Disability Hate Crime but emphasized his view that the judiciary were alert to issues of vulnerability involving disabled victims of crime and conveyed how a vulnerability focus was increasingly institutionalized in court processes. During the interview, this judge's thinking evolved regarding the focus on vulnerability compared to the lack of a focus on hostility.

The judge initially reflected that the judicial institutionalization of a focus on disabled people's vulnerability can deliver the same result as a judicial institutionalization of a focus on hostility:

'It's a distinction (between vulnerability and hostility) without much of a difference, isn't it? ... That's a point more easily taken by someone who doesn't have to do the sentencing exercise. Show me the difference in reality ... it'll lead to the same end result. That's why I said "distinction without a difference" from the sentencer's point of view. ... But I can see from the disability rights' community where that may be an interesting contrast.' (R33)

This judge reflected that:

'I think that spotting it and, more seriously than spotting it, is getting the judiciary to take it seriously ... is even more difficult ... because I think there are people who don't accept it as a concept ... or shrug it off ... I'm not entirely satisfied that each and every one of my judicial brothers and sisters take this as seriously as I think they should.

I think racist and homophobic is easy. Easier to recognise, to deal with, to prepare for, to cope with and, if necessary, to punish in respect of. ... It [Disability Hate Crime] is difficult because I think the nuances and the subtleties of it are simply something that generally passes you by.' (R33)

In terms of the overall judicial response to Disability Hate Crime to date, he said: "It's probably not good generally ... I think there are those who don't take it seriously enough, don't recognize it when it's staring them in the face and equally, importantly, don't know where to look for it" (R33). Judges also highlighted the need for judicial training and awareness raising on Disability Hate Crime if institutionalization progress is going to be achieved. A district level judge agreed that: "You have to get it onto the agenda and keep it on the agenda somehow" (R31). One Crown Court judge commented: "I think the best and most effective way of bringing this issue on to the agenda is to feed it into the Judicial College training" (R33).

Significantly, disability has since been addressed in the Judicial College's updated edition of the Equal Treatment Benchbook (Judicial College, 2018). This is, in significant aspects, an impressive 400-page-plus guidance document for the judiciary. It sets out equality and diversity issues for consideration when judges are hearing cases. It reflects contemporary understandings of issues such as racism, antisemitism and Islamophobia. It also has a substantial section on Disability. The section on Disability is first, completely framed within first a focus on disabled people as vulnerable and, second, on providing guidance to make reasonable accommodations in court cases involving disabled people. It is totally silent on Disability Hate Crime. The *Equal Treatment Benchbook* reflects and reproduces a conception of disabled people as inherently vulnerable. Given the extent of engagement and progress in other parts of the criminal justice system in the past 20 years with the Disability Hate Crime agenda, this judicial

Equal Treatment Benchbook is indicative of the lack of judicial engagement with the issue to date. It has not moved on in its understanding of disabled people's experiences from the earlier edition of the *Equal Treatment Benchbook* published in 2008.

It is clear that there has been limited judicial engagement with the Disability Hate Crime agenda to date. This reflects both a rarity feature and an institutionalized judicial focus on vulnerability and non-recognition of disability hostility. This is accentuated by the nature of the legal provision on Disability Hate Crime, namely Section 146, as simply a sentencing enhancement construct. There are very few examples of appellate courts addressing Section 146 – it is the decisions of appellate courts that form the basis of legal guidance to lawyers and judges in these cases. This is reflected in the CPS legal guidance for prosecutors on Disability Hate Crime (CPS, 2007a) in which all the case studies are based on racially and religiously aggravated appellate court decisions. While understanding the legal reasoning for basing legal guidance on appellate court decisions, it carries a significant negative risk for Disability Hate Crime cases. Given that some of its features manifest differently to racially and religiously aggravated crimes, disability hostility cases are in a sense appraised against an earlier settled framework that can inadvertently prevent Disability Hate Crime cases from meeting the appraisal criteria (Crown Prosecution Service Legal Guidance on Disability Hate Crime, 2007).

This hurdle to institutionalization of Disability Hate Crime is further accentuated by the fact that the issue of hostility under Section 146 arises only at the stage of sentencing. Finding an opportunity for Section 146 issues to ever be considered by a higher court is likely to prove more difficult than it has been to secure higher court consideration of aggravated offences in terms of race and religion. The most likely route to secure judicial clarification is through application for leave to review a sentence on behalf of the Attorney General on the basis that it was unduly lenient. This would most likely be heard by three senior judges who could then contribute to the further institutionalization of Disability Hate Crime through producing 'an authoritative statement of law and principle' on Disability Hate Crime (Crown Prosecution Service Legal Advice on Section 146 of Criminal Justice Act 2003, June 2015). That very important institutionalizing moment in 'the legal construction of hate crime' (Grattet and Jenness, 2001a, p 103) has yet to occur in respect of Disability Hate Crime. In the meantime, Disability Hate Crime cases are appraised against a racial hostility model and set of race case precedents. In this respect, the judiciary are yet to institutionalize Disability Hate Crime in the judicial realm on its own terms. Judges as criminal justice system actors are yet to reach a consensus with other criminal justice system actors and for the concept to become 'more settled'. Disability Hate Crime is ripe for 'judicial meaning making'

(Grattet and Jenness, 2001a), given that, for them, it is still a comparatively new and unsettled concept.

Conclusion

While policy agenda status was secured in the aftermath of the Pilkington case and its focusing impact, the Disability Hate Crime agenda has continued to journey towards institutionalization from 2009 onwards. Significant questions remain: has institutionalization occurred as one might expect; and what is the nature and extent of institutionalization to date? Institutionalization of a policy agenda is regarded as a process that involves development of a policy domain, with shared definitions, ways of responding and discourse; a diminution in the need for collective action over time and an embedded taken-for-granted approach (Powell and DiMaggio, 1991). Compared to this policy institutionalization template, it is clear that, while elements of institutionalization are underway in respect of Disability Hate Crime, institutionalization has yet to deliver an agreed settled approach to this policy agenda.

Clearly, significant institutionalizing efforts and achievements have occurred in establishing common definitions and annual reporting within the criminal justice system, all of which are essential institutional steps in making the Disability Hate Crime agenda operable and 'real' for police, prosecutors and communities on a daily basis.

While common definitions and annual reporting constitute a significant step in institutionalization of the Disability Hate Crime agenda, this chapter shows how they also foregrounded the dilemma of difference that sits within Disability Hate Crime. Recording and annual reporting has brought to the fore both the commonalities across hate crime strands and the specifics of Disability Hate Crime. In doing so, these institutionalization efforts have helped surface a further institutionalization challenge – can the differences which Disability Hate Crime brings to the hate crime domain be accommodated within this domain? The evidence indicates that the differences in Disability Hate Crime continue to pose challenges to its institutionalization within the wider hate crime domain. Twenty years on from agenda triggering, despite considerable criminal justice system institutional efforts, it remains an unsettled concept pushing at the boundaries of possibility in the hate crime domain.

Further institutionalization efforts were manifest in the wide-ranging EHRC Inquiry into Disability Related Harassment that took place after the Pilkington Inquiry. This Inquiry helped to further institutionalize Disability Hate Crime in that it helped to delineate the contours of the problem, it questioned the framing of the issue to date by the public sector, and it challenged institutional responses, and constituted a call to action for improved institutional responses. It was a significant agenda-setting initiative in an agenda-institutionalization period, and it highlighted some shortcomings that others pursued.

A spotlight has been shone on institutionalization efforts and failures to embed Disability Hate Crime in the criminal justice system through several criminal justice inspections. These thematic inspections seriously questioned the extent of substantial institutionalization of Disability Hate Crime that has occurred to date. Inspections pointed to a lack of shared definitions and understanding, varied ways of responding by agencies and a far-from-settled policy formula and way of working to address Disability Hate Crime. The reports point to continuing basic agenda-setting challenges in the period of agenda institutionalization.

Such are the institutional challenges posed by the Disability Hate Crime agenda that the government first requested the Law Commission (2014) to conduct a review as to whether the existing aggravated offences should be extended to cover disability and other strands. The Law Commission concluded that there were strong equality arguments for doing so. However, due to the narrow parameters of that review the Law Commission could only make recommendations within the existing legal framework. Despite an expected government response within one year, no substantive response has been forthcoming. It took five years for any further action from government. The Law Commission was then requested to undertake a more fundamental review of hate crime law. The Law Commission has undertaken a comprehensive review and embarked on a wide-ranging consultation on Hate Crime law reform in England and Wales. We await their concluding report and recommendations, which we can expect to be well evidenced and argued. However, we can be less confident of the current Conservative government responding positively in terms of progressive hate crime law reform. In the absence of progress on the hate crime legal provisions in place, institutionalization challenges for Disability Hate Crime persist and limited institutionalization is occurring in the criminal justice system.

This chapter has highlighted how, in contrast to the US, where the judiciary were among the first criminal justice actors to engage with hate crime, in terms of the institutionalization of its meaning and boundaries, in England and Wales, active judicial institutionalization is yet to commence. This study found shared views across activists, police and prosecution respondents that judicial engagement is central to further institutionalization. However, the judiciary are engaged with, sensitive to, and committed to institutionalizing a vulnerability focus regarding disabled victims of crime. Again, for Disability Hate Crime, the construct constraints posed by Section 146 in terms of securing authoritative judicial judgements on the meaning of the statute pose a significant challenge to furthering institutionalization of this policy agenda. The context is ripe for judicial awareness-raising to enhance judicial engagement and potentially further institutionalization.

This chapter has examined a wide range of evidence on institutionalization of the Disability Hate Crime agenda. I would argue that institutionalization of Disability Hate Crime is underway but far from achieved. The criminal justice system's journey towards institutionalization itself faces challenges based on institutionalized constructs of hate crime, reflected in law, in policy and practice. Disability Hate Crime has required and secured considerable national criminal justice system institutional effort to institutionalize it within the hate crime domain and progress has been made (for a summary see Figure 6.1). Yet, close on 20 years on from legislating to address Disability Hate Crime, instead of becoming a settled concept, business as usual, it remains unusual business in the criminal justice system. Disability Hate Crime continues to push at the boundaries of possibility in the hate crime domain, reflecting both unique challenges that it raises and the broader conception of hostility and discrimination, themes considered in the next two chapters.

TOWARDS AGENDA INSTITUTIONALIZATION?

Figure 6.1: Diagram of Phase 3 developments

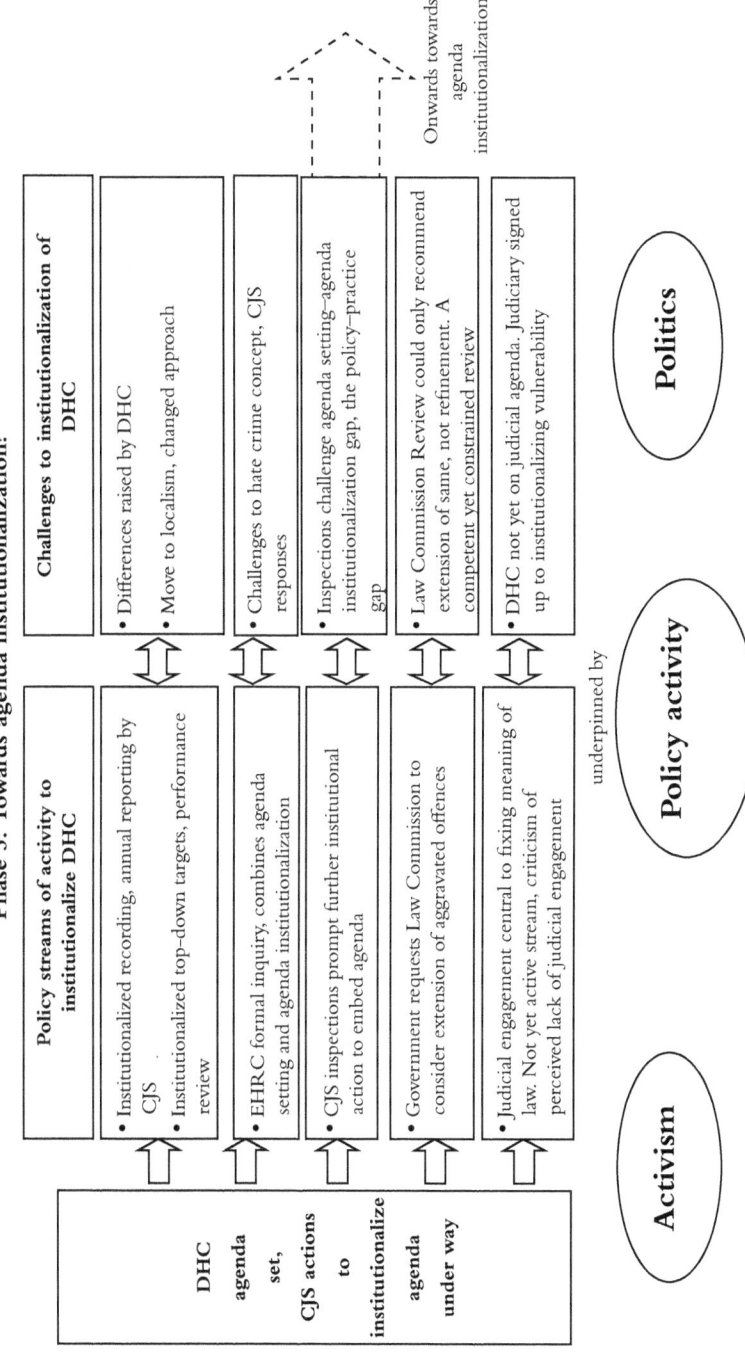

7

The Problem with the Current Agenda: Focus on Vulnerability

Key points

The issue of vulnerability has posed significant challenges to agenda institutionalization of Disability Hate Crime. It has functioned to substitute protection and safeguarding for rights, justice and equality. At other times, it has been suggested to better capture the range of disabled people's experiences of victimization. It is argued that vulnerability is embedded as the master stereotype of disabled people in criminal justice policy and practice and that this undue focus on vulnerability is impeding delivery of justice in Disability Hate Crime cases. This chapter analyses the three streams of activity in relation to vulnerability – the political, the policy and the activist streams. The shifting understanding of vulnerability in relation to Disability Hate Crime is evolving largely in response to activists' concerns and reviews external to the criminal justice system. Recent policy statements from the criminal justice system presents what is still an unsettled position in relation to vulnerability.

Introduction

In each stage of the journey in the development of Disability Hate Crime policy, one issue has been continuously present: the issue of vulnerability. It has at times emerged onto the Disability Hate Crime agenda, only to be silenced. On some occasions, it has been seen as an alternative representation of the 'problem' of Disability Hate Crime, eliciting a different set of responses focused on protection and safeguarding rather than rights, justice and equality. At other times, it is presented as complementary to the hate crime problem representation, with vulnerability presented as better capturing the range of disabled people's experiences of victimization. What is clear is that the issue of vulnerability has posed challenges to agenda institutionalization of Disability Hate Crime.

This chapter analyses the issue of vulnerability as it has impacted upon the construction and institutionalization of Disability Hate Crime in the criminal justice system. The emphasis is on understanding the vulnerability focus in the criminal justice and its application to disabled people. How does a vulnerability focus impact upon Disability Hate Crime policy and pose challenges to institutionalization? It is argued that the shifting understanding of vulnerability in relation to Disability Hate Crime is evolving largely in response to activists' concerns and reviews external to the criminal justice system.

This chapter's analysis also focuses on the three streams of activity in relation to vulnerability – the political, the policy and the activist streams. The focus is more so on the policy and activist streams as these are where most activity on vulnerability has, and continues to, occur.

The rise of vulnerability in public policy

In the last two decades, a discourse and set of practices has emerged in public policy in relation to vulnerability, including in criminal justice policy in England and Wales (Brown, 2014a; Thorneycroft, 2017). Various population groups have been problematized as vulnerable for policy purposes. Some authors have linked this to the rise of the so-called 'therapeutic state' and an attendant therapy culture (Furedi, 2004). Others view it as potentially linked to a recasting of long-standing notions of deserving and underserving groups in society for policy purposes (Roulstone and Prideaux, 2012). Others again view it as linked to the deepening of inequalities associated with neoliberal economies which, it is argued, can accentuate the vulnerability of some groups who are seen as less autonomous (Fineman, 2012). In recent years, the concepts of vulnerability and difference together have been proposed as offering a lens for better understanding hate crime victimization (Chakraborti and Garland, 2012).

In some respects it reflects a moving away from the policy discourse associated with identity equality movements which focused on equality target groups of women, LGBT people, disabled people, Black and minority ethnic people and other groups. It can be argued that it reflects a recasting by state actors of equality rights focused groups into more passive vulnerable groups, whereby they become the focus of policy protection, care and control. In some ways, the politics and policies of vulnerability indicate a more cautious, conservative and paternalistic turn and an attempt to reframe identity politics for policy purposes. It somewhat neutralizes rights focused movements into vulnerable groups warranting the state's paternalistic and protective policy gaze at best. Alongside this some other scholars have emphasized the vulnerability in all human living and seek to decouple the concept from minoritized experiences (Fineman, 2012; Thorneycroft, 2017).

Groups constructed as vulnerable in policy discourse can include children, young people, older people, women, LGBT people, migrants, ethnic minorities and, in this context, disabled people. In many instances, the attribution of a vulnerable categorization to a group is taken to indicate a lack of agency to act as free rational adults exercising autonomy. For many public service providers, it implies a commitment to protection of those deemed vulnerable and intended to imply access to protective supports. It is clear from the research for this book and others (Brown, 2016) that, for many policymakers and service providers, a focus on vulnerability is a well-intentioned approach in public policy. It is also an embedded approach seldom subjected to interrogation. This flows from an ethos focused more on a paternalist concern for the vulnerable rather than rights for citizens. Such a vulnerability focus can facilitate access to supports for some people experiencing varying levels of risk and need. As one senior criminal justice system official reflected: "The assumption around vulnerability is, in a way, a kind of shorthand that acts as a trigger for services that you might need" (R23).

This vulnerability categorization is so pervasive within public policy today that the disability movement and NGO sector themselves both critique and deploy it in different arenas. It is often rejected in pan-disability rights and Disability Hate Crime arenas while deployed by disability NGOs to argue for much-needed welfare services. This was noted by respondents as indicative of the sheer pervasiveness of the vulnerability framing and how the disability movement can hold itself back as a fully-fledged equal rights movement by playing a 'pity card' or 'vulnerability card'. One respondent referred to the disability movement wanting it both ways in terms of embracing and rejecting the vulnerability categorization (R27).

Critical consideration indicates that in public policy discourse and practice, the vulnerability categorization has been used increasingly but without general consensus on a shared meaning. Almost all vulnerability categorizations include disabled people regardless of their views as to whether they regard themselves as vulnerable. Indeed, almost all usages of the vulnerability categorization imply inherent weakness and reduced capability. Vulnerability has become a malleable concept in policy and practice that lends itself to rhetorical use and, indeed, to challenge and change. This malleability has provided the context within which the understanding of vulnerability applied to Disability Hate Crime has evolved in parts of the criminal justice system in England and Wales.

In terms of influence on policy discourse in England and Wales, the vulnerability focus gained prominence in social care policy from the late 1990s to early 2000s. The focus was on protecting vulnerable adults with national policy initiatives, such as 'No Secrets' (Department of Health policy on safeguarding of vulnerable adults), increasingly using vulnerable adult categories and implementing adult safeguarding structures at local level. This care and protection focus became the dominant frame within which the 'problem' of disabled people was represented and responded to (Bacchi, 2009; EHRC, 2011a). It is noteworthy that, in the more recent 2014 Care Act, there was a moving away from the language of vulnerability in terms of groups of people and more focus on situations that can accentuate risk and vulnerability (HM Government, 2014; R34). In the intervening years, there had been critique of the vulnerable adult categorization in social care, from service user groups and, reflected in, a shift in Department of Health social care categorizations.

This chapter analyses whether this problem representation and discourse on vulnerability has impacted on policy and practice in the criminal justice system. If so, has this problem representation and policy discourse in turn impacted on agenda setting and institutionalization of Disability Hate Crime? What is the situation now and what may require future focus? In this analysis, this study draws upon Bacchi's analytical framework: the What is the Problem Represented to be Framework (WPR) (Bacchi, 2009).

The impact of vulnerability on the criminal justice system

In recent decades, there has been a focus on the vulnerability of victims in criminal justice policy in England and Wales. Scholars trace this increased prominence to the first New Labour government's justice and equality reform agendas, which contained a dual focus on vulnerability and rights as they addressed disabled people (Dunn et al, 2008). New Labour simultaneously spoke to civil rights for disabled people while also pursuing a well-intentioned, albeit paternalistic vulnerability focus. The latter was reflected in both law and criminal justice system guidance. For instance, the Youth Justice and Criminal Evidence Act 1999 defines a vulnerable person as a person, in this instance a victim or witness, who 'suffers from mental disorder within the meaning of the Mental Health Act 1983 or otherwise has a significant impairment of intelligence and social functioning or has a physical disability or is suffering from a physical disorder' (Youth Justice and Criminal Evidence Act, HM Government, 1999). This definition was significant as it inadvertently institutionalized a stereotype of disabled people as inherently vulnerable within the legal framework and that continues to pose challenges and constraints for those working within the legal system in England and Wales.

As an example, analysis of the guidance issued by the Sentencing Guidelines Council illustrates the pervasiveness of this inherent vulnerability focus. Thirteen different sentencing guidelines identify a whole range of crimes (ranging from robbery, fraud, assault and so on) where the vulnerability of the victim based on disability is an aggravating feature. A vulnerability focus is thus part of the criminal justice system' architectural framing of disabled victims and pervades the possible criminal justice responses to disability victimization. Alongside these sentencing guidelines, Section 146 of the Criminal Justice Act 2003 refers to aggravation based on disability hostility, and there are no specific sentencing guidelines on hate crime.

This embedded focus on vulnerability in criminal justice policy and practice, which equates disability and vulnerability, has not gone unquestioned (Roulstone et al, 2011; Quarmby, 2011). Although a vulnerability focus first became dominant in the social care domain, and remains prevalent in health care, the social care domain has embraced other categorizations of disabled people which focus more on 'situational risk', as this study found. However, there has been a significant time lag between shifting understandings in the social care domain and the continued pervasiveness of a vulnerability problem representation in the criminal justice system. A senior policy official in the Department of Health (R34) was critical of the pervasive use of the vulnerable person categorization in public policy; she referred to a process to 'cleanse' social care policy of the vulnerability categorization while that categorization persists in criminal justice policy and practices. In reflecting on the current position, this official commented:

> 'While I think we've pretty well knocked it on the head in social care policy, our battle is trying to get the Ministry of Justice, the Home Office, the police, housing to do this because they all have a vulnerable-person category ... so there's a multi-prong attack needed. ... It is just so ingrained and, of course, it's easy because actually thinking of an alternative to describe what you mean can be quite challenging. It's easier to say, "vulnerable people", it rolls off the tongue, it's just not helpful.' (R34)

There is a varied, somewhat complicated and shifting situation in relation to a vulnerability focus in the criminal justice system. Alongside the embedded focus in criminal law and supporting guidelines, which equate vulnerability and disability, there is an increasing desire to focus on vulnerability among the judiciary and parts of the police. In a context of declining policing resources, increased demand and critique of police handling of cases such as the Pilkington case, the police have moved to a revised national policing model where vulnerability is a key criterion guiding policing interventions. The rationale for centring vulnerability in guiding future police interventions is not wholly clear. This is now to be mirrored in national policing inspection frameworks (R23). This potentially constitutes a further institutionalization of a vulnerability focus in the criminal justice system.

At the same time, the research for this book found clear evidence of a shifting understanding of the vulnerability problem representation as applied to disabled people among senior CPS and national police leads involved with the hate crime agendas. These 'progressive' shifts in problem and policy representation appear to be occurring in parts of the criminal justice system in response to disability activists' critique, performance challenges, external inspections and internal reflection based on case experiences. However, these 'progressive' changes exist within the CPS and parts of the police alongside a continued pervasiveness of vulnerability focus across the criminal justice system more widely.

Does a vulnerability focus matter?

The research for this book has found that the policy discourse on vulnerability has been palpably present in the development of Disability Hate Crime policy in terms of problem representation and policy responses. At times, it has been subject to policy silence or a competing problem representation; most recently, it has been included in policy initiatives aimed at a more overarching representation of disability victimization referred to as Disability Hate Crimes and other crimes against disabled people (CPS, 2017; Bacchi, 2009). In this analysis, the focus is on the salience of this shifting vulnerability focus.

It is possible, over the past 20 years, to identify three phases in the developing construction of vulnerability as it relates to Disability Hate Crime. These are a Policy Silence Phase, a Disability Hate Crime plus Vulnerability Phase and, most recently, an all-embracing Disability Hate Crime and other Crimes against Disabled People Phase. Chapter 4 on Agenda Triggering notes that, in 2003, government officials' initial drafts of a disability hostility aggravation amendment to the Criminal Justice Act 2003 focused on vulnerability aggravation rather than hostility aggravation (R6). This suggested that the vulnerability focus was the default setting in the policy mindset. Thus, the issue of vulnerability in Disability Hate Crime was present from the very outset of this agenda. However, as was noted in Chapter 4, given that the activist and political streams were in the ascendant at that stage, the activists' focus on disability hostility per se prevailed and the vulnerability issue was subject to policy silence for a period (Bacchi, 2009).

Given the policy construction of targeted crimes against disabled people as either vulnerability or hostility based, a focus on one has inhibited movement on the other. In such an either/or policy construction, this initial period of policy silence on vulnerability in relation to hate crime was of sufficient duration to secure the legal amendment known as Section 146 (Criminal Justice Act 2003), focused solely on disability hostility. However, as Bacchi (2009) notes, policy silences do not necessarily resolve the duality in issues masked by the silence: silences can stand as pointers to ongoing challenges and can emerge, or indeed erupt, at later stages in the policy process. This occurred in the subsequent development of Disability Hate Crime policy.

Having secured Section 146, the agenda increasingly moved from the activist stream to the policy stream. Policy officials were now in the lead and managing the responses to activists' demands. A focus in this agenda-setting period was the fleshing out of the two-sentence legal provision in Section 146 into what it would mean in operational terms for the CPS and the police. Much of this activity took place around the framing of a CPS public policy statement on Disability Hate Crime in 2007 (CPS, 2007b). This activity, as noted in Chapter 5 on Agenda Setting, was led by criminal justice system officials and involved inputs from disability organizations and activists.

Analysis indicates that, in terms of problem representation, this original CPS public policy statement was perhaps more accurately described as a Disability Hate Crime plus Vulnerability policy statement. The 2007 public policy statement states that, for its purposes, some crimes against disabled people are hate crimes and 'some crimes are committed because the offender regards the disabled person as being vulnerable and not because the offender dislikes or hates disabled people' (CPS, 2007b, p 9). Thus, the criminal justice system constructed a focus on disability hostility and a focus on disability vulnerability as completely mutually exclusive (Roulstone et al, 2011, p 352). Respondents who were involved in the development of the Disability Hate Crime policy highlighted the challenges in arriving at this distinction. In contrast, criminal justice system officials indicated more ease with this distinction. Disability organizations indicated less ease and a sense of less ability to influence the final focus of the public policy statement. There was a sense that this dual focus was solely what was on offer and, although less than appropriate, there appeared a reluctant resigned acceptance (R3).

This framing of the problem potentially provided perpetrators with a get-out clause where their targeting of disabled victims because of their disability could go unrecognized. It set a high threshold for Disability Hate Crime to meet, constructing crimes perceived to be based on vulnerability targeting as not hate crimes. This was to pose fundamental and far-reaching challenges given the pervasiveness of the stereotype of disabled people as vulnerable.

Having a public policy statement on Disability Hate Crime that distinguished so emphatically between crimes based on hostility and those based on vulnerability begs the question: Do these separate problem representations matter? What has it meant in practice? My analysis for this book indicates that this separating out of a hostility and vulnerability focus in Disability Hate Crime cases has had significant impacts at the levels of both recognition and redistribution (Fraser, 2003), which I address here.

The evidence in this study points to significant impacts at the level of overall recognition, in the sense of group recognition, affirmation and response to minoritized experiences (concepts elaborated by scholars such as Fraser (2003) and Taylor (1994)). Impacts in terms of recognition of crimes have had implications for crime reporting, monitoring and response. As reflected by some respondents, the Disability Hate Crime agenda is fundamentally an issue of recognition-based justice. In terms of identity recognition, the disability movement in recent decades has emphasized the quest for independent living as exemplifying full citizenship. Within this emphasis, a policy focused on disabled people as vulnerable runs directly contrary to how many disabled people define their situation. Part of the objection is to the very use of the term 'vulnerable' and its conjuring up of an inferior weak status. A focus on vulnerability is seen as a deficit concept that limits the capacity for full citizenship and independent living. It places the focus on the individual disabled victim rather than on disability prejudice in society and disablist perpetrators. A focus on vulnerability in targeted disability crimes is viewed by many disabled activists as an act of serious misrecognition, as social justice subordination with significant consequences for individual and group esteem and justice (Taylor, 1994). A senior independent researcher involved in research on this topic reflected:

> 'Implicit within the vulnerability focus is that the answer to the problem (of disability victimization) lay in the group itself. This plays into the more medical–personal tragedy model of disability … the focus on disabled people's vulnerability is really a lever that causes people to look at disabled people with the attendant implications that it is their vulnerability that explains why they experience different kinds of hate crime. So, your interest is in who experiences what and where rather than actually tackling the wider societal structures that reproduce vulnerability.' (R14)

He concludes that an undue focus on vulnerability in disability victimization leads to: "a lot of responses focused on managing the disabled person – and the issue of vulnerability becomes ultimately a shorthand for depriving disabled people of rights" (R14).

In fact, the research for this book found that the vulnerability categorization as reflected in the original public policy statement on Disability Hate Crime was rejected by all disability activist respondents and by others in the equal rights sector and some in the criminal justice system. Considering that the issue of self-definition is a defining feature of the identity-based equality movements and acknowledged as central to minority respect and recognition (Taylor, 1994), it is striking how a policy categorization of disabled people as vulnerable became so embedded in policy discourse and practice. Regardless of how disabled people view themselves, and how much they reject the vulnerability categorization, it is a categorization placed upon them. Relatively recent research on young people in contact with social care agencies in England and Wales found similarly to this study (Brown, 2016).

The research for this book found that the problem representation of disabled people as vulnerable evoked strong views among respondents, and that the issues revolve around recognition-based justice for disability activists and for some others involved with this agenda.

A member of the Equality and Human Rights Commission said the focus on vulnerability in considering Disability Hate Crimes was "unfortunate and regrettable": "For a start, it immediately puts the focus on the victim as the person who needs to fix themselves or be protected or saved and it draws attention away from the acts of the perpetrators" (R28).

Some disability activists were more forthright about the use of the vulnerable person problem representation to refer to disabled victims of hate crime. A former director of a disability NGO commented:

'If you have a narrative of vulnerability and people who are deserving only of our pity and our patronage and our kind of patting them on the head and saying, "Oh well, it's terrible, terrible, terrible", that's less challenging than accepting that people are equal to us and are worthy of our respect, our recognition, and our support. And, therefore, when crimes happen to them, they need to be dealt with on an equal footing to us. But, if we see people as vulnerable, that's less challenging to our notion of difference, they're vulnerable, they're to be pitied.' (R26)

She added that a vulnerability focus simply evokes a pity response rather than a rights and justice response.

Recognition of how a problem representation of disabled people as vulnerable can cloud issues of hostility in what are Disability Hate Crimes goes to the heart of the challenges in the institutionalization of the Disability Hate Crime agenda in the criminal justice system. This was recognized by a range of respondents within the criminal justice system.

One former criminal justice system leader said:

'We have to be very careful here with the language we use and the approach that we take. Disabled people are not by definition vulnerable but, like all people, they may get into vulnerable situations, and it is someone in a vulnerable situation who is very often taken advantage of. So, it doesn't mean that they are, and I think it is wrong to say they are, as it were, in a constant state of vulnerability, because they're not. It's just that they may find themselves in vulnerable situations more often than other people, and that's what is exploited. ... But it is quite important in this context to make sure we are talking about the situation that somebody finds themselves in rather than vulnerable by characteristics. … And it may be that some groups find themselves in vulnerable situations more often, but it's still wrong to say they're always vulnerable.' (R19)

Another former criminal justice system leader elaborated on the consequences of a vulnerable-person focus in Disability Hate Crimes:

'There's an overarching point which is that it's demeaning … it can be demeaning language. The problem with using it (using the vulnerable-person label) in an overarching way is that it fails to mark the essential gravity of the offence. It's obviously bad to pick on someone because they're vulnerable. In some circumstances, it can be extremely bad, and it seems to me that a crime which is additionally motivated by hostility towards the disability … that is bound to represent an aggravating feature … what an undue focus on vulnerability does is that it denies that additional aggravating feature of hostility and it means that society isn't marking its disapproval of that form of hostility. So much of this crime is, in truth, motivated by hostility … whether the judges and prosecutors recognize it or not, it seems to be the truth.' (R30)

This respondent identified wider consequences that can flow from this overfocus on the vulnerable victim to the neglect of a focus on disability hostility:

'What becomes the exclusive attention of the court is the situation of the victim. So, the crime is situated within that vulnerability context, and it stops short of analysing and taking proper account of the motivation of the offender in all its wickedness. Because, obviously, the hostility element is an additional element of wickedness which, if you focus on the victim and the victim is in a vulnerable state, is simply ignored and then it's ignored for sentencing purposes which is bad. But just as bad and perhaps worse is it's ignored in terms of marking the seriousness of the offence which is what flows from sentencing. So, then, there's no acknowledgement on the part of society of the true gravity of the conduct.' (R30)

He reflected, based on his experience, that the greatest challenge to establishing an appropriate criminal justice system response to Disability Hate Crime was:

'The dual problem of the excessive focus on vulnerability and the inability to move away from an idea that this is not a wider social problem, wider than the idea that the problem is contained within the people who are disabled. So, I think these two are linked and I think that is the biggest challenge to progress on Disability Hate Crime.' (R30)

He reflected that this excessive focus on vulnerability raised challenges for the justice system that were still not appropriately recognized and addressed, resulting in Disability Hate Crime lagging behind other hate crime strands in terms of recognition and response:

'It was almost as though the justice system saw disabled people as bringing their problems on themselves by being disabled. In other words, this is a problem because you are disabled. Now, we'd never these days say to a black person or to a gay person, "This is your problem because you're black or you're gay". I think we still say this to disabled people, it's seen as a problem for them because they're different and because they raise feelings of fear or hostility. ... So, there's a sense that there's a problem that emanates from disability, in a way that you no longer ever say, "This is a problem that emanates from your ethnicity or your sexuality". We would say, "This is a problem because we have homophobic people" or "This is a problem because we have racists". We're still not saying, "This is a problem because we have people who are hostile towards disabled people".' (R30)

A former senior criminal justice system manager reflected how a focus on the vulnerability of disabled victims rather than a focus on the hostility of perpetrators in hate crime cases: "puts Disability Hate Crime on the margins of hate crime and, even in terms of the approach, it becomes a social care issue; it's not even a serious criminal justice issue" (R15).

A senior independent researcher involved in hate crime research reflected that the issue of vulnerability was sensitive and challenging in terms of disability victimization. He reflected that, depending on the nature of people's impairment, it can: "Influence the fact of their ability to cope. Now it is not just situational, that is, it is to some extent intrinsic, but only at the individual level, not at the group level" (R35). Recognition-based justice, for many respondents, is what the Disability Hate Crime agenda is fundamentally about. It is about recognizing the harms, including hostility, that can be attendant with living with a minoritized disability identity. It can be argued that failure to recognize disability hostility in the criminal justice system is a breach of recognition-based justice. It is a failure to afford parity of esteem to a legally protected characteristic, a failure to extend in practice the protection of the hostility victimization framework to a victimized group.

However, the research for this book found that this failure is also often a breach of substantive or redistributive justice. It is not only a recognition failure. It is about naming the experience in a victim-centred way (recognition) to enable the criminal justice system to deal with it substantively and justly within the criminal justice system (redistribution). It can also lead to a failure to mark the substantive gravity of the crimes committed in all their dimensions through failing to materially address the hostility dimension in the sentence handed down a redistribution failure. Thus, full justice is not being delivered. Recognition and redistributive justice are intertwined here. This can lead to a sense of double victimization by the criminal justice system for disabled people: the insult of non-recognition together with the injury of failure to deliver substantive justice (Fraser and Olsen, 2008).

The recognition–redistribution template as devised by Fraser is a useful reminder of the significance of both identity and material dimensions of inequalities. As with any heuristic framework, it risks over-compartmentalizing identity and material dimensions of inequalities in ways which may neglect how they flow into each other, such that there are material dimensions to identity inequalities and identity dimensions to material inequalities. There are very real material consequences to recognition-based failure. There also are the real psychological–material gains that may accrue to a perpetrator in a hostility-based crime that, through a single incident, can contribute to reproducing an unequal social order with material consequences flowing from identity (Perry, B., 2001). To the extent that Disability Hate Crime is recognized at all, it is more readily recognized as a recognition-based inequality, but it is not solely that. If Disability Hate Crime is misrecognized as hate crime, this can flow on to material–substantive injustice where the actual penalty handed down not only fails to recognize the identity aspect at all but also fails to materially reflect that in an enhanced penalty. That is the failure of redistributive justice linked to what starts out as recognition inequality.

A case analysis of the vulnerability focus

As part of the research for this book, I analysed 15 cases in which disabled people had been victims of targeted incidents and crimes, all of which could be regarded as hate incidents or hate crimes. In Chapter 2, there is a description of each case, together with an indication of the case outcomes in terms of whether they were successfully prosecuted as Disability Hate Crimes. As indicated, 12 of these cases were accessed via the criminal justice system and three via NGOs or the independent statutory sector. All 15 cases involved targeted victimization of disabled people linked to their disability status. In selecting and analysing these cases, the aim was to explore the range of cases that feature in both officially recorded and non-crimed cases. Notwithstanding the current limitations of Disability Hate Crime data, this marked a unique analysis of Disability Hate Crime cases.

It is striking that all 12 cases accessed via the criminal justice system were identified by the police and the CPS as involving a vulnerable victim. It is as if the identification of a disabled victim of crime automatically leads to a vulnerability categorization, indicating an embedded equating of disability and vulnerability in the criminal justice system. Consistent with the insights of Lipsky on street level bureaucracy and discretion, this study has found in its analysis of individual cases, a clear tendency to 'routinize, simplify and differentiate' Disability Hate Crime cases based on a vulnerability categorization-stereotype. There is, as Lipsky noted, an institutional receptivity to differentiate the victim population by informed prevalent attitudes and prejudices, in this instance, into a vulnerability categorization. To the extent that discretion was exercised in these cases the research for this book found that it was exercised in an institutionally patterned way that helped divide up the victim population for case management and response purposes. This can and did lead to stereotyping and was in turn to impact the delivery of substantive justice (Lipsky, 2010).

As this analysis found, this vulnerability categorization influenced subsequent experiences, some positive, some less so, for the delivery of justice. This automatic categorization of disability victimization under a vulnerability category, it could be argued, is understandable given the surrounding legal architecture on vulnerability within which criminal justice system practitioners operate. While this categorization may be intended to lead to supports in the criminal justice process, the research for this book found that special measures were provided in only three of the 12 cases identified with a vulnerability categorization. These included the use of court intermediaries and in-court reading of impact statements rather than direct giving of evidence by victims. These measures helped to secure justice based on vulnerability in these three cases.

However, in the other nine cases, the vulnerability categorization had no identifiable positive influence on the consideration of or use of special measures. My analysis has found that, in the more serious offences where a vulnerability categorization was identified, it served to occlude a focus on hostility, particularly during the court process and at sentencing stage (see Chapter 2, Cases 8, 'Enslavement case', 9, 'Sunset View care home' and 14, the murder of Brent Martin). In many cases where the police and prosecutors used dual-case categorizations – vulnerability focused and hostility focused – the vulnerability focus became the master categorization as these cases journeyed through the criminal justice system, with the disability hostility focus silent or slipping from consideration at key criminal justice stages. In other analysed cases, where the vulnerability focus emerged as the master category at the outset, a disability hostility focus was unlikely to feature at all. This is highlighted particularly in the enslavement case. Furthermore, this analysis – and this study's key informant interviews – found that there are issues in relation to the judiciary's embracing of the vulnerability categorization, and their under-recognition and, in some cases, rejection of a hostility dimension as applied to crimes targeting disabled people (see Chapter 2, Cases 5, 'Skate park case' and 9, 'Sunset View care home'). As key actors in the criminal justice system, the judiciary's problem recognitions, case categorizations and, as a corollary, their problem silences have consequences for both recognition and redistributive justice for victims of Disability Hate Crime. These consequences arise, first, in terms of recognizing the hostility aspect of the crime and, second, in terms of marking the substantive harm of the hostility dimension in the penalty handed down.

This book's analysis of the 15 cases supports the view of a range of this book's key informants that Disability Hate Crime and vulnerability do not exist wholly as free-standing phenomena. Rather, they are constructed daily through the decisions, categorizations and mis-categorizations made by criminal justice system officials. This case analysis supported the view that Disability Hate Crime cases were frequently constructed to involve 'competing' problem representations as cases of vulnerability or hostility, leading to case framings that failed to deliver full justice for disabled victims of hate crimes.

An undue focus on vulnerability in the cases analysed occluded a legitimate focus on disability hostility. Indeed, a Disability Hate Crime dimension is often recognized and acknowledged in the criminal justice system only in cases involving more accepted manifest verbal hostility (see Chapter 2, Cases 1, 'Downtown, 3, 'Valetown' and 6, 'Visiting mates'). This means that serious offences up to and including murder have gone unrecognized as they have not fitted the prevalent hostility frame (see Chapter 2, Cases 8, 'Enslavement, 9, 'Sunset View care home' 14, the murder of Brent Martin). This augments a finding from the EHRC Formal Inquiry where the dominant framing of disabled people as vulnerable allowed targeted murders to be treated less seriously than warranted, dealt with as a social care review and ending in denial of full justice (EHRC, 2011a). The received messaging about lives lesser valued has been felt acutely among disabled people (Quarmby, 2011).

In the evidence gathered for this book, I found that targeted crimes that arise in the contexts of an imbalance in power relations and abuse of power also featured among Disability Hate Crimes (see Chapter 2, Cases 2, 8, 'Enslavement, 10, 'Domestic Violence and 11, 'Church warden). This raised questions about Disability Hate Crime and its relationship to the wider hate crime domain. It raised a question as to whether all hate crimes involve some acting out of imbalanced power relations, a particular form of 'doing difference' (Perry, B. 2001, pp 4–5). Might such imbalances of power arise much more frequently and explicitly in Disability Hate Crimes, given disabled peoples often increased structured and situational vulnerability?

It is noteworthy that almost all the successful Disability Hate Crime cases occurred outdoors (five out of six) and almost all the failed Disability Hate Crime cases occurred indoors (eight out of nine). This is perhaps reflective of some insensitivity to the different geography of segregation impacting on disability and, in turn, on Disability Hate Crime (Roulstone et al, 2011).

Indeed, the manifestations of some Disability Hate Crimes appear to sit at the intersection between violence against women and what may be termed the more classic racist, religious and homophobic crimes. Some Disability Hate Crimes that I analysed display characteristics of hostility and violent discrimination, accompanied by verbal abuse often associated with classic racist, religious and homophobic crimes (see Chapter 2, Cases 1, 'Downtown', 2, 'Supported Housing', 3, 'Valetown' 4, 'Spitting cyclist' and 6, 'Visiting mates'). On the other hand, other Disability Hate Crimes reflect manifestations of the abuse of power more akin to violence against women, including crimes of exploitation (see Chapter 2, Cases 8, 'Enslavement', 9, 'Sunset View care home', 10, 'Domestic Violence' and 11, 'Church warden'). The evidence from this study and from criminal justice system data points to heightened levels of sexual offences and criminal damage in both Disability Hate Crimes and crimes of violence against women (CPS, 2010b, 2010c). The research for this book points to the need for both to be regarded as manifestations of hostility. Given disabled people's disadvantaged social positioning, some experience an imbalance of power in relationships with families, friends, peers, communities, and in relation to state agencies and other institutions. There exists the potential to abuse and exploit these imbalances of power and there is a need to be equally alert to the discriminatory violence manifestations and the abuse-of-power manifestations because of 'disability vulnerability' in Disability Hate Crimes. Balderston (2012; 2013), in ground-breaking research on disabled women and violence, recognizes this issue but also the very limited recognition of and response to the intersectionality of disabled women's experience of targeted violence. The research for this book also found that cases involving abuses of power in relation to disabled people were not being recognized and responded to in terms of the hostility that underpins these cases. In this context, substantive justice was not being delivered. The implications of this are expanded on later in this chapter where I make the case for a refined legal model of disability hostility.

At the outset of this analysis, I queried whether the focus on vulnerability in Disability Hate Crime cases had any real impact. It is evident that this focus has had significant impacts at the levels of both recognition and redistributive justice. An undue focus on vulnerability in Disability Hate Crime cases has led to a strong sense of social justice subordination for disabled people and the denial of substantive justice which marks the gravity of hostility-based crimes for disabled victims. In the face of such misrecognition, disability activists, parts of the criminal justice system itself and others have challenged this perceived justice failure.

Moving away from a vulnerability focus

In the years following the 2007 publication of the first public policy statement on Disability Hate Crime, disability activists questioned the criminal justice system's performance in investigating and prosecuting such cases. As indicated in Chapter 5, they articulated their challenge both in response to individual cases of perceived criminal justice system failure and in campaigning reports highlighting inappropriate responses. At the heart of the activists' concerns lay a critique of an undue focus on vulnerability. These criticisms were shared, at least in part, by some in the criminal justice system. This led, in the first instance, to the previously mentioned keynote speech by the then Director of Public Prosecutions in October 2008, when he acknowledged that a widespread undue focus on vulnerability in the criminal justice system was 'clouding the issues' of hostility in Disability Hate Crime cases, and that the poor performance in handling these cases stood as 'a scar on the conscience of the criminal justice system' (Macdonald, 2008). This informed the issuing of supplementary guidance on distinguishing between issues of vulnerability and hostility in such cases (CPS, 2010b).

The case failures continued, however. The issue was given impetus by the serious case failures profiled in the EHRC formal inquiry in 2011, which highlighted both problems with recognition and substantive–redistributive justice because of an undue focus on issues of vulnerability. The issue was given further impetus by two critical criminal justice inspection reports on the criminal justice system's handling of Disability Hate Crime (2013 and 2015, considered earlier). These reports highlighted the criminal justice system's ongoing failure to define and operationalize an appropriate definition of Disability Hate Crime.

These critiques and reflections led, in 2015, to a CPS review of the original 2007 public policy statement on Disability Hate Crime. This review also involved the police and a national advisory group, including activists and the independent statutory sector. In August 2017, the updated Public Policy Statement on Disability Hate Crime and other Crimes against Disabled People was published. This public policy statement indicated shifting conceptualizations of Disability Hate Crime and of vulnerability since the first Statement was issued in 2007.

The publication of the revised draft public policy statement on Disability Hate Crime for consultation marked the entry into what I identify as the third phase in the journey to managing vulnerability and Disability Hate Crime. I identify this as the Disability Hate Crime and other Crimes against Disabled People phase, drawing from the title of the 2017 public policy statement. This shift in language is not without significance and reflects changes, continuities and ongoing challenges in the conceptualization of Disability Hate Crime. It appears to imply a broader set of crimes against disabled people, of which hate crimes are a part. There is something of a naming and content disconnect between the earlier and the latest public policy statements. The original 2007 public policy statement, while foregrounding hate crime in its title, actually foregrounded vulnerability in its substantive content. The latest public policy statement mentions hate crime in its title and immediately balances the title with reference to 'other crimes against disabled people', while its content substantially heightens the focus on disability hostility and significantly reduces and critiques any undue focus on vulnerability in Disability Hate Crimes. However, in the policy journey to resolve the challenge of vulnerability in Disability Hate Crime cases, there seems to remain an alignment gap at the level of policy naming and policy substance, indicating the continuing unsettled nature of this policy agenda.

The 2017 public policy statement at one level signals significant gains for activists and others in terms of their critique of an undue focus on vulnerability. It acknowledges that vulnerability is a problematic categorization, that it is unacceptable to many disabled people and others, and it commits to interrogating this notion. It reads: 'When presented with cases that involve disabled people, we will be aware that the stereotype-based belief that disabled people as a group are somehow inherently vulnerable, weak and easy targets is an attitude that motivates some crimes against disabled people' (CPS, 2017, p 1). It acknowledges the link between a wider disability prejudice and Disability Hate Crimes when it states that:

> When presented with cases that involve disabled people, we will be aware that the prejudice, discrimination and social exclusion experienced by many disabled people is not the inevitable result of their impairments ... but it rather stems from specific barriers they experience on a daily basis: this is known as the social model of disability. (CPS, 2017, p 1)

Most significantly, the latest public policy statement states that, while there will not be an undue focus on vulnerability in such cases in future, this exists within a legal framework which identifies disabled people as vulnerable, and the criminal justice system must and will work within that framework. Therein lie ongoing challenges and constraints, not least that significant positive efforts of prosecutors and police nationally are constrained by the wider legal framework.

So, is the 2017 public policy statement on Disability Hate Crime a significant milestone towards the institutionalization of the Disability Hate Crime agenda? Or does it represent a continued clash of problem representations? It contains elements of both, according to this book's analysis. In a positive development, it marks significant shifts in the conceptualization of disability hostility and of vulnerability for policy purposes. Its shifting title could also indicate, at one level, a bilocation of Disability Hate Crime half inside, half outside the hate crime domain. Moreover, it still focuses significantly on a wider set of 'other crimes' experienced by disabled people, which it regards may be opportunistic or vulnerability based and that these are non-hostility based crimes. This is most stark when it states:

> It's important to make a distinction between a disability hate crime and a crime committed against a disabled person because of his or her disability ... crimes are committed because the offender perceives the disabled person to be vulnerable and not because the offender dislikes or hates the person or disabled people. (CPS, 2017, p 2)

Among the examples of crimes that are committed against disabled people because they are disabled but are not regarded as hate crimes include 'mate crime' and crimes where there is a relationship and expectation of trust. Here the 2017 public policy statement replicates – and amplifies – the most problematic part of the 2007 public policy statement with examples of targeted hostile crimes against disabled people, albeit in relationships of trust, which my research concludes should be regarded as fitting the hate crime definition, but which are now not to be regarded as such. Much of the scaffolding in the 2017 public policy statement on Disability Hate Crime appears to have been altered to reflect longstanding critique but a core policy distinction remains largely unaltered. Inevitably, it also remains located within the current wider legal framework, which conceives of disability and vulnerability as coexisting statuses. It continues to straddle the competing representations of vulnerability and hostility but in ways that now seek in part to positively rebalance the policy focus. The result is a mix of progress and confusion, a policy scenario marked by one policy step forward and one step back. Thus, the ongoing unsettled nature of Disability Hate Crime continues to be manifest in this significant policy pronouncement from the criminal justice system. This is likely to persist without a legal reframing of the issue.

Analysis for this book concludes that sustained progress on vulnerability in the context of Disability Hate Crime is only likely to be realized in the context of moving to a more far-reaching alternative understanding of disability hostility. This would require a shift in the legal framing of disability hostility. Currently, the criminal justice system is constrained because it operates on a model of disability hostility that is based on hostility motivation and/or hostility demonstration. That is all that Section 146 is designed to address. Indeed, in analysing 15 cases, this study has found that such a model only captures some Disability Hate Crime cases (see Chapter 2, Cases 1, 'Downtown', 2, 'Supported housing', 3, 'Valetown', 4, 'Spitting cyclist', 5, 'Skate park' and 7, 'Homeless hostel'). In the main, it captures cases that involve manifest verbal hostility together with base criminal offences. It does not capture Disability Hate Crimes where people are targeted because of their disability and that often involve serious disability-based harassment, abuses of power including exploitation (often over time) and, in some instances, murder. The research for this book has found that these cases are reframed as occurring 'because of' vulnerability rather than 'because of' disability and are responded to as such. Having analysed many cases, one disability campaigner reflected that these crimes against disabled people were not attacks on vulnerable people per se, but targeted attacks on disabled people first and foremost. She concluded that this pervasive problem representation as vulnerable was leading to a lack of justice:

> 'This doesn't just happen because you're a so-called vulnerable person ... and that was the thing that I wanted to get out into the media, that this is not that people attack people because they're vulnerable, they're attacked *because they are disabled*. These are hate crimes; they are not attacks on a vulnerable person.' (R12)

This insight was echoed by a former senior criminal justice system manager. She concluded that lawyers can tend to adopt an 'easy' vulnerability focused mindset in these cases:

> 'Why do I have to go through the intellectual debate on this? I can just put it to the judge that this is a vulnerable victim, and they've got powers to enhance sentence because the victim is vulnerable, so why go through the mental gymnastics? ... And that is where you run into difficulties with the disabled community because it does matter. It is about disabled people's rights, and the prosecutors, they just don't get it. They think it's a prosecution, a person's been sentenced, and there's been an uplift of a sort. The fact that it was not under Section 146, that it has not been for disability hostility, they're not losing sleep over it, but the disabled groups are. They are saying, "You're not recognizing our rights and the fact that we are being targeted *because of* our disability". So therein lies the problem.' (R15)

She goes on to conclude that this undue focus on vulnerability and the inextricably linked failure to recognize crimes committed *because of* disability led to Disability Hate Crime being placed at the edge of the hate crime domain. This has led to a reframing of disability hostility as a social care issue rather than a criminal justice issue, she said.

A respondent involved with the agenda over many years and across sectors reflected on the undue vulnerability focus in Disability Hate Crimes as one that "constitutes both a barrier and also an opportunity" (R3). She identified the barrier as the challenge of proving hostility in Disability Hate Crime cases when the pervasive embedded perception is that this all happened because "they are vulnerable, not hated" (R3). "Being called vulnerable, being perceived as vulnerable is actually a stereotype and when expressed … it is what we would call a bias indicator. It can help prosecutors actually recognise Disability Hate Crime and help make the case that it is a hate crime" (R3).

The analysis of cases for this book allows me to concur with that reflection and go further. Indeed, the vulnerability categorization–stereotype is, in a sense, the master stereotype that floods the disability experience with an almost automatic equating in the criminal justice system of seeing disability and perceiving vulnerability. If, as this study found and outlines, the vulnerable-person stereotype is the most pervasive stereotype of disabled people, then it can be viewed that targeting disabled people for crime *because of* their perceived vulnerability is a hostile act and can be regarded as such. Directly related to this, targeting of disabled people for crime because of perceived vulnerability is a discriminatory selection. Indeed, the case analysis I conducted shows that targeting disabled people for crime *because of* their perceived vulnerability often simply provides the cover through which hostility can be expressed (Chapter 2, Cases 2, 'Supported housing', 4, 'Spitting cyclist', 5, 'Skate park', 7, 'Homeless hostel', 8, 'Enslavement', 9, 'Sunset View care home', 10, 'Domestic violence' and 11, 'Church warden'; Faye Waxman, 1991).

This book and others have found that targeting of disabled people because of their perceived vulnerability has been popularly linked to what are termed opportunistic crimes. However, as Thomas (2011) has indicated, these crimes are often calculating, in the choice of target. Discriminatory calculation rather than a passing opportunism often guides these crimes with that discriminatory calculation reflected in the selection of a disabled person as a target (Chapter 2 case profiles).

On the basis of the research for this book, I concluded that the issues of perceived vulnerability and hostility are not separate in Disability Hate Crime cases. Thomas (2011) has previously proffered the view that targeting vulnerability might well be a more complicated expression of hostility. The analysis for this study went further and concluded that targeting vulnerability and targeting hostility are not opposite sides of the same coin in Disability Hate Crime; they are, in fact, very often the same sides of the Disability Hate Crime coin. Targeting vulnerability and targeting hostility are almost always variations in the expression of hostility. In this context, I argue that, as one of this book's key respondents reflected, interrogating vulnerability is central to advancing Disability Hate Crime "and must always be analysed and addressed where it's raised" (R3).

This raises a wider implication arising from this book's analysis. If Disability Hate Crime victimization requires recognition that it be identifiable through either demonstration of hostility, a hostility motivation, or targeting *because of* a victim's disability, then the existing legal framework falls short of what is required to capture the nature and range of Disability Hate Crimes. The current legal framework, the demonstration–motivation model embodied in Section 146 of the Criminal Justice Act 2003, is limited in the range of disability hostility cases it can capture. No matter how enlightened the criminal justice system policy initiatives are, no matter how many times vulnerability is revisited, without a change in the law that enables capturing victimization *because of* disability vulnerability, this book concludes that only limited justice can be delivered on Disability Hate Crime. Concurrent with the research for this book, research led by Professor Mark Walters at Sussex University concluded similarly that hate crime law requires reform to capture targeting by reason of disability or other protected characteristics. Deploying similar methods, Walters, Wieldlitzka and Owusu-Bempah's research (2017) conclusion adds weight to the conclusion reached here in respect of disability targeting. The conclusion reached in this book goes further than recommendations made by Walters et al as I argue for a three-limbed legal test of proof to be applied in Disability Hate Crime, namely a hostile motivation test, a demonstration of hostility test and/or a by-reason-of disability test.

That said, there are provisions in jurisdictions which can be appraised and considered, particularly in US states which operate a 'because of' or discriminatory selection model of hate crime law. On the basis of my research, I would not simply conclude in favour of replacing the current demonstration–motivation model as exists in England and Wales with a discrimination-selection model imported from the US. Rather, this study points to the need to appraise a hybrid model in respect of Disability Hate Crime which can capture motivation, demonstration and discriminatory selection-based hostility. In this way, the vulnerability targeting challenge can be included within the Disability Hate Crime framework. Given the different histories and 'geographies of segregation' (Roulstone et al, 2011) of the different discriminations such as racism, homophobia and ableism, different manifestations of discrimination have developed, and these merit a varied geometry in terms of legal, policy and practice responses. Failure to recognize and respond to these differences risks ongoing failure to deal appropriately with Disability Hate Crime through requiring this specific form of hate crime to conform to a legal model of hostility devised 20 years earlier to respond to racist and religious crimes. Indeed, failure to respond to these differences in manifestations of disability hostility relegates Disability Hate Crime to the status of an unsettled and unsettling concept – largely because of the ongoing failures to revisit and reconstruct the vulnerability/hostility nexus, and the pervasive hegemonic notions of what can constitute hostility and prejudice in targeted violence and harassment based on identity discrimination.

Conclusion

While considerable activist, policy and political stream activities have contributed to the emergence and development of a Disability Hate Crime policy agenda in the criminal justice system, the issue has not yet become institutionalized as business as usual. It remains an unsettled and unsettling agenda. Central to the ongoing unsettled and unsettling nature of this agenda are the questions posed by the issue of vulnerability.

This chapter identified and analysed three phases in the problem representation of vulnerability in relation to Disability Hate Crime. These are an initial Policy Silence phase; a second phase, the Disability Hate Crime plus Vulnerability phase lasting ten years; and now the most recent phase, which I identified as the Disability Hate Crime and other Crimes against Disabled People phase (2016–to date). I conclude that it marks both further progress towards institutionalization and indicates ongoing policy challenges. The most recent policy statement from the criminal justice system presents what is still an unsettled position. This is reflected in a policy name change that, at one level, bi-locates Disability Hate Crime inside and outside the hate crime domain.

At the same time, the substantive policy content significantly foregrounds the focus on hostility and in part critiques the focus on vulnerability. There also remain unsettled issues in terms of how this revised public policy statement sits alongside existing criminal justice system legal guidance including senior counsel's guidance that foregrounds the issue of vulnerability. And all of this policy activity, including considerable positive developments, are taking place within a wider legal framework which still equates disability and vulnerability, which operates competing problem representations. Now, a gap may be emerging between parts of the criminal justice system vision and policy on this agenda and the constraints of the existing legal framework. In this regard, Disability Hate Crime, through forcing consideration of vulnerability targeting on to the policy agenda, is pushing at the boundaries of possibility within the current hate crime domain and highlighting its constraints.

This chapter's analysis leads to the conclusion that an ongoing vulnerability focus remains the policy challenge in the journey towards the institutionalization of Disability Hate Crime. Analysis for this book leads to the conclusion that vulnerability is embedded as the master stereotype of disabled people in criminal justice policy and practice. Vulnerability has proven the most contentious concept in seeking to institutionalize Disability Hate Crime in the criminal justice system. Its uncritical application to disabled people as if it were an inherent group attribute and without disabled people's agreement go to the heart of the challenges and has served to impede the institutionalization of the Disability Hate Crime agenda. This ensures that Disability Hate Crime continues to be an unsettled and unsettling concept.

The analysis in this chapter, however, also identified a possible way forward towards progressive institutionalization of Disability Hate Crime. This could be addressed in short- to medium-term legal reform. The research for this book found that the legal framework for addressing Disability Hate Crime is limited in the range of disability hostility cases it can capture. That framework is Section 146 of the Criminal Justice Act 2003, which sets out what is known as a demonstration–motivation model, The fundamental challenges lie not in the nature of disability discrimination, which can be expressed as classic violent discrimination and as abuses of power in imbalanced power relationships, but in the limitations of the available legal framework to address it. What is required is a legal framework for disability hostility that includes hostility based on demonstration, motivation and/or by reason of disability. Vulnerability and hostility should not be hermetically sealed off in crimes against disabled people. They should be considered and interrogated together and vulnerability in criminal acts recognized for what it is, a discriminatory and hostile targeting of disabled people.

Given the different natures of the different discriminations, it is warranted that a variable geometry of legal responses to the different hate crime strands be put in place. There is a need to appraise a hybrid model in respect of Disability Hate Crime that can capture motivation, demonstration and discriminatory selection-based hostility. In this way, the vulnerability targeting challenge in disability victimization and wider policy challenges posed by vulnerability can be addressed within the Disability Hate Crime framework, and further progress towards institutionalization can hopefully occur. In the absence of such a change in the legal framework, notwithstanding the good intentions and significant positive efforts of criminal justice system agencies, in particular the CPS and parts of the police and activists' campaigning, the policy challenges of vulnerability are likely to continue and to impede institutionalization of this policy agenda.

As I write this book the British Criminology Society has recently established for the first time a Vulnerabilities Research Network to advance understanding and to stimulate debate on vulnerability across spheres of research, policy and practice. It is a welcome development but early days in the work of this new network. It remains to be seen the extent to which it's work will subject the concept of vulnerability to critical analysis (British Criminology Society, 2020). At present the British Criminology Society is calling for a critical analysis of the use of the term vulnerability while at the same time it is calling for the promotion and inclusion of vulnerability and its manifestations in the criminal justice process.

8

An Agenda Item Yet to Fully Speak Its Name: Ableism and Disability Hate Crime

Key points

This chapter assesses the context of disabled people's experience of disadvantage and discrimination, and the persistence of prejudice against this population today in a wide range of social and institutional contexts. The dual problematization of welfare versus rights by state institutions gives a framing to Disability Hate Crime, which sets a high standard for considering ableist crime. This chapter explores the extent to which this prejudice is reflective of the ableism impacting the Disability Hate Crime agenda itself. It is argued that in failing to recognize disability prejudice and ableism and their impacts on Disability Hate Crime, there is a failure to recognize and name the issue appropriately and, as a consequence, to deal with Disability Hate Crime justly.

Introduction

The previous chapter analysed a unique challenge in Disability Hate Crime, the challenge of vulnerability targeting and how it is an unsettling feature of this policy agenda. This chapter analyses another unsettling and closely linked feature of Disability Hate Crime and that is, an aspect of this agenda that is yet to 'fully speak its name'. This chapter analyses issues of recognition of disability prejudice, ableism and disablism as they affect the development and institutionalization of Disability Hate Crime policy making in the criminal justice system.

In the hate crime policy domain, as indicated in earlier chapters, it is commonplace to speak about racist crime, antisemitism, homophobic crime, Islamophobic crime and transphobic crime. In doing so, there is an implied acceptance of the link between ideologies of racism, antisemitism, homophobia, transphobia and hate crime. There is a recognition of the ideological diminution that minoritized identities experience. Indeed, this is taken as a defining feature of hate crimes.

However, it is not yet commonplace to speak about ableist crime. Thus, ableist crime is usually referred to as Disability Hate Crime. This sets a high threshold for ableist crimes. It begs the question whether there is recognition of the prejudicial ideology of ableism that underpin ableist incidents and crimes. It also raises the further question as to why there may be this lack of recognition of a diminished minoritized identity based on a prejudicial ideology that inferiorizes disability identity. What alternative explanations exist and what, if any, are their impacts on Disability Hate Crime policy and practice? This emerged as one of the key topics for consideration in the analysis underpinning this book.

The focus in this chapter is first on understanding the context of disabled people's experience of disadvantage and discrimination over time and in England and Wales today. The discussion then moves to the recognition of systemic or institutional discrimination experienced by disabled people in wider society and in the criminal justice system. I analyse the gaps between recognition of institutional discrimination experienced by disabled people and lack of recognition of ableism influencing Disability Hate Crime. I explore whether, yet again in the disability domain, competing accounts of disabled people's experiences in terms of welfare or rights occlude recognition of both disablism and ableism. I examine the roles played by state institutions and by disability organizations in constructing a dual problematization of welfare versus rights, and explore the shifting understandings and challenges in locating Disability Hate Crime within a wider prejudicial ideology frame of understanding. Is a frame of disablism, ableism, impairmentism or a blended frame most appropriate? Why does the conceptualization of disability prejudice remain unsettled? What impact does the use of one term instead of another make in this context? Why is it that academia, particularly outside of Britain, appears more willing to engage with ableism? This chapter concludes with thoughts on how disability prejudice, in the form of ableism, is a prejudice that is yet to fully speak its name in England and Wales.

The intersection with experiences of disadvantage

As previously mentioned in Chapter 2, scholarly accounts of the social situation of disabled people in Britain point to varied experiences influenced by issues of class, gender and impairment (Borsay, 2005; Braddock and Parish, 2001; Oliver and Barnes, 2012). There is, however, recognition of a patterned basis of disadvantage and discrimination experienced by disabled people (Oliver and Barnes, 2012; ODI, 2012 EHRC, 2017a).

Available evidence indicates that across key indicators of disadvantage and discrimination disabled people remain among those experiencing particularly significant levels of disadvantage and discrimination (EHRC, 2017a). A comprehensive profile of the social situation of disabled people in Britain, 'Being disabled in Britain' and aptly subtitled, 'a journey less equal' charted this patterned pervasive disadvantage in education, work, standard of living and experience of poverty, health and care, transport, housing, justice and detention, and inclusion and participation in civic and political life (EHRC, 2017a). The consistency of this disadvantage is demonstrated by the results of the 2021 UK Disability Survey (Disability Unit, 2021).

The EHRC highlighted the fact that, in education, disabled students in England and Wales are more likely to be bullied, excluded from school and have nearly three times lower educational attainment levels than non-disabled children (EHRC, 2017a).

The report also showed that disabled people are much less likely to be employed than non-disabled people. In 2015–16, 47.6 per cent of disabled adults were working in England and Wales, compared to 80 per cent of non-disabled adults (EHRC, 2017a). In 2021, 47 per cent of working-age disabled adults were working (Disability Unit, 2021). There is also a disability pay gap akin to gender and ethnicity pay gaps: in 2015–16, disabled people's median hourly take-home pay amounted to £9.85, compared to £11.41 for non-disabled people (EHRC, 2017a).

Significantly, more disabled people in England and Wales live in poverty than non-disabled people. In 2014–15, 30 per cent of working-age adults in households with at least one disabled household member were living on incomes below 60 per cent of median income, compared with 18 per cent of households with no disabled household members (EHRC, 2017a). In 2021, 33 per cent of households with a disabled adult experienced poverty, and 40 per cent of households with a disabled child experienced poverty, more than twice the rate where there is no disability (JRF, 2020). Before COVID-19, 42 per cent found paying their usual living expenses 'quite difficult' or 'very difficult', most frequently due to limited income (Disability Unit, 2021).

Disabled people in England and Wales are more likely to have major health conditions, to experience health inequalities and are more likely to die younger than non-disabled people (EHRC, 2017a; Disability Unit, 2021).

Disabled people also face a range of physical, attitudinal and institutional barriers in attempting to participate in society (EHRC, 2017a; Disability Unit, 2021). These include seeking to vote, under-representation in public appointments and in political office. In addition, there remains inadequate access to transport and other services that can affect the quality of life of disabled people: during 2012–14, 45 per cent of disabled adults in England

and Wales reported difficulties in accessing basic services in transport, health, benefits, culture and leisure, compared with 31.7 per cent of non-disabled adults (EHRC, 2017a).

Disabled people continue to face difficulty in finding appropriate housing, with less than 17 per cent of housing authorities having strategies in place to build disabled access-friendly homes (EHRC, 2017a). The high cost and low availability of accessible housing are often prohibitive (Disability Unit, 2021).

Disabled people also experience disadvantage and disproportionality in terms of justice and detention (Disability Unit, 2021), with an over-representation of people experiencing mental health difficulties and learning-disabled people in the prison population. Prisoners are not only more likely to have a mental health difficulty compared to the general population, but 70 per cent of prisoners who died by suicide from 2012–14 had identified mental health difficulties (Disability Unit, 2021).

In addition, disabled people are disproportionately represented as victims of crime, with disabled people feeling a heightened lack of safety, compared to non-disabled people (EHRC, 2017a). These areas of victimization are reinforced by analysis of crime survey data in England and Wales (Iganski et al, 2011b), by the work of Emerson and Roulstone (2014) on disability violence and by two systematic reviews of disabled people's experience of targeted violence (Sin et al, 2010b).

The EHRC (2017a) also pointed to the growing body of evidence on the specific theme of this book, namely Disability Hate Crime. It highlighted increased recording of Disability Hate Crimes by the police in recent years, possibly reflecting improved recording and increased reporting. In 2021, 45 per cent of disabled people reported feeling unsafe in their neighbourhood, 54 per cent worry about being insulted or harassed in the street or any other public place and 45 per cent worry about being physically attacked by strangers, at least 'some of the time' (Disability Unit, 2021). More than half (58 per cent) of respondents in the 2021 UK Disability Survey reported people mistreating them because of their disability, 33 per cent reported people being hostile to them online because of their disability, and 15 percent reported experiencing violence because of their disability (Disability Unit, 2021). A fifth (21 per cent) reported feeling unsafe inside where they live at least 'some of the time', and among those, the most frequently reported reasons for feeling unsafe inside where they live were worries about intruders (48 per cent) and difficulty accessing immediate help (37 per cent) (Disability Unit, 2021). Wilkin (2020) has described, on the basis of interviews with victims of Disability Hate Crime, that abuse and humiliation are everyday occurrences, and these are disabled people occupying public spaces on public transport.

Of the disabled people who had experienced events related to bullying, harassment, or violence based on their disability, just 29 per cent had officially reported it, and only 15 per cent of those were 'satisfied' or 'very satisfied' with the end result of the reporting (Disability Unit, 2021). Wilkin (2020) describes addressing Disability Hate Crime as 'low priority' for transport regulators and local authorities.

The EHRC (2017a) concluded that "negative attitudes towards disabled people remain prominent in Britain" (p. 12) and this patterned disadvantage can be more fully understood in that context. Aspects of the contemporary manifestation of these negative attitudes were highlighted and analysed by Burch in the context of the recent climate of austerity and the construction of disabled people as a 'drain on so-called hard-working taxpayers' (Burch, 2017, p 392).

This evidence base in relation to the disadvantage experienced by disabled people in England and Wales raises the question: how have we understood and responded to this phenomenon? Responses have shifted over time. At various times, official responses have included banishment, concealment, institutionalization, segregation and onwards to welfare, care and protection, rights and justice (Braddock and Parish, 2001; Borsay, 2005; McDonnell, 2007). The result is a mix of policy and practice problematizations and paradigms in response to disability. As the EHRC identified in its 2011 formal inquiry into harassment of disabled people, there are two main paradigms affecting policy responses to disability in Britain today: the Welfare Model and a Rights Model. Taking a longer view of policy and practice responses, the Welfare Model and its earlier relatives (the Pity and Charity Model) and its sibling, the Medical Model, have tended to prevail in terms of official responses to disability. The dominance of the Welfare Model has led to the highlighted areas of disability disadvantage being explained away in terms of individual tragedy requiring a support-based response of individual welfare, care and protection. The ideology of welfare interpellates disabled people as individual tragic subjects (Althusser, 1969).

However, a Rights Model of disability has emerged in disability activism and in academia which seeks to shift the problematization of disability. In the British context, this has largely taken the form of a Social Model of Disability and emerged as a corrective to the dominance of the Welfare Model in the late 1960s and 1970s. The Rights Model shifts the gaze from the individual disabled person to the disabling society – a society that, in terms of attitudinal and physical barriers, disables people who are different simply by virtue of impairment. The focus shifts from care and containment of the individual to transforming social structures to better include everyone, including people with impairments. This Rights–Social Model has begun to influence government policy in a range of contexts. As the dominant counter model, it is questionable, however, whether it offers an over-socialized corrective to the Welfare Model (Shakespeare, 2006).

In terms of understanding and responding to disability in Britain today, the Welfare Model tends to predominate, tempered somewhat by the influence of the Rights–Social Model. It is as if a 20th century paradigm and problematization of welfare, care and control in relation to disability in Britain overshadows a 21st-century shift to rights and justice. This forms the context within which this book analyses this topic.

Confronting institutional discrimination

In the research for this book, respondents acknowledged the disadvantage and discrimination experienced by disabled people. They acknowledged that there are systemic disadvantages impacting disabled people that go beyond the experience of an individual impairment and have a basis in the structural positioning of disabled people in society. This recognition was shared by disability activists, other rights advocates and some criminal justice system leaders and officials.

One former criminal justice system leader reflected that institutional discrimination "is particularly stark in the area of disability", and went on to reflect: "I think institutional discrimination is probably starker in Britain in respect of disabled people than any other group actually" (R30). He concluded that:

'I think it is a very fundamental societal mindset which sees disability as a problem, and you see it everywhere. ... It is not seen as an issue for liberation, it is seen as a problem ... I think it is a fundamental mindset about disability ... and, as a result ... the country is full of barriers to disabled people.' (R30)

Other criminal justice system leaders tended to emphasize institutional failure to respond appropriately to diverse needs, in this instance disabled victims. Their views reflect in part the emphasis in the earlier Lawrence Inquiry (1999) on a failure to provide an appropriate service to people based on their cultural background.

One HMIC inspector reflected that she believed institutional discrimination existed in respect of disabled people in the criminal justice system, and, in particular, she spoke about policing:

'Institutions that have a lot of cases, and where there's a big-volume business (like the police), the way to deal with a big-volume business is to do exactly the same thing for everybody and to manage your demand ... and there's maybe an unconscious management of demand when more difficult, more complex cases (eg some Disability Hate Crime cases) are required to be dealt with. They require you to get off the conveyor belt and not do everything in the same way again. I think that is a big challenge corporately for an institution that it can adapt to do that (in this instance, for disabled people) because, quite often, institutions are not made up of wicked people determined to do a bad job. They are made up of good people who are sometimes frustrated by volume demands.' (R23)

She concluded that this can lead to a failure to provide an appropriate service, which amounts to institutional discrimination.

This view of how institutional failure and discrimination can inadvertently become a feature of volume business in the criminal justice system was echoed by a national policing hate crime lead: "We are OK when it is a vanilla service you require, the same for everyone … the criminal justice system is not good at responding to subtlety, to anything beyond a black and white service" (R36). While leaders in the criminal justice system recognized the issue of institutional failure and institutional discrimination as experienced by disabled people, policy officials, disability rights activists and independent statutory sector respondents more readily identified specific aspects of institutionalized discrimination, which they recognized.

One former criminal justice system senior manager reflected that:

'The whole system [and] the criminal justice system makes assumptions which, of their very nature, discriminate against disabled people. There is an assumption of certain types of mental illness impacting on your ability to tell the truth. There are lots of assumptions within our whole system that I think do discriminate against disabled people. There is an assumption, "Oh, you won't be able to do this; and if you cannot stand up to cross examination, you're not a reliable witness; and if you need an intermediary, will your evidence be so powerful?" So, the system is, I think, quite heavily loaded against the disabled victim.' (R15)

One criminal justice system hate crime champion went further, asserting that, in the area of hate crime, parliament and legal statute has an inbuilt institutional bias towards disabled people in that:

'For racial and religiously generated offending, we have specific offences, whereas we don't have these for homophobic or disability (hate crimes) and that makes a significant difference to how victims of these offences are treated within the criminal justice system. Parliament has legislated that the same behaviour done to somebody who is black will have a different sentencing outcome and be treated in a different way in the criminal justice system than exactly the same offence committed against somebody who is homosexual or has a disability. So, if I punch you in the eye and you have a black eye and I say something racist at the same time which is aggravated, that becomes an either-way offence, two years. If I do the same thing, punch you in the eye, call you a "spastic" or something that can only be dealt with in the magistrate court, maximum sentence six months. I can invoke Section 146 all I like, but it still won't make it more than six months and so, actually, parliament and the statute itself has an institutional bias.' (R22)

This recognition of institutional bias and failure in the criminal justice system to provide disabled victims of crime with an appropriate response as victims and as victims of Disability Hate Crime was also recognized by lead officials who felt somewhat uncomfortable with the language of institutional discrimination. One hate crime policy official, with long-standing involvement, reflected: "Unwittingly offering a lesser service because of disability, I think, is probably commonplace" (R8).

The absence of disablism and ableism from consideration of institutional discrimination

Notwithstanding the widespread recognition of institutional discrimination, fewer respondents in the research for this book named a prejudicial ideology such as disablism or ableism as underpinning such discrimination. Respondents said they viewed it as significant, yet puzzling, that we readily speak of racist crime or homophobic crime but not disablist crime or ableist crime. They tended towards the view that this failure to link targeted crimes against disabled people to a wider disability prejudice, and not recognizing it as disablism or ableism, goes to the heart of understanding the challenges to the development of Disability Hate Crime within the hate crime policy domain.

One respondent identified a serious risk in failing to link Disability Hate Crimes to a wider prejudicial ideology (such as disablism or ableism), which is the "real risk of motivations being disregarded in any crime that is experienced by disabled people. We have lost the inference in language linking back to intent and motivation" (R7).

One former criminal justice system leader reflected on this non-recognition of disablism and the non-use of Disablist Crime:

'That just says everything about the history of this issue. There is not the understanding (of ableism or disablism). It is a very modern concept, whereas racism is not really such a modern concept. People just have not thought in those terms about disability ... I think it has always been seen as a problem emanating from and owned by disabled people. And so, there isn't a word for it, is there? To talk about disablism or ableism doesn't yet mean anything.' (R30)

A disability activist added that wider society and the criminal justice system are yet to make the links between disability discrimination, Disability Hate Crime and wider disablism or ableism because "we're still arguing in the pity place" (R10). She further reflected that: "The oppression that faces disabled people (ableism) is still not being recognized ... and we have to struggle very hard for people not to feel sorry for us. ... There is something different about the oppression that faces disabled people" (R10). Not all respondents were quite so unambiguous in their recognition and naming of ableism or disablism as oppressive ideologies affecting disabled people's daily lives and experiences of hate crime.

Some activist respondents said they recognized ableism and disablism but were hesitant to name them in seeking social change. Indeed, some involved with the EHRC inquiry into disability related harassment reflected that institutional ableism was the underpinning issue implied in that Inquiry, but that this language was avoided because of the negative reaction to the issue of institutional racism after the Lawrence Inquiry. There was fear of a similar reaction in the context of disability as well as wider non-recognition of the term (R28; R20).

Respondents reflected that Disability Hate Crime is not linked to a wider disablism or ableism in part because of the impact of the Social Model view of disability. Given this model's distinction between impairment (a given) and subsequent disability (a social construct), for some social model adherents the issue is not disablism or ableism but impairmentism. These conceptual challenges were reflected in respondents' views:

> 'I'm personally not a fan of the phrase "disablism". It sort of jars with how I regard things. If you're being accurate (in terms of Social Model analysis), it would probably be impairmentism ... within the way we have constructed disability rights, and see disabilities as socially constructed rather than of the individual. ... And I think that's been the whole basis of our analytical framework with the Social Model. ... I would say there is institutionalized prejudice towards disabled people.' (R7)

Another strong Social Model adherent reflected that "if you follow the Social Model, it gets complicated" (R2), while another long-standing national disability activist reflected: "I don't like that term (disablism) but there is discrimination and some of it arises in institutions. But it is more than that, it's also about society and how we work and the way that those in power use that power" (R37).

She further reflected:

> 'We have worked so hard to get the Social Model integrated into society and, unfortunately, that has been pulled back recently and the Medical

Model is coming back in. The Social Model is what we are about, and that is about recognizing that we have impairments and that we are not disabled so much by our impairments as through the ways society performs and reacts to our impairments. So, when you talk about disablism, it is sort of a negative word, it has negative connotations. I mean, in a way, you could say the issue is impairmentism.' (R37)

Other respondents, less wedded to a purist version of the Social Model of Disability, were more embracing of the links between Disability Hate Crime and wider prejudicial ideologies of disablism and ableism. They also recognized the challenges in seeking to advance understanding of disablism and its clear underpinning of Disability Hate Crime in the current context.

A former senior criminal justice system manager reflected:

'If you said, "This [i.e., Disability Hate Crime] is due to disablism", staff would say, "What do you mean?" If you said, "This is due to racism or sexism", they get it. I think we are not there yet. Our language has not even evolved to the point where we talk about disablism or disablist. I think this just shows something around where we are in our maturity around understanding the issues.' (R15)

Other respondents reflected that they observed a situation in society today where institutional disadvantage based on disability may be recognized but there remains a failure to link up the dimensions of disadvantage, together with a failure to locate them in a coherent understanding of disability prejudice, disablism, or ableism.

One senior independent researcher reflected that, based on his research, disability "stereotypes and prejudices are widely prevalent, widely accepted, and they contribute to the climate in which hate crime happens" (R35).

He further reflected that these stereotypes and prejudices contribute to widespread institutional discrimination experienced by disabled people in employment, service provision and: "In the absence of a challenge to institutional discrimination, all these prejudices and stereotypes travel unimpeded into the general ether of society (and impact on hate crime)" (R35).

Other respondents more directly involved in criminal justice system service delivery also reflected on the implications of a failure to link up the dimensions of disability disadvantage and discrimination. One reflected on the significant implications of not locating Disability Hate Crime within a wider understanding of disablism:

'If you do not situate Disability Hate Crime in the broader context of disablism and ableism, then you are not going to be able to deal with Disability Hate Crime in the round. You may get your head around proving disability hostility. You may then fail when it comes to actually meeting the access needs of victims and witnesses and all the rest of it, as they can arise from institutional arrangements that exclude disabled people and can arise from institutional discrimination. So, disability hostility has to be understood in the context of wider structural discrimination experienced by disabled people in order to be addressed appropriately.' (R3)

She went on to reflect:

'If you take initiatives like the Section 95 Report on Race and the Criminal Justice System in England and Wales ... they situate race hate crime figures in the broader context of race discrimination and disadvantage, linking to issues such as staff perceptions, stop and search, all these things that affect success or failure of, actually, what is quite a specific policy area (ie hate crime). We need an equivalent broader context of understanding for Disability Hate Crime. Progress will happen with the growth of such understanding of ableist advantage and discrimination and dismantling of systemic barriers.' (R3)

These points regarding the need to situate Disability Hate Crime cases in a broader context of understanding of disability prejudice, disablism and ableism are considered through the critical analysis of a range of cases in the section which follows.

Notwithstanding this recognition of institutional disadvantage experienced by disabled people and, indeed, its underpinning by a prejudicial ideology, there remains an under-articulation of disability hostility as ableist crime and an under-articulation of disablism and ableism. Indeed, the most recent criminal justice system policy statement on Disability Hate Crime makes one reference to disablism (CPS, 2017). All this begs the question as to why, in the face of evidence of significant disability disadvantage and discrimination, a failure to locate and understand such disadvantage and discrimination within contexts of disablism and ableism persists?

Delivering justice: does disability prejudice matter?

As outlined in Chapter 7, as part of the research for this book, I analysed cases in which disabled people had been victims of targeted incidents and crimes, all of which could be regarded as hate incidents or hate crimes. Analysis of these cases indicates the importance of recognizing disability prejudice, disablism, or ableism for the delivery of full justice. The importance of recognizing disability prejudice is highlighted in some of the serious cases considered in this research, including those involving enslavement, murder (Brent Martin) and murder–suicide (Pilkington-Hardwick case).

In the investigation and prosecution of the murder of Brent Martin a learning-disabled man with mental health difficulties, there was no identification of a disability prejudice dimension by the police, prosecutors or the judge involved. At sentencing, the judge spoke of a senseless attack on "an extremely vulnerable victim". The investigating police officer was reported as saying, "There is no motive for this assault but children often bully people with learning difficulties." At the sentencing hearing, one of the defendants said in open court that he was "not going down for a muppet".

This case appeared 'senseless' and 'without motive' because the decision makers did not locate the facts of the case within a wider understanding of disability prejudice, disablism or ableism. A rereading of this case in the context of disability prejudice, disablism and ableism charts a history of targeted ableist abuse of the victim going back to primary school. This targeted abuse first led to the victim being moved from mainstream to special education, enforcing educational segregation. Then a targeted assault on him as a teenager culminated in a mental breakdown; he was sectioned and spent seven years in psychiatric care. Upon discharge, he was targeted by a group of teenage 'mates' based on his disability, and he 'lost' his money to this group. The teenagers knocked him unconscious, culminating in a final assault involving head-butting and banging the victim's head against a parked car. The victim died three days later in hospital.

Long-standing targeted abuse, exploitation and violence, based on a victim's disability identity, were identified as manifestations of ableism in the previous chapter. In this case, disability prejudice and underpinning ableism were present throughout, but never recognized or named. It could be argued that the police, prosecutors and the judiciary involved saw what their limited view of disability hostility could reveal – the disability hostility and prejudice was simply 'hidden in plain sight'. There was no consideration of disability aggravation because no one in a decision-making capacity in relation to this case ever identified it as such. No one named the case in all its dimensions of both hostility and vulnerability and, as a consequence, full justice was not delivered (Bennett 2017).

In the aftermath of this case, disability activists argued that there was a strong sense of injustice in the failure to recognize and address the disability prejudice dimension (Quarmby, 2011). For a period of time, the case became a litmus test of the criminal justice system's failure to recognize disability prejudice and its failure to deliver both symbolic and substantive justice for disabled people.

The Pilkington–Hardwick case involved sustained disability related harassment of a family comprising a disabled adult and two disabled children over a ten-year period and that culminated in a murder-suicide. A series of targeted disability related incidents were reported to the police, yet none of the reported incidents were formally crimed. To the extent that they were noted at all, they were classed as anti-social behaviour incidents and closed. This case is detailed earlier in Chapter 5 where it was analysed as a focusing event that led to Disability Hate Crime securing agenda-setting status in the criminal justice system.

Over the course of ten years approximately, the family reported incidents of ableist verbal abuse including terms such as 'mong', 'spastic', 'freaks', 'Frankenstein', 'perv', 'nutcase', 'spazzo' and 'lunatic', alongside window breaking and damage to the family's car and garden. On one occasion, the disabled boy was taken captive, locked in a shed and held at knifepoint. This sustained harassment culminated in a situation where the bodies of the mother and daughter were found in a burnt-out car in a lay-by in Leicestershire. Two years later, an inquest found that the mother unlawfully killed her daughter and died by suicide herself. The inquest found that the inappropriate response by the police and the local council to the disability harassment reports made to them by the family contributed to the decision made by the mother to act as she did.

In this case, neither the police nor other agencies recognized or named the incidents as hate incidents or hate crimes linked to disability prejudice, disablism or ableism. If noted at all, the incidents were termed 'anti-social behaviour', which became the prevalent frame for interpreting what happened to the family. Yet the sustained disability harassment based on manifest disability prejudice was again present throughout but never recognized or named. Again, full justice was denied to this family with particularly tragic consequences through a failure to recognize and name their experiences in the round and to respond appropriately (Capewell et al, 2015).

Analysis of the 15 cases in Chapter 2 indicates that not only is recognition of disability prejudice, disablism and ableism significant in individual cases, it also indicates that a shared understanding of the disability prejudice dimension of cases needs to exist across decision makers at each key stage in the criminal justice process. It is not enough for police and prosecutors to recognize and name this prejudicial dimension – the judiciary must recognize and respond appropriately to the prejudice dimension of such cases. Analysis of failed Disability Hate Crime cases points to the judiciary's non-recognition of disability prejudice, disablism or ableism as significant factors impacting the delivery of full justice for victims of Disability Hate Crime.

The significance of this judicial lack of recognition is highlighted by a number of the cases analysed in the research for this book. In the 'Skate park case', where a learning-disabled man was attacked in a skate park, the judge at the sentencing stage rejected the prosecutor's argument that the targeted abuse was due to disability prejudice. Fred was a 29-year-old learning-disabled man who also had significant physical impairments including partial sight, profound deafness and a speech impairment. Described as having 'a mental age of 15', he lived with his mother and frequently went for a walk in the local skate park. One Saturday evening, when Fred visited the skate park for a walk, a number of young people were throwing branches and twigs around. They were verbally abusive, demonstrating manifest hostility towards Fred. He remonstrated with these young people and was upset with them. A short time later, three young men came into the skate park in a van, and one of them proceeded to assault Fred. They punched, kicked him, caused a bump to the side of his head, cuts to his mouth and ear, and bruising to his back and legs. Fred got away and, although injured, he was able to get home with his bike. He immediately told his mother about the incident, and she contacted the police. Fred identified the young men who attacked him because one of them had assaulted him previously.

From the outset, the CPS recognized and identified this as a case of potential Disability Hate Crime. They pursued a proactive case-building approach to secure evidence in relation to the disability hostility dimension of the case, and the prosecutor raised this dimension with the sentencing judge. However, the judge did not accept the disability hostility dimension and stated in open court that this was not a case of disability hostility. He said he knew what type of individual the defendant was. He said that the defendant knew that the victim was a vulnerable person (that is, because he was disabled) and that there was a previous incident where this defendant targeted a vulnerable victim. The judge indicated that this case was about an attack on a vulnerable person and 'not your argument of hostility'.

This case highlighted that a shared understanding and recognition of disability prejudice and ableism by all decision makers in the criminal justice system is crucial. It highlights that full justice can be denied in practice through non-recognition of disability prejudice in such cases. It also highlighted that criminal justice system officials, in a sense, find what they go looking for in these cases. As a corollary, they cannot find what they are not alert to and do not look for in these cases. This can have consequences for both symbolic and substantive justice in targeted crimes experienced by disabled people.

As mentioned in Chapter 6, 'Towards Agenda Institutionalization?', the impact of judicial non-recognition and non-naming of disability prejudice is a matter of ongoing concern (mainly outside the judiciary).

It is clear from consideration of cases analysed for this book that a lack of alertness to and focus on disability prejudice and ableism across the criminal justice system matters in the delivery of both symbolic and substantive justice in Disability Hate Crime cases. Cases have been non-crimed because of a lack of alertness to disability prejudice with a resultant lack of substantive justice. And cases have been crimed solely in one dimension to the neglect of a disability prejudice dimension with a resultant lack of both symbolic and substantive justice (see the enslavement case, Sunset View care home case, Brent Martin case and Pilkington–Hardwick case in Chapter 2).

This analysis of individual Disability Hate Crime cases that highlights the under-recognition of disability prejudice, ableism and disablism underpinning these cases reflects again the issues raised and insights of Lipsky (2010) and Hall (2013) on street-level bureaucracy and the exercise of desertion. These cases reflect Lipsky and Hall's insights on how prevalent attitudes to responding to particular types of cases or victim groups can become routinized in day-to-day policing such that a victim group response became day-to-day policing practice. This research for this book found this in the analysis of individual cases where clear disability hostility was present and relevant but not recognized. The research for this book found in the analysis of individual cases a prevalent response to what were constructed as vulnerable victims, and how this was constructed such that other responses could not easily be countenanced. This reflects the often-well-intentioned response to managing caseloads identified by Lipsky in agencies such as the police, but as seen in the research for this book, it can lead to failures to deliver substantive justice (Lipsky 2010; Hall 2013).

Competing paradigms and problematizations

This research provides evidence of the continued existence of two paradigms that frame disability and responses to disability in England and Wales today. These paradigms – the Welfare, Care and Protection paradigm, and the Rights and Justice paradigm – were referred to earlier in this chapter and in Chapters 2 and 7.

As mentioned previously, within the Welfare, Care and Protection paradigm, disability is constructed as an individual condition that can best be addressed with the interventions of medical and welfare professionals deploying various care, control and protection mechanisms. This paradigm has evolved over time and has, more recently, incorporated aspects of 'users' voices', mainstreaming and normalization in responses to disability.

The Rights and Justice paradigm, in contrast, places the emphasis on disabling attitudinal, institutional and physical barriers, which discriminate against disabled people and prevent them from having equal opportunities to live independent lives. This model places emphasis on removing these systemic barriers. Under the Welfare Model, a disabled person who is a victim of targeted hostility may get a social care plan designed for a vulnerable person. At most, the issue may become recognized as abuse. Under the Rights Model, a disabled person who is a victim of targeted hostility gets justice on the basis of Disability Hate Crime.

Today, aspects of both the Welfare Model and the Rights Model can be seen to influence public policy and practice, including criminal justice policy and practice. While the Welfare Model remains embedded as the dominant policy and practice response, aspects of the Rights Model have become incorporated in international conventions (UN Convention on the Rights of Persons with Disabilities, 2007), in domestic legislation (Equality Act 2010) and in policy documents (ODI, July 2017). Parts of the disability movement have campaigned over considerable time to make these inroads into the previous hegemonic positioning of the Welfare Model (Quinn, 2015).

Research for this book not only points to these two 'competing' paradigms existing in relation to disability, it also points to the dominance of the welfare paradigm occluding recognition of disability discrimination and ableism. This dominance acts as a barrier to the recognition of Disability Hate Crime as a serious issue underpinned by the ideology of ableism. Because the welfare paradigm focuses so readily on individual tragedy and is so shrouded in the rhetoric of protection, it can be inattentive to the hostility that exists towards disabled people and that can manifest as Disability Hate Crime. The research for this book has found that an overly welfare focus is holding back the securing of justice for disabled people in hate crime cases. This is an inadvertent 'benign bigotry', form of paternalistic ableism towards disabled people as vulnerable, which has the malign impact of denial of justice and rights (Nario–Redmond, 2019).

Research for this book indicates that, while the emergence and dominance of the Welfare paradigm, linked to the rise of medical and caring professions and increased state interventions in managing 'social problems', can be traced over a considerable time period, its articulation and reproduction today cannot be ascribed to state institutions and welfare professionals alone. The disability movement plays some part in reproducing the Welfare Model, which may hold back justice for disabled people in the longer term.

A director of a national disability NGO reflected on these competing paradigms in respect of disability:

'I think the whole discourse on disability does get muddied; it's complicated by the fact that there is a lot in public discourse about disabled people requiring support, and that is what a lot of people are campaigning for. There is sort of a care paradigm. So, although the Social Model of Disability has been taken on to some degree by government, and we have, obviously, got legislation in terms of barring discrimination and it puts in place positive duties. I think that, because some of the campaigns are about. … "We need our benefits", "Don't take our benefits away", that is not an anti-discrimination message or at least it is not framed as such. It is much more a "We need to be looked after" kind of paradigm and I think that is very challenging.' (R21)

This respondent captures the dilemma that the disability movement finds itself in the position of disabled people in terms of disadvantage left her wondering if articulating the experience of disablism is "tactically the best way to go" (R21). The disability movement finds itself sometimes caught between a welfare problematization and the desired end place of rights and justice. Given the structural discrimination experienced by disabled people outlined earlier, disabled people find themselves disproportionately marginalized and in need of various supports to survive in an ableist world. As a result, disabled people find themselves frequently having to work the Welfare or pity problematization in order to survive. But, in doing so, this can restrain articulation of rights-based issues such as independent living and hate crime.

Some respondents were more openly critical of the role played by the disability movement itself in terms of the competing paradigmatic accounts of welfare and rights. A leader in the equality rights sector reflected:

'I think the disability movement completely failed to develop a theory of disability-based prejudice. So, the dominant notion about attitudes towards disability, they are still medical, they are still deficit-based. They are still really about pity, sorrow, and all of that. Whereas, of course, in race, you've got a very clear, I mean contested, but nonetheless sort of very clear theoretical landscape where you can say, "Actually, we have a view about why this action, performed to the harm of a black person or a white person, is based on an idea about race, a theory about race".' (R27)

This respondent reflected further that, "because the basic notion about disability is that there's a deficit, then the kind of dominant cultural attitude is pity and sorrow" (R27). He goes on to reflect that the disability movement became "too fixated on physical disability" and physical barriers in society, neglecting the difference raised by learning disability and mental health. He concludes that there is not yet "a powerful overarching narrative about disability prejudice" reflecting an over-concern with the Social Model focus on barriers and a consequent failure of "the disability movement to develop a theory about the effect of disability difference and disability prejudice" (R27).

These issues of competing Welfare and Rights models, together with an under-developed theory of disability prejudice, are inextricably linked. Furthermore, the challenge in understanding disability prejudice is complexified by the simultaneous powerful appeal and limitations of the Social Model of Disability. Given the structural positioning of disabled people in England and Wales as a disadvantaged group, the disability movement's campaigning efforts around survival supports and the theorization around disability need, poverty, education and employment (Roulstone and Prideaux, 2012) has somewhat neglected wider discrimination impacting on disabled people. Understandably, the focus of the disability movement often has to be on quantity of life issues (for example, benefits to address poverty) rather than quality of life issues (for example, addressing a life lived with respect through tackling issues such as hate crime). In focusing on survival issues, the disability movement, given the wider dominance of the Welfare Model, finds itself playing the pity and vulnerability card in order to secure much-needed welfare supports from government. In doing so, the disability movement may inadvertently contribute to limiting the longer-term advancement of disability rights. Research for this book found the understandable yet contradictory situation where some disability activists strongly articulated a rejection of the vulnerability label in the context of hate crime policy making yet deployed the vulnerability label in other arenas when arguing against changes to disability benefits.

And while the Social Model has the appeal of a simple, powerful explanatory framework, attractive in part as a form of liberation framework focused on dismantling physical and attitudinal barriers, research for this book indicates that it has simultaneously advanced and constrained the disability movement from even further progress. Its incompleteness as a full account or theory of disability prejudice in contemporary society has been acknowledged by its academic proponents who have described it as a model rather than a theory for understanding disability (Oliver, 2009; Cameron, 2014). It neglects the stubborn fact of people's impairments and, more so, the accompanying pain that some disabled people experience (Shakespeare, 2006). It shifts the entire gaze from the individual to the structural and, in doing so, occasionally proffers an over-materialist account of disability.

Furthermore, the research for this book found that some proponents of the Social Model found it difficult to accommodate challenges that do not fit this heuristic framework. Thus, it is with accounts of disability prejudice in England and Wales today. Given the Social Model's emphasis on distinguishing so starkly between impairments and disability, it has encountered difficulties in articulating and accommodating the discourse and language of disability prejudice such as disablism and ableism. Given its origins and near-dominance in Britain as a powerful counter framework, there is, with few notable exceptions, under-theorizing and under-recognition of disability prejudice in terms of understanding the ideologies of disablism and ableism in Britain (Goodley, 2014; Iganski and Levin, J., 2015). In contrast, a developing body of theorizing on ableism and disablism is emerging internationally (Kumari Campbell, 2009, 2015; Watermeyer, 2013; Nario-Redmond 2010, 2019) and it is commonplace to find chapters on ableism in international textbooks on identity-based inequalities, sitting alongside equivalent chapters on racism, sexism, ageism and homophobia (Adams et al, 2007; Adams et al, 2013).

It could be queried what difference the absence of an articulation of disablism or ableism makes for the recognition of and response to Disability Hate Crime? One respondent, as mentioned earlier in this chapter, reflected that, by not linking considerations of Disability Hate Crime to wider ableist prejudice, there is a "very real risk of losing the inference in language linking back to intent and motivation" (R7). Research for this book finds that, in losing the connection to wider disability prejudice and ableism, the hate crime itself can easily be lost. There is an initial failure to recognize the crime as a crime informed by a wider prejudice. Then, as a direct consequence, there is a failure to respond to the crime appropriately. Finally, there can be a failure to deliver justice.

In this context, there is a need for wider work to be undertaken that articulates and advances an understanding of disability prejudice and, within this, to advance understanding of disablism and ableism. Barbara Perry, in a critical account of theorizing in the field of hate crime, identifies common threads among contemporary theoretical accounts, including the tendency to locate hate crime as part of 'broader social patterns of oppression and disadvantage' (Perry, B., 2009b, p 72). Related to this, she points to the tendency for theorists to emphasize how dominant cultural imaging and ideologies contribute to dehumanization, demonization and stigmatization of a group and how, in this context of cultural-ideological inferiorization, it 'becomes very easy to then justify their victimisation' through hate crimes (Perry, B., 2009b, p 72). In the research for this book, I have found an under-articulation of such an understanding of Disability Hate Crime, particularly prevalent in policy and practitioner domains, more than in academia. This is somewhat more challenging in the British context, given the near-dominance of the Social Model as the counter-framework of understanding and the challenges it poses for due focus on disablism and ableism conceptually and in terms of discourse.

Articulating disablism and ableism

In recent years, there has emerged a small but significant body of work on disablism and ableism, in particular the work of Nario-Redmond, Watermeyer and Kumari Campbell internationally, and Goodley and Thomas in the British context. Goodley (2014) helpfully considers disablism and ableism in terms of exploring how both disability and ability are co-constructed and the extent to which a critical consideration of disability requires us to 'think simultaneously about disability and ability' (Goodley, 2014, p xi).

It is interesting that as recently as 2010, the term ableism was not yet circulating in the social sciences as a construct to be studied (Nario-Redmond, 2019). According to Harpur, writing in 2012, a next great step in disability scholarship is to harness the power of the term ableism to signify disability discrimination and disadvantage (Harpur, 2012; Nario-Redmond, 2019).

It is argued that what is needed now are not Disability studies but Dis/Ability studies. Goodley argues that a consideration of ableism requires a turning away analytically from disability to ask: What do we mean by being able? He argues that disability and ability, and disablism and ableism, can really only be understood in relation to each other. He concludes with a case for Dis/Ability studies which always holds disablism and ableism, disability and ability in co-consideration, so as to interrogate 'their co-construction and effect upon one another' (Goodley, 2014, p xiii).

Kumari Campbell (2009) takes a different and philosophically informed approach, arguing for a fundamental shift in the gaze from disability to ability, from disablism to ableism. She argues for a reproblematization away from welfarist approaches to a focus on deeply embedded ableist underpinnings in society (Bacchi, 2009). Disability studies, she argues, have been over-preoccupied with analysing the attitudes and barriers that contribute to the subordination of disabled people (Kumari Campbell, 2009). In this context, disablism 'is a set of assumptions and practices that promote the differential or unequal treatment of people because of actual or presumed disabilities' (Kumari Campbell, 2009, p 4). She argues that, informed by a disablism focus, 'the strategic positions adopted ... essentially relate to reforming these negative attitudes, assimilating people with disabilities into normative civil society, and providing compensatory initiatives and safety nets in cases of enduring "vulnerability"' (Kumari Campbell, 2009, p 4). In this context, Kumari Campbell argues that the challenge is to 'reverse, invert this traditional approach, to shift our gaze and concentrate on what the study of disability tells us about the production, operation and maintenance of ableism' (Kumari Campbell, 2009, p 4).

Kumari Campbell argues that some researchers mistakenly use disablism and ableism as interchangeable terms. She views ableism as more deeply embedded and as existing in 'the arena of genealogies of knowledge' (Kumari Campbell, 2009, p 5). Although she acknowledges that there is limited consensus on what constitutes ableism, she states that ableism 'refers to a network of beliefs, processes and practices that produce a particular kind of self and body (the corporeal standard) that is projected as the perfect, species-typical and therefore essential and fully human. Disability then is cast as a diminished state of being human' (Kumari Campbell, 2001, p 44: Ralph et al, 2016). Kumari Campbell regards ableism as having a function in 'inaugurating the norm' (Kumari Campbell, 2009, p 5) where 'the essential of ableism is the formation of a naturalized understanding of being fully human' (Kumari Campbell, 2009, p 6).

It can be argued that Kumari Campbell rightly shifts the problematization gaze from disability disadvantage to ableist normativity. She outlines how ableist normativity is so pervasive and naturalized in society, including in the legal system (for example, the notion of the competent credible victim–witness and initiatives such as special measures that compensate for disability deviance from the able-bodied norm) that it simultaneously constructs disabled people as diminished, different and deviant, and sets them up for disadvantage and discrimination including the violence of hate crime.

A significant contribution to advancing contemporary understanding of ableism is to be found in the work of Michelle Nario-Redmond (2010, 2019). Writing within social psychology, Nario-Redmond provides a critical account of the nature, causes and consequences of ableism in contemporary western societies. She views ableism as an analytical construct that emerged to explain enduring disability disadvantage and discrimination. She views ableism as an 'analytical parallel' of the concepts of racism, sexism and heterosexism. She writes of how like racism, sexism and ageism, ableism is replete with assumptions about what it is to be normal and able, and how those deemed not to be able are to be protected, controlled and treated socially including harshly and with hostility on occasions (Nario-Redmond, 2019). Nario-Redmond refers to ableism as ideas, practices, and ways of relating in society that privileges able-bodiedness, and in doing so, simultaneously constructs and marginalizes disabled people. Ableism she argues is 'simply prejudice and discrimination towards people simply because they are classified as disabled' (Nario-Redmond, 2019). She helpfully elaborates on the varied manifestations of ableism that can be identified in contemporary western societies today. She identifies benevolent, paternalistic, ambivalent and hostile ableism. This is a helpful continuum for understanding ableism's varied manifestations. While this book is focused on hostile ableism as expressed through hate crime, having an appreciation of the varied manifestations of ableism is helpful as these different manifestations of ableism can flow into each other, and paternalism, ambivalence and hostile ableism can be evident in a single hate incident or hate crime.

It is clear that disablism and ableism are central issues in developing and articulating a contextual understanding of Disability Hate Crime. However, it is equally clear that there is significant work yet to be undertaken on both and their inter-relationships. It is also clear from earlier analysis that neither concept has everyday currency in hate crime policy.

In ways, this indicates the evolving adolescent state of analysis in this area. For now, I tend towards the view that the concepts of disablism and ableism, particularly ableism, are helpful in developing a fuller theoretical account and understanding of Disability Hate Crime. This relatively early stage of understanding does not make the challenge of policy making and practice easier. In time, the concept of ableism may well emerge as the more overarching conceptual narrative, it being a 'higher level' ideology within which may be nested meso-level ideologies such as disablism. In this developing context, I tend towards a view of ableism as a prejudicial set of ideas, an ideology that normalizes and naturalizes an able-bodied norm and inferiorizes disabled people who are regarded as not matching up to that able-bodied norm (Figure 8.1). It embeds an ableist normativity in society that serves to negate disabled identity. It has manifestations and impacts in terms of the advantages experienced by the able bodied, and the disadvantage and discrimination experienced by disabled people at structural, cultural, institutional and individual levels. In advancing an understanding of Disability Hate Crime in terms of this book, I would suggest that much can be gleaned from the work of scholars on identity inequalities and wider equality studies, including the work of Young (1990) in the US context and

Figure 8.1: Ideologies of ableism and disablism

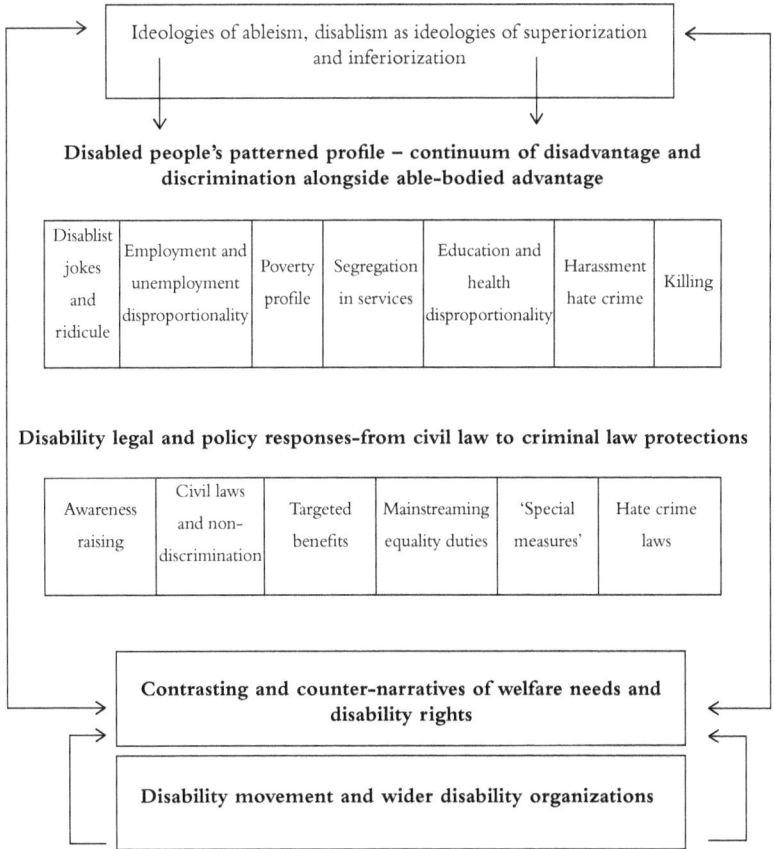

Figure 8.2: Disability Pyramid of Hate

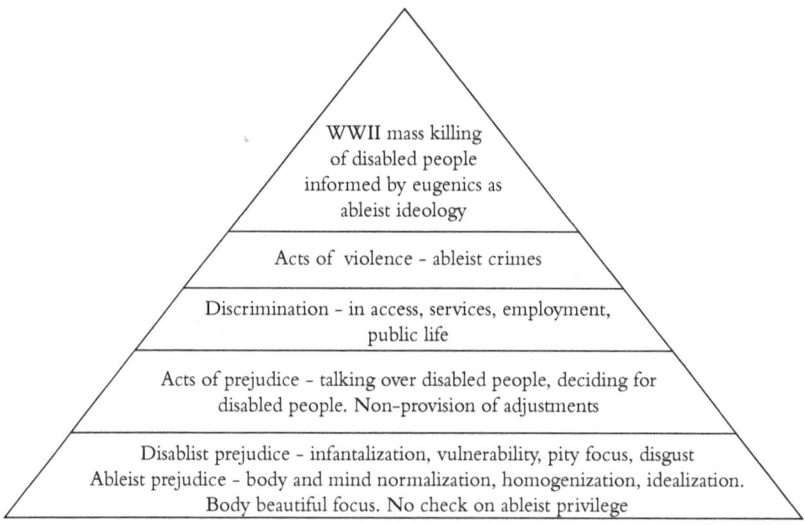

Thompson (2011) in the British context. Informed by these scholars and based on critical engagement and reflection on the issue, I would proffer the following as tentative building blocks towards a framework of fuller understanding for disability prejudice, disablism and ableism.

Such a framework for understanding disability prejudice provides a context within which individual Disability Hate Crimes can potentially be more fully contextualized, recognized and understood. The further development and promulgation of such a framework potentially provides a way forward for identifying and responding to Disability Hate Crime and further institutionalizing Disability Hate Crime in the wider hate crime domain. It may be further enhanced by considering it alongside an adapted application to Disability Hate Crime of Levin's Pyramid of Hate (Levin, B., 2009), which was itself informed by Allport's earlier work on the scale of prejudice (Allport, 1954).

A disability adapted Pyramid of Hate reflecting impacts of disablism and ableism may be conceived of (Figure 8.2). Why does an existing framework for understanding prejudice warrant consideration anew and adaptation? The research for this book has found that there is a need to both state and elaborate on what can be seen as obvious for other prejudices when considering Disability Hate Crime because of the pervasive non-recognition of disability prejudice and ableism. Indeed, this was why Mark Sherry decided to title his book on Disability Hate Crime as 'Does anyone really hate disabled people?' (Sherry, 2010) or what Digranes has termed 'an unthinkable hatred' (2016). A conceptual analysis that develops a fuller understanding of the nature and manifestations of disability prejudice and ableism is an important part of understanding the wider context for Disability Hate Crime. However, it will not in itself provide a full theoretical account and its socio-cultural focus needs to be complemented with a focus on understanding individual perpetrators or groups of perpetrators and the influence of factors of human agency in hate crime perpetration (Levin, J. and McDevitt, 2002; Iganski and Levin, J., 2015). I would, however, argue that, through pursuing and promulgating such a critical understanding of the context of Disability Hate Crime in terms of wider disability prejudice and ableism, the phenomenon can begin to be better recognized as part of the hate crime domain, and policy and practice institutionalization can potentially progress. To paraphrase Bacchi (2009), it is through pursuing such a wider theoretical framing and problematization of the Disability Hate Crime problem that the challenges to policy institutionalization can be questioned. Then, in time, it can be disrupted and replaced by a framing that more appropriately 'fits' the problem to be addressed.

Conclusion

In this chapter, I have analysed a further aspect of the Disability Hate Crime agenda that is impacting negatively on agenda institutionalization: the non-articulation and promulgation of an understanding and acceptance of wider disability prejudice and ableism. Ableism is an agenda item yet to fully speak its name in Disability Hate Crime.

This chapter locates its analysis within a recent profile of socially patterned disability disadvantage and discrimination. This yields a picture of disability marginalization, exclusion and deprivation. The analysis considers the varied responses to disability disadvantage and focuses on the competing problematizations and paradigmatic responses of Welfare, Care, and Protection and Rights and Justice, and notes the dominance of the Welfare, Care and Protection paradigm.

The analysis found recognition of institutional disadvantage and discrimination experienced by disabled people, including within the criminal justice system. At the same time, this research found non-recognition of disability prejudice, disablism or ableism. It noted a missing link between patterned disability disadvantage and discrimination, and the recognition of underpinning ideologies of disablism and ableism.

This research concludes that the existing competing paradigms of Welfare and of Rights impact on disability responses and occlude recognition of disablism and ableism and consequent problematizations. The situation is complexified by the simultaneous dominance of the Welfare paradigm and the constraints of the Social Model counter framework in conceptually and discursively embracing disablism and ableism. An impact of these complexities is that the prejudice in Disability Hate Crime is not recognized for what it is, that is disability hostility. In the absence of a context for understanding disability prejudice and ableism, Disability Hate Crime gets lost in individual hate crime cases and, more broadly, as a conceivable form of hate crime.

There is a small but significant and growing body of understanding articulating the significance of ableism and its impacts. However, that understanding is at an early stage of development compared to other identity oppressions. There remain issues of conceptual and discursive understandings to be further explored and fleshed out. Notwithstanding this early evolving analysis of disability prejudice, disablism and ableism, criminal justice system policy and practice is advancing in what is still an area of some contention and contestation.

In this context, I proffer a tentative framework for understanding Disability Hate Crime within a wider ideology of ableism and, in doing so, link it both to earlier work on identity inequalities and on the Pyramid of Hate. This is a contribution to articulating a link between Disability Hate Crime and theoretical accounts of social patterns of oppression and disability. In doing so, I point towards ways in which both academia and activism might contribute to the further institutionalization of Disability Hate Crime within the wider hate crime domain. In the continuing absence of recognizing disability prejudice and ableism and their impacts on Disability Hate Crime, there is a risk of failing to recognize and name the issue appropriately. In failing to name all the dimensions appropriately, there is also a risk of failing to deal with Disability Hate Crime justly as evidenced in the cases analysed in this chapter. In this context, it will remain a prejudice that is yet to fully speak its name and remain an unsettled and unsettling agenda.

In this chapter, I have sought to provide the elements of a framework through which ableism might be better recognized, named and responded to in Disability Hate Crime, and thereby enhance the delivery of justice for disabled people.

9

Conclusion

Key points

This chapter notes that Disability Hate Crime remains to this day an unsettled and unsettling policy and practice agenda. However, the chapter also notes the potential to make progress through adopting a more inclusive legal policy response to Disability Hate Crime. Through such an inclusive legal policy response, the book concludes on a cautiously optimistic note. This chapter also argues that Disability Hate Crime exists within a wider context of disabled people's experience of disadvantage and discrimination across most areas of social life. A Disability Hate Crime focus should be located within an understanding of disability prejudice and ableism and within a focus on rights and justice. In such a policy context, and underpinned by appropriate legal provisions, Disability Hate Crime can contribute to realizing a society where disabled people can live more dignified lives, freer from fear, and with the potential for enhanced human flourishing based simultaneously on recognition of human difference and common humanity. Pursued in isolation, it risks becoming an over-individuated response to wider structural injustices.

Introduction

The starting point for this book was the expansion of the criminal justice system hate crime domain in England and Wales in 2003 to include Disability Hate Crime. While there has been some significant scholarship on the establishment and expansion of the overall hate crime domain as discussed in Chapter 3, prior to this book there had not yet been a study devoted specifically to the emergence and development of Disability Hate Crime policy. One book on an important aspect of this topic, namely hate crime on transport, two edited collections, a few book chapters and journal articles have been published on aspects of Disability Hate Crime in England and Wales to date. These are very insightful, interesting and valuable, but they do not attempt to provide a comprehensive analysis of the topic as a policy agenda. What this book provides for the first time, is a comprehensive analysis of the emergence and development of Disability Hate Crime as a policy agenda within the criminal justice system in England and Wales over the past 20 years. As outlined in Chapters 1 and 3, this book addressed these questions: How did Disability Hate Crime emerge and develop as an area of policy and practice within the criminal justice system of England and Wales and why did Disability Hate Crime emerge and develop as an area of criminal justice policy as and when it did? In answering these exploratory questions, this book adds to the multidisciplinary field of hate crime studies more broadly and on hate crime policy making in particular.

Employing a qualitative methodology, informed by grounded theory and public policy perspectives on problematization and agenda setting, this book provides a multi-layered account of the ongoing journey of Disability Hate Crime from agenda invisibility towards agenda institutionalization in the criminal justice system in England and Wales. It draws upon a range of key informant interviews in the fields of activism, policy making and politics, exploring the factors influencing Disability Hate Crime policy emergence and development, together with an analysis of a range of Disability Hate Crime cases. These are complemented by an interwoven analysis of policy documents that set out criminal justice system policy on Disability Hate Crime.

Existing scholarship on hate crime as discussed in Chapter 2 has tended to find that, once the hate crime domain was established, it was relatively easy to 'add to the list' of protected characteristics. However, this study has found that, after an initial embrace of Disability Hate Crime into the 'hate crime family', this agenda's institutionalization has faced significant challenges at each stage of agenda triggering, agenda setting and agenda institutionalization. The result is that institutionalization of Disability Hate Crime remains some way off close on 20 years after the issue was legislated for. Rather than institutionalization of Disability Hate Crime within the hate crime domain as day-to-day hate crime business, it remains unusual business to this day. Based on the research for this book, my concluding argument is that Disability Hate Crime is a case of an unsettled and unsettling policy agenda within the hate crime policy domain in England and Wales. Furthermore, Disability Hate Crime will only move beyond its unsettled and unsettling status when there is a shift in policy approach, from an undue focus on vulnerability to a due focus on ableism, and when this shift is threaded through and reflected in hate crime law.

An unsettled agenda

What does it mean to conclude that Disability Hate Crime is an unsettled policy agenda in the hate crime domain today? This book noted the features that a settled policy agenda is expected to display, including development of the policy domain with shared definitions, shared ways of responding, a shared discourse on the problem, a diminution in the need for strategic action over time, an embedded taken-for-granted approach and a predictable area of practice that has become routine business for the criminal justice system and other stakeholders. Appraised against these features, this book has found that policy making and practice on Disability Hate Crime was –and continues to display – an unsettled approach with limited policy institutionalization.

An unsettling agenda

This book also concludes that the Disability Hate Crime agenda is an unsettling agenda. It is unsettling in that it questions and disrupts prevalent constructions of the problem of disability as a welfare issue and seeks to replace them with a construction based on justice and rights. It questions understandings of disability prejudice, disablism and ableism hostility and, indeed, understandings of hostility more widely in the hate crime domain. It shows how non-recognition of disability prejudice, disablism and ableism impacts delivery of justice in hate crime cases. It questions the uncritical use of the vulnerability categorization in targeted crimes experienced by disabled people and challenges us to reconceptualize of what is meant by targeting on the basis of vulnerability. It pushes at the boundaries of possibility in the hate crime domain. However, while it questions and disrupts these prevalent constructions, it is yet to replace them. Thus, it is an unsettling agenda as well as being an unsettled agenda. The unsettled stage of this policy agenda's journey to institutionalization is closely linked to its unsettling features.

In identifying my argument regarding the unsettled and unsettling features of Disability Hate Crime policy, it begs the question as to what extent, if any, the other hate crime strands are unsettled and unsettling. Respondents in the research for this book highlighted the unsettled and unsettling features of Disability Hate Crime in contrast to how they experienced other hate crime strands as more settled in terms of established shared discourse, ways of working and day-to-day practice. In those other hate crime strands such as racist crime, homophobic crime or transphobic crime, there are no significant competing problem representations operating. This is what makes Disability Hate Crime unusual.

Unsettled and unsettling features present from outset and in each stage of the policy process

The unsettled and unsettling features of the Disability Hate Crime agenda were present from the first triggering of this agenda, as noted in Chapter 4. The Disability Hate Crime agenda was triggered in 2003 when an alliance of activists, a cabinet minister and the then Disability Rights Commission coalesced around a legislative window of opportunity in the form of an amendment to the Criminal Justice Act 2003. At that agenda-triggering stage, an approach to Disability Hate Crime as hostility was formally adopted. A temporary policy silence was imposed on a prevalent alternative problem representation held by policy officials who proffered a view that such targeted crimes were based on vulnerability rather than hostility. Although the agenda was triggered by the amendment, it was another four years before the policy agenda could be said to be well established on Disability Hate Crime.

The unsettled and unsettling nature of the Disability Hate Crime agenda was again evident in its agenda-setting journey from 2004 to 2008. The agenda shifted from the political into the policy arena and, crucially, there emerged a new Disability Equality Duty in 2004, which shaped the 'discovery' of Disability Hate Crime as a shared priority of both disability activists and criminal justice agencies. A coupling of the hate crime solution and the Disability Hate Crime problem occurred using the equality duty as a lever. A largely off-the-shelf hate crime template was placed around Disability Hate Crime, with very limited attention paid to disability difference and its unsettling features were temporarily downplayed to secure hate crime agenda status.

Policy stream activity on a cross-government programme of work on hate crime and, crucially, a stream of work to agree a common definition of monitored hate crime constituted further steps in the development of the Disability Hate Crime agenda. This study concludes that it marked a very significant moment in the formal construction of the Disability Hate Crime agenda.

Another significant moment in the construction of the Disability Hate Crime agenda was the development of a CPS public policy statement on Disability Hate Crime (2007). This policy statement again reflected the unsettled and unsettling nature of the agenda through breaking the policy silence on vulnerability and hostility in Disability Hate Crime. It surfaced and fore-grounded vulnerability – a significant challenge and alternative problematization in the Disability Hate Crime area. In effect, it constructed the Disability Hate Crime agenda as speaking to two problem representations simultaneously, namely hostility and vulnerability. In doing so, it spoke to the heart of the unsettled and unsettling nature of this policy agenda in its attempt to construct the problem. It spoke to the unsettled features through bi-locating targeted disability crimes with some inside and some outside the hate crime domain. It spoke to the unsettling features of Disability Hate Crime through surfacing in a significant way the issue of vulnerability-based targeting.

Alongside these policy stream activities, disability activists were active in exposing the unsettled nature of the Disability Hate Crime agenda.

While contributing to developments designed to settle the agenda, they were acutely alert to putting policies to the test. While the criminal justice system was working on settling this new policy agenda, activists spotlighted poor criminal justice system performance on cases and gained traction with a narrative around a lack of recognition of disability hostility, lack of appropriate criminal justice system responses and shocking failures to deliver justice in individual cases. This exposed the unsettled nature of the agenda as it was being implemented. However, in doing so, they contributed to the development of agenda setting at this time.

From 2006 to 2008, the unsettled and unsettling aspects remained present alongside increased coupling of the policy, the activist and political streams. This coupling was enabled by the influence of a focusing event, albeit a second-order focusing event, the Pilkington case. The aftermath of this case created another policy window of opportunity through which Disability Hate Crime emerged (again) and, this time, policy agenda status was secured. However, the Pilkington case also spoke to the unsettling features of the agenda in that it contained two competing problem representations, namely in this instance, anti-social behaviour and hate crime.

As the research for this book has shown, the unsettled and unsettling nature of Disability Hate Crime was present in this entire policy agenda-setting activity. Competing problem representations of welfare and rights, vulnerability and hostility, breaking policy silences on vulnerability, and the issues of disability difference lurked within all this policy agenda-setting activity. These competing problem representations were to become more prominent as policy stream efforts increasingly turned towards institutionalizing this agenda.

Ongoing journey towards policy institutionalization

Efforts to settle Disability Hate Crime within the criminal justice system hate crime domain were well underway in 2009 and continue to this day. These efforts included seeking to implement common definitions, a shared response, annual reporting on performance, an EHRC formal inquiry, a number of criminal justice system-wide inspections, two Law Commission reviews, prosecution guidance on hostility and vulnerability in these cases and a revised policy statement on Disability Hate Crime. As noted earlier, institutionalization of a policy agenda also includes a shared discourse regarding the problem, a diminution in the need for strategic action and the transition to an embedded taken-for-granted business-as-usual approach. Appraised against these features of a settled policy agenda, there is not yet a single settled shared discourse regarding the issue of Disability Hate Crime. In fact, there are at least two problem discourses in operation. Furthermore, the judiciary are not in any significant way engaged with the Disability

Hate Crime agenda and discourse, although they are increasingly alert to a vulnerability discourse. This book concludes that there remains an ongoing need for significant criminal justice system strategic action on Disability Hate Crime. Furthermore, there is not yet a taken-for-granted business-as-usual approach.

While the police and prosecution leadership nationally have commendably prioritized Disability Hate Crime over a 15-year period, the criminal justice system overall has yet to deliver an agreed settled approach with the leadership evident upstream yet to be reflected in downstream settled practice. The considerable criminal justice system leadership efforts to institutionalize Disability Hate Crime internally face institutional challenges based on established taken-for-granted constructs of hate crime reflected in law, policy and practice. Almost 20 years on from legislating for Disability Hate Crime, it remains unsettled and unsettling. This is the case, in large part, because of unique challenges around vulnerability and understanding of disability hostility and because Disability Hate Crime requires that a broader, more inclusive conception of hostility, prejudice and discrimination be considered to enable settlement within the hate crime domain. There is a pressing need for a shift in policy approach from a vulnerability to an ableism approach.

From vulnerability to ableism

This book has found that the questions posed by the issue of vulnerability are central to the ongoing unsettled and unsettling nature of the institutionalization of Disability Hate Crime in the hate crime domain. A significant challenge here is that the legal framework in England and Wales in large part equates disability and vulnerability. In the context of considering Disability Hate Crime, this leads to competing problem representations around vulnerability and hostility. A vulnerability focus has proven to be the most challenging and contentious concept in seeking to settle Disability Hate Crime in the criminal justice system. The uncritical application of a vulnerability categorization to disabled people, as if it were an inherent group attribute, has served to impede substantive policy and practice progress. Vulnerability floods disability as a policy area, such that we see disability and perceive vulnerability. If, as this book has found, the vulnerable-person stereotype is the most pervasive stereotype of disabled people, then it can be viewed that targeting people because of their perceived vulnerability is a biased, hostile act.

This book concludes that, while benign in intent, a form of systemic 'benevolent prejudice' within the criminal justice system in the uncritical use of the vulnerability focus has withheld justice for disabled victims of targeted crime. This impedes institutionalization of the Disability Hate

Crime agenda. An undue focus on vulnerability has led to a strong sense of social justice subordination for disabled people and the denial of substantive justice which marks the gravity of hostility-based crimes for disabled victims. This book furthermore concludes that, in the hate crime domain, which is marked by victim-centred definitions of hostility, it is highly questionable to place (even benignly) a vulnerability categorization on a group of people who reject both the categorization and its potentially malign impacts on the delivery of justice.

Notwithstanding this conclusion, it should be recognized that vulnerability, as currently constructed as a minoritized identity, conveying weakness, wound and deviation from the capable able-bodied norm, is not the only possible construction of vulnerability. There can also be a recognition of vulnerability as part of the human condition for all people – in the longer term, a radical recasting of vulnerability away from a minoritized identity towards a shared human condition identity may be possible (Fineman, 2012). This would require widespread positive recognition, regard and respect for the vulnerability in all humans, and that vulnerability may be accentuated at different life stages or with different life experiences. Given the current pervasive negative connotations of vulnerability in relation to disability and given the disability movement's current stage on the journey to equality and social justice, such a restructuring is, I suggest, a very considerable way off in the area of disability, if it ever might be appropriate.

Interrogating vulnerability and hostility together

A further conclusion informed by the research for this book is that, in Disability Hate Crime, considerations of hostility and vulnerability should not be hermetically sealed off from each other but should be interrogated together. Vulnerability targeting in criminal acts should be recognized for what it is, as hostile and discriminatory selection and targeting of disabled people. Sustained progress on the challenge of vulnerability in Disability Hate Crime and on resolving the unsettled and unsettling features of Disability Hate Crime are only likely to be realized in the context of moving to a more holistic understanding of disability hostility. This study makes direct recommendations in terms of legislative change to address this issue here.

Recognizing ableism to settle the agenda

Alongside the agenda challenge of addressing vulnerability in Disability Hate Crime, there is an inextricably linked agenda item that is yet to fully speak its name in Disability Hate Crime: that is a developed and shared understanding of disability prejudice and discrimination and how they link to the ideology of ableism. This book found a ready naming of race hate crime as racist crime and of LGB hate crime as homophobic crime. There was a ready linking of these hate crime strands to ideologies of racism and homophobia. However, the research for this book found virtually no identification of Disability Hate Crime as ableist crime, while finding an acceptance of institutional disadvantage and discrimination experienced by disabled people. Notwithstanding this, this book also found an underdeveloped sense of what underpins the patterned basis of disability disadvantage and any relationship toa wider prejudicial ideology. This goes to the heart of the unsettling features of Disability Hate Crime and the existence of competing problematizations of disability issues as either one of welfare and care or rights and justice. Given the dominance of the welfare and care problematization, it is counterintuitive almost to countenance the existence of disability hostility given that the prevalent narrative is one of care, protection and, at worst, pity. Indeed, viewed critically, the dominant narrative could be described as a 'benevolent prejudice', albeit one that this study demonstrates has significant malign impacts. Crucially, this book has found that the competing problematizations of welfare and care and rights and justice occlude recognition of disability prejudice and ableism and that this lack of recognition matters in the delivery of justice in Disability Hate Crime cases. It has led to failures to deliver recognition justice and substantive justice in Disability Hate Crime cases. It is essential to recognize Disability Hate Crime as ableist crime fuelled by a wider prejudicial ideology of ableism if the hate crime policy and practice agenda is to be implemented effectively.

Moving beyond dual problematization to settle this agenda

The research for this book demonstrated the roles played by activism, politics and policy making in the emergence and development of Disability Hate Crime in England and Wales over the past 20 years. It has demonstrated that activists have contributed significantly to agenda setting and played a larger role than is often recognized. And it has demonstrated that politicians intervened at strategic moments to 'make it [the agenda] happen' and that, without a significant early political intervention by a senior minister, this agenda might not have emerged as and when it did. This study has demonstrated that policy officials played a particularly significant role in defining and institutionalizing the agenda in the hate crime domain. In very large part, policy officials hold the ring on the Disability Hate Crime agenda today. Significantly, this study has demonstrated that the focus on activism, politics and policy making needs to be underscored by a focus on problematization to understand the journey towards and the challenges in the institutionalization of Disability Hate Crime. The fundamental challenge in institutionalizing Disability Hate Crime in the criminal justice system is the challenge flowing from the dual and simultaneous problematization of disability as a welfare, care and protection issue, and as a rights and justice issue.

These two problem representations intersect in the area of Disability Hate Crime where the issue is constructed as two things at once, vulnerability targeting and hostility targeting. The policy domain is unsettled whenever an issue is constructed as two things simultaneously. This study provides an alternative problematization approach that enables a more overarching problem representation to be considered – a framing of the issue as hostility *including* vulnerability. This alternative framing is not an either/or problematization of hostility or vulnerability. It is not a problematization of hostility and vulnerability. This is an alternative problematization of hostility *including* vulnerability, which recognizes the targeting of disabled people for crimes based on vulnerability as a biased hostile act, a discriminatory selection and, in this way, a hate crime. Herein lies the origin of the title of this book, Disability Hate Crime: from vulnerability to ableism.

Overall contribution of this book

Arguably, this book makes a number of significant contributions to the field of hate crime studies and hate crime policy making studies in particular.

First, the book addresses a gap in existing hate crime studies, by providing the first comprehensive analysis of policy emergence and development of Disability Hate Crime in England and Wales. It augments earlier work by Mason-Bish who charted the emergence and development of the hate crime domain overall and who indicated the need for studies in respect of each hate crime strand. That specific knowledge gap in respect of Disability Hate Crime is addressed in this book.

Second, the analysis of the focus on vulnerability in the context of Disability Hate Crime is a dimension of the originality of this book. This book addresses the challenge of vulnerability in Disability Hate Crime and provides a unique analysis of a vulnerability focus as a dimension of hostility in Disability Hate Crime. In doing so, it provides a reconceptualization of disability hostility in a way that can include vulnerability-based targeting. It breaks the conceptual and policy logjams posed by this issue, building on this with clear legal and policy recommendations outlined. These recommendations can contribute to settling the agenda and resolving its unsettled features within the hate crime domain. This book extends our understanding of hostility in the legal and policy context in England and Wales by taking hostility beyond a solely motivation–demonstration continuum to also include hostility by reason of disability. In doing so, this study contributes to our understanding of the case for a varied geometry of legal provisions to reflect different histories, segregations, geographies and manifestations of the different hate crime strands.

The book augments the body of case studies on the public policy making process, through a refinement of the policy stream's emphasis on activism, politics and policy making with the fundamental emphasis placed here on problematization and also through uniquely introducing the pre-policy agenda-setting phase that I termed 'agenda triggering'. In doing so, this study addresses a shortcoming in Kingdon's policy stream approach, which focuses on the role that streams play in policy agenda setting and how it may pay limited attention to problem definition and problem representation. Thus, this book strikes a balanced understanding between agenda setting and the social construction of the problem of Disability Hate Crime by underscoring the role played by problematization in this domain, as informed by Bacchi's concept of problematization as a continuous process of construction (Barbehon et al, 2015). This study refines the policy stream heuristic with the addition and foregrounding of problematization and, in doing so, reflects calls in critical public policy studies to build on existing understandings of agenda setting. Uniquely, I also introduce the concept of agenda triggering as a refinement of the policy streams approach to help capture those policy situations where an issue is formally triggered but does not yet constitute an active policy agenda and the distinction between these. This was devised as a way of understanding what occurred in relation to targeted disability victimization, which I argue was ahead of its time in 2003 when the agenda was triggered and whose time was to come – four years later – with active agenda setting.

The book also addresses the influence of wider equality law on the development of the Disability Hate Crime agenda, especially the public sector positive duties' approach to equality. In particular, it provides an insight into the influence of the Disability Equality Duty in the criminal justice system. This gap was identified in earlier scholarship (Mason-Bish, 2009) and is addressed by this book. This book's findings of the influence of the Disability Equality Duty as a positive lever for agenda development contrast with the disability movement's scepticism about the impacts of this duty. This positive influence was largely due to the equality receptive climate in the criminal justice system in the early 2000s following the Lawrence Inquiry. This analysis provides a unique insight into how these statutory duties to mainstream equality worked positively in practice in some parts of the criminal justice system, in particular the police and prosecution services in the early to mid-2000s. This book demonstrates how, at a moment in time, the specific duty to involve disabled people in policy consultation enabled a coupling of disabled people's priorities along with public sector organizations duties and facilitated Disability Hate Crime to emerge.

Recommendations

Based on this research study, I make two sets of recommendations: for further research and legal and policy change.

Future research recommendations

This study focused on policy emergence and policy making on Disability Hate Crime. Its focus is on the policy process, not on different victim groups that may experience Disability Hate Crime. In this regard, there is a need to consider research which focuses on the experience of Disability Hate Crime by different impairment groups, namely learning-disabled people, physically disabled people and people experiencing mental health difficulties. Some of this research is underway and is to be encouraged and supported in order to develop a fuller understanding of the phenomenon.

I would recommend that research is undertaken on:

- The experience of Disability Hate Crime by a range of impairment groups including learning-disabled people, physically disabled people and people experiencing mental health difficulties.
- The profile and social situation of perpetrators in Disability Hate Crime cases to identify possible early interventions with those identified as at risk of such offending and thereby help inform strategies to reduce the risks of targeted disability victimization.
- The emergence and development of policy agendas in respect of each of the hate crime strands, namely scholarly studies – monographs in the areas of racist and religious crimes policy development, homophobic and transphobic crimes policy development.

Legal and policy recommendations

As outlined earlier, there is a developing debate on hate crime law in England and Wales. This developing debate is focused on issue of how effective the hate crime law is, how equitable it is and whether it remains fit for purpose. In recent times this debate has been led by the Law Commission and the work of the leading hate crime scholar, Professor Mark Walters. Within this debate there is a recognition of the challenges posed for effective prosecution of Disability Hate Crime within the constraints of the current legal framework. This has led some scholars, including Walters, to favour a discriminatory selection test of legal proof as appropriate to apply to Disability Hate Crimes. The research for this book also leads me to support the use of a discriminatory selection test in Disability Hate Crimes. In fact, I go further to argue that, if we are seriously committed to addressing Disability Hate Crime, it warrants a triple lock legal test of proof:

1. That the government amend the hate crime legal provisions addressing disability hostility, namely Section 66 of the Sentencing Act 2020 (Section 146 of the Criminal Justice Act 2003). In doing so, that the government introduce a legal provision on disability hostility that recognizes that disability hostility can be identified on the basis of a demonstration of hostility, a hostility motivation and/or targeting by reason of a person's disability.
2. That policy statements and guidance within the criminal justice system be reviewed following on such change in legal provision to reflect the range of grounds impacting disability hostility.
3. That the Judicial College engages with the Disability Hate Crime agenda, collaborates with the police and prosecution services in developing a shared understanding, embarks on judicial training on Disability Hate Crime and reflects best practice guidance on Disability Hate Crime in the Equal Treatment Bench Book.

Concluding comments

Throughout this book, there has been one overall aim in the exploration of activist, political and policy stream contributions and strengthened by the focus on problematization in the analysis of cases and policy statements: to provide an analysis of the emergence and development of Disability Hate Crime in the criminal justice system hate crime domain in England and Wales.

Through the application of a hybridic framework of agenda setting and problematization, this book has shown how Disability Hate Crime emerged and developed. It has shown how Disability Hate Crime remains an unsettled and unsettling agenda arising from its dual construction as either hostility or vulnerability targeting which itself flows from the wider dual problematization of disability as either an issue of welfare, care and protection or an issue of justice and rights.

This book provides a way through this either/or problematization in the hate crime domain, specifically through an alternative construction of Disability Hate Crime as disability hostility *including* vulnerability. This alternative construction has practical legal and policy implications. In doing so, this book has made a contribution to empirical reality and existing theory. There remain many issues for further exploration in relation to Disability Hate Crime, but this book should make it possible to deepen both the theoretical and empirical investigation of other aspects of this topic, perhaps not only in the context of England and Wales, but more generally.

Disability Hate Crime has emerged into the hate crime domain in England and Wales and developed within it – it is now a firm policy agenda. However, it is yet to become settled as part of consistent day-to-day practice in the delivery of justice to disabled people. Nonetheless, a way forward is possible, within the hate crime domain and with active judicial engagement, through a legislative change and building on the considerable efforts of police and prosecutors spurred on by activists and politicians. That said, while progress in the Disability Hate Crime domain is required at best it can replace the undue vulnerability focus with a due focus on ableism, in the hate crime domain, it is not going to significantly disrupt and replace the wider dual problematization of disability as issues of welfare, care and protection or an issue of rights and justice. That is a wider challenge of which the challenges in relation to institutionalizing Disability Hate Crime are simply manifestations.

Recognizing and responding to Disability Hate Crime is just one element in a wider strategy required to deliver social justice for disabled people in England and Wales. Taken alone, a Disability Hate Crime focus or, indeed, almost any hate crime focus is, in a sense, a tertiary social policy intervention. It is not a primary social policy intervention (as in education) or a second-level social policy intervention (as in welfare benefits). It is attempting laudably, to secure an element of justice far along the human need and discrimination continuums. Pursued in isolation, it risks becoming an over-individuated response to wider structural injustices.

This study has pointed to clear evidence of Disability Hate Crime existing within the wider context of disabled people's experience of disadvantage and discrimination across most areas of social life. When located within an understanding of disability prejudice and ableism and within the context of a rights and justice-focused national strategy to advance disabled people's social situation in England and Wales, a Disability Hate Crime focus, underpinned by appropriate legal provisions, can contribute to realizing a society where disabled people can live more dignified lives, freer from fear and with the potential for enhanced human flourishing based simultaneously on recognition of human difference and common humanity.

APPENDIX

Research Design and Methods

Introduction

The research for this book was based on a qualitative methodology and informed by a grounded theory approach (Charmaz, 2014). It was based on a case study design with an extended unit of analysis covering the criminal justice system, political and community sector activity. The design was underpinned by mixed research methods comprising key informant interviews, document analysis and analysis of individual hate crime cases. A triangulated methodology was used to understand the lived experience of Disability Hate Crime, provide an analysis of the embodiment of policy and reflect the empirical reality of policy being transferred into practice.

The selection of a case study design was informed by the need to explore specifically how Disability Hate Crime policy emerged and developed, the distinctiveness of Disability Hate Crime within the hate crime policy domain and the fullest range of contributory factors and challenges to the development of Disability Hate Crime policy and practice (Swinbourn, 2010; Thomas, 2011). Case study design was particularly suited to this research topic because it fitted well with this research study's focus on process tracing, the exploration of the policy process, in this case between criminal justice agencies, other parts of government and the activist-community sector leading to the emergence and development of Disability Hate Crime policy.

This case study spans 1997–2020: 1997 marks the election of the first New Labour government in Britain, and 1998 marked the introduction of criminal law provisions on hate crime in England and Wales. It considered developments up to 2017 when a significant update of Disability Hate Crime policy occurred (CPS, 2017) and considered more recent inspections tracing some improvements in the area and a more recent Law Commission consultation review on Hate Crime legal provisions in England and Wales. This case study focuses on England and Wales as they form a unified criminal justice system, with shared ministerial leadership, a single prosecution service, linked police services and a unified courts system. There is a single criminal law system, which is different from Scotland and Northern Ireland. The same criminal law provision on Disability Hate Crime exists in England and Wales. The research for this book considered the Wales dimension in each aspect of the research including key informant interviews, documentary research and case analyses. The research found no substantive difference in policy and practice between England and Wales. This is not surprising given that it forms an integral part of a unified legal policy domain.

Distinguishing features of this research study are its exploratory nature and its inductive approach. The study explored, from multiple perspectives, how and why Disability Hate Crime emerged as and when it did.

Key informant interviews – semi-structured

Interviews were conducted with 55 key informants, outlined in Table A.1, drawn from among activists, criminal justice practitioners, policy officers and politicians. They are identified by role here. Interviews lasted between 35 minutes and two hours approximately, with the majority lasting approximately 70 minutes. The broad interview topics are outlined here:

- What is hate crime and how it is conceived?
- Disability Hate Crime and how it relates to hate crime.
- Contributory factors to the emergence and development of the Disability Hate Crime agenda.
- Challenges to the emergence and development of the Disability Hate Crime agenda.
- Vulnerability and hostility in relation to the Disability Hate Crime agenda.
- Activism, politics and policy activity in the emergence and development of the Disability Hate Crime agenda.
- Role of wider legislative context on Disability Hate Crime policy agenda.
- Discussion of disability discrimination and relationship to Disability Hate Crime.

Table A.1: List of key informants

Respondent number	Role descriptor
R1	Director, disability NGO
R2	National disability activist
R3	Former NGO and CJS official
R4	Senior staff, LGB NGO
R5	Cabinet minister, HM government
R6	Senior official, DRC

(continued)

Table A.1: List of key informants (continued)

Respondent number	Role descriptor
R7	Senior manager, DRC
R8	Hate crime policy official, HM government
R9	Member, House of Lords
R10	National disability activist
R11	Senior manager, London Met Police
R12	National disability activist
R13	Top tier civil servant, hate crime
R14	Senior independent researcher
R15	Former senior CJS, manager
R16	Policy official, CJS
R17	Policy official, CJS
R18	Former senior manager, CJS
R19	Former CJS leader 1
R20	Senior EHRC official
R21	Director, national disability NGO
R22	Hate crime champion 1, CJS
R23	Inspector, HMIC
R24	National disability activist
R25	Hate crime champion 2, CJS
R26	Former director, disability NGO
R27	Senior leader equality rights
R28	EHRC commissioner
R29	Chief prosecutor, CPS
R30	Former CJS Leader 2
R31	District judge
R32	Judge, Central Criminal Court
R33	Judge, Crown Court
R34	Senior policy official, Department of Health
R35	Senior independent researcher
R36	ACPO hate crime lead
R37	National disability activist
R38	Senior official, Welsh govt
R39	Policy officer, Welsh NGO
R40	Policing hate crime adviser
R41	NGO case worker

Table A.1: List of key informants (continued)

Respondent number	Role descriptor
R42	Policy official disability, HM Government
R43	Policy officer, disability NGO
R44	Policy official VAW, CJS
R45	Member of Parliament
R46	Policy official, CPS
R47	National disability activist
R48	Policy officer, disability NGO, Wales
R49	Senior policy official, CJS
R50	Senior prosecutor, CPS
R51	Director, national NGO
R52	National disability activist, Wales
R53	Member, House of Lords
R54	Inspector, HMCPSI
R55	Appeal court judge

Documentary analysis

Documentary research can add value both in terms of researching a new area and adding further insights to existing topics. Documentary research crucially contributes triangulation to projects based on other data collection methods. A range of documents have been produced on Disability Hate Crime from 1997 to 2017. In this study, I analysed key documents in terms of their genesis in the Activist–Problem Stream, the Policy Stream and the Politics Stream. Each selected document was considered under three overall headings: Context, Thematic Analysis and Critique. Context is very significant in obtaining a critical understanding of documents. Documents are not free-standing neutral texts, free from wider organizational and political assumptions. They can be better understood when the context in which they emerge is considered and understood.

Selected documents were appraised in terms of the following questions:

- What are the key themes in the document? Are there implicit themes?
- Does the document relate to a genre of documents and, if so, what genre and how?
- How does the document conceive of and problematize disability and disabled people?
- Does the document address and problematize the issue of vulnerability? If so, how?

- How does the document conceive of and problematize hate crime? And Disability Hate Crime?
- What are the silences in the document, if any?
- Are there other ways of conceiving of the issues addressed in the document and, if so, what are they?

The titles of the documents analysed are set out here:

- CPS, Disability Hate Crime – guidance on the distinction between vulnerability and hostility in the context of crimes committed against disabled people, 2010;
- CPS, Legal guidance on Disability Hate Crime, 2007;
- CPS, public policy statement for prosecuting cases of Disability Hate Crime, 2007;
- CPS, public policy statement on Disability Hate Crime and other crimes against disabled people, 2017;
- EHRC, Hidden in Plain Sight, inquiry into disability related harassment, 2011;
- HHCPSI, HMIC, HMSP, Joint Inspection of the Handling of Cases involving Disability Hate Crime, 2018;
- HM Government, Action Against Hate 2016–2020, 2016;
- HM Government, Challenge it, report it and stop it, delivering the governments hate crime action plan, 2010;
- HM Government, Hate Crime – the cross-government action plan 2009–10;
- HMCPSI, HMIC, HMIP, Joint review of Disability Hate Crime follow-up, 2015;
- HMCPSI, HMIC, HMIP, Living in a different world: joint review of Disability Hate Crime, 2013;
- Judicial Studies Board, Equal Treatment Bench Book 2008;
- Law Commission, Hate Crime Laws: A consultation paper, Consultation Paper number 250, 2020;
- Scope, Getting away with murder 2008;
- UK HM Government, The Care Act 2014;
- UK HM Government, Youth Justice and Criminal Evidence Act 1999.

Analysis of individual cases of Disability Hate Crime

Individual case histories in this study provide another rich form of research data. If a strength of the key informant interviews lies in building understanding through the perspective of living experts and that of documentary analysis lies in building understanding of codified representations of the issue in policy and so on, then a key strength of individual cases lies in advancing understanding through an analysis of the empirical material contained in a diversity of individual cases perceived as Disability Hate Crimes. In a study focused on policy and practice, it enabled a critical consideration of issues in practice.

In this study, I considered but also went beyond consideration of what are termed 'serious cases'. Such incidents are regarded as 'the tip of the iceberg' (EHRC, 2011b). Available evidence indicates that the majority of recorded cases are 'lower to mid-level' in terms of seriousness although clearly not in terms of impact. I negotiated access to the CPS computerized case management system of prosecution cases.

As part of the research for this book, I analysed 15 cases (12 from the CPS system) in which disabled people had been victims of targeted incidents or crimes, all of which could be regarded as hate related.

Table A.2 provides a headline description for each of these cases, together with a brief indication of the case outcomes in terms of whether they were successfully prosecuted as Disability Hate Crimes. It also contains illustrative case profiles. All cases were anonymized in terms of personal details. All 15 cases involved targeted victimization of disabled people. A descriptive name has been given to each case for readers' easy reference.

The cases secured via the CPS were accessed in the following way: the CPS provided data on all Disability Hate Crime-flagged defendant prosecutions for 2013–14 set out by principal offence category, court centre and mode of trial. This showed 548 Disability Hate Crime-flagged defendant prosecutions during the 2013–14 reporting period. Twelve cases were selected from this data, six having been successful and six unsuccessful. The final three were accessed via NGOs and the independent statutory sector which was a purposeful extension to the sample to secure non-crimed cases. Notwithstanding the current limitations of Disability Hate Crime data, this was an early and significant analysis of Disability Hate Crime cases. It represented, in a sense, the best that could be done in the data context.

The analysis of individual cases also allowed for integration with the emerging findings from other research methods. The individual cases were analysed against approaches set out in key policy documents. This analysis was informed by themes emerging from the key informant interviews. The individual cases also illuminated the features of Disability Hate Crime, helping to advance our understanding of its commonalities with wider hate crimes and its specificities.

NVivo analysis of key informant interviews

The 55 key informant interviews underpinning the book were analysed using NVivo qualitative research software. I compared findings between

Table A.2: Headline details of Disability Hate Crimes cases analysed

Case	Case description	Outcome
The Downtown case	Ongoing neighbour harassment of disabled man on social housing estate involving abusive language. 2013–14	Disability Hate Crime recognized by court and uplift given and recorded.
The supported housing case	Ongoing harassment of two learning-disabled men in a supported housing scheme by local youth. 2013–14	Disability Hate Crime recognized by court and uplift given and recorded.
The Valetown case	Abusive behaviour towards learning-disabled man by neighbour involving abusive language. 2013–14	Disability Hate Crime recognized by court and uplift given and recorded.
The spitting cyclist case	Common assault on disabled wheelchair user in Oldtown. Involved abusive language. 2013–14	Disability Hate Crime recognized by court and uplift given and recorded.
The skate park case	Attack on a learning-disabled man involving abusive language. 2013–14	Disability Hate Crime recognized by CPS. Disability Hate Crime rejected by judge and verdict was 'an attack on a vulnerable victim'. No uplift.
The visiting mates case	Harassment and abuse of disabled man in his flat and on street by able-bodied associate. Involved use of abusive language. 2013–14	Disability Hate Crime recognized by court and uplift given and recorded.
The homeless hostel case	Common assault of disabled man in a hostel by fellow resident. Involved abusive language. 2013–14	Disability Hate Crime recognized, uplift given and recorded.
The enslavement case	Targeted enslavement and exploitation of young disabled woman over many years. 2013–14	Disability Hate Crime aspects not recognized. Identified as vulnerable victim case only. No hate crime dimension in sentence.
The Sunset View care home case	Targeted ill-treatment of learning-disabled residents revealed by undercover reporter. 2013–14	Disability Hate Crime aspects recognized by CPS and police, rejected by judge in favour of Mental Health Act offences.
The domestic violence case	Husband abuses wife with vascular dementia. 2013–14	Disability Hate Crime aspects initially identified. Case had multiple identifications as domestic violence, vulnerable victim. Disability hostility not raised in court.

Table A.2: Headline details of disability hate crimes cases analysed (continued)

Case	Case description	Outcome
The church warden case	Church warden's targeted abuse of two disabled churchgoers. 2013–14	Disability Hate Crime identified initially but not raised at sentencing stage. Focus on victim vulnerability.
The neighbours' dispute case	Neighbours' dispute that evolved into targeted disability hostility. 2013–4	No-crimed case. Did not enter CJS. Resolved through advocacy and liaison.
The noise nuisance case	A case categorized as noise nuisance of targeted harassment. 2013–14	No-crimed case of noise nuisance, later recognized as disability hostility.
The murder of Brent Martin	Learning-disabled man with mental health difficulties murdered in Northumbria. Brent Martin. 2007 (for comparison)	A case categorized as involving extremely vulnerable victim. No Disability Hate Crime aspect recognized.
The Pilkington case	Sustained harassment of family with disabled children culminates in murder-suicide, Pilkington–Hardwick case. Occurred 2007, IPCC report 2009.	A series of incidents that were reported to police but non-crimed. Classed as series of anti-social behaviour incidents.

key informant responses by interviewee roles in activism, policy or politics, drawing on the constant comparative method. NVivo was used to analyse the text of the interviews using an open coding approach. This resulted in the identification of approximately 170 open codes, reduced to approximately 30 categories and then to six themes. These six themes formed the basis of this book's thematic chapters.

Illustrative extract from NVivo data analysis codebook

- Codebook Phase 1 – generating initial codes (open coding) (Table A.3)
- Codebook Phase 2 – axial coding (developing core categories) (Table A.4)
- Codebook Phase 3 – focused coding (Table A.5)

Given the focus of this research study on the emergence and development of policy on Disability Hate Crime, this study used an adapted version of US public policy academic John Kingdon's policy streams approach (2001, 2011) as an organizing framework and analytical tool as the study developed. The policy streams approach is set out in Chapter 1. In this study, an adapted version of Kingdon's framework was used in a tentative, critical and reflective way to

Table A.3: Codebook\\Phase 1 – generating initial codes (open coding)

Phase 1 – 171 open codes developed	Code definitions for coding consistency	Interviews coded	Units of meaning coded
Disability movement uses competing frames of disability.	This refers to perceptions that for a variety of reasons the disability movement uses competing frames of disability, in particular a pity/vulnerable frame and a rights frame.	5	9
Disability raises difference principle and substantive equality.	This refers to perceptions that disability raises the difference principle in equality and linked to this raises substantive equality and these pose challenges for the development of the DHC policy and practice agenda.	1	2
Disabled people fear consequences of reporting DHC.	This refers to the perceptions that disabled people can fear the consequences for their independence if they report DHC.	1	2
Disablism and ableism – issues and concepts.	This refers to perceptions that the issues of disablism and or ableism are significant in understanding the experience of DHC and the development of the DHC policy agenda.	16	31
DPOs raise awareness.	The role played by disabled people organizations in raising awareness of Disability Hate Crime.	39	74
Early origins of hate crime agenda in Britain.	This refers to the early origins of the hate crime legislative, policy and practice agenda in Britain.	1	8
EHRC inquiry issues and impacts.	This refers to perceptions of the issues raised and the impacts of the EHRC Inquiry into Disability Related Harassment.	21	77

inform the study's development and to explore whether it provided a valuable analytical framework in this case. The elements of Kingdon's framework became ever more evident through the three cycles of encoding that moved me as the researcher from the descriptive (open coding) to the interpretive (developing core categories) to the abstract (focused/theoretical coding). Through this process, it became increasingly apparent that the primary data gathered in this research persistently revealed categories of codes consistent with an adapted version of Kingdon's model as an analytical lens (Figure A.1).

APPENDIX

Table A.4: Codebook\\Phase 2 – axial coding (developing core categories)

Phase 2 – axial coding – 171 open codes collapsed and mapped to 6 axial codes (core categories) supported by 26 subcategories	Code definitions for coding consistency	Interviews coded	Units of meaning coded
1.0 – DHC and the wider hate crime domain	This refers to the overall hate crime domain and how DHC relates to that domain.	50	536
Adopting Hate Crime language enabled progress	This refers to perceptions that the adoption by disability activists of the language of DHC enabled progress on the emergence and development of the DHC policy and practice agenda.	3	4
Developments in human rights and equality thinking and law	This refers to the perception that developments in human rights thinking and law in recent decades enabled progress to occur on the DHC policy and practice agenda.	6	9
Differences between DHC and other hate crimes	This refers to the perception of differences between DHC and other hate crimes.	19	30
DHC similarities to VAW	The refers to the perceptions that there are similarities between DHC and violence against women as well as similarities to other hate crimes.	15	20
Disability hostility can vary by impairment	This refers to the perception that disability hostility can vary by impairment, that is whether an impairment is a physically disabled person, a learning disabled person or a mentally disabled person.	1	1
Disability lags behind other equality strands	This refers to the perception that disability equality lags behind other equality strands in terms of protection.	10	16

(continued)

Table A.4: Codebook\\Phase 2 – axial coding (developing core categories) (continued)

Phase 2 – axial coding – 171 open codes collapsed and mapped to 6 axial codes (core categories) supported by 26 subcategories	Code definitions for coding consistency	Interviews coded	Units of meaning coded
Disability raises difference principle and substantive equality	This refers to perceptions that disability raises the difference principle in equality and linked to this raises substantive equality and these pose challenges for the development of the DHC policy and practice agenda.	1	2
Hate crime domain existed and DHC perceived to fit	This refers to the perception that a hate crime domain is firmly established in Britain and DHC when it emerged was perceived to fit into that policy domain alongside racist, religious and homophobic crimes.	38	78
Hate crime focus shifts minorities relationship with CJS	This refers to the ways in which a policy and practice focus on hate crime can shift minorities' wider relationships with the CJS.	1	2
Hate crime most associated with racist crimes historically	This refers to the phenomenon historically of thinking and considering hate crime as equating to racist crime.	33	64
Hostility, a daily occurrence	This refers to the ongoing day-to-day experience of hostility by disabled people.	9	14

Researcher issues – professional and personal

As a previous Director of Equality and Diversity at the CPS for England and Wales, I was able to negotiate access to documentation and key informants through existing networks and relationships of trust already established. Agreement to access CPS documents and cases was obtained together with agreement to participate in key informant interviews. Agreement was also secured from the relevant ACPO lead. Contact was made and engagement agreed with key disability community sector leads. Contacts were made with a number of politicians involved, including the lead Cabinet minister who contributed to this agenda.

APPENDIX

Table A.5: Codebook\\Phase 3 – focused coding

Phase 3 – Focused coding – 6 core categories and 26 sub-categories conceptually mapped and collapsed to 6 themes (focused codes)	Interviews coded	Units of meaning coded
T1 – From hate crime to DHC	50	536
T1.1 – DHC and the wider hate crime domain	50	536
T2 – Agenda triggering – agenda setting	48	1423
T2.1 – Contributory factors to policy development on DHC	48	1423
T3 – Agenda challenge vulnerability in DHC	49	402
T3.1 – Vulnerability label is problematic	49	402
T4 – Competing framings of the disability experience	44	759
T4.1 – 6 Towards agenda institutionalization	40	207
T4.2 – Agenda challenge – vulnerability in DHC	32	101
T4.3 – Agenda item yet to come – ableism, disablism and DHC	24	125
T4.4 – An unsettled and unsettling agenda	44	326
T5 – Challenges to policy development and implementation on DHC policy development	45	399
T5.1 – Challenges to policy development and implementation on DHC policy development	45	399
T6 – Agenda Item yet to come – ableism, disablism and DHC	41	206
T6.1 – Disability discrimination and disablism – issue, challenges and concepts	41	206

Note: Codebook – Phase 3 – focused coding involved conceptually mapping and collapsing categories into a broader thematic framework.

The effects of the author's five-year work at the CPS, some directly relating to hate crime, are difficult to gauge. The aim was to use the insights obtained positively. The researcher contributed to and witnessed the community engagement process informing hate crime policy development, and the challenges in implementation including recording and reporting on cases. I also witnessed the community sector campaigning on the issue. It is difficult to ascertain the impact of such close involvement in terms of potential bias. However, there is little doubt that it was valuable experience in understanding the policy making and institutionalization process and the contribution of various actors to these processes. To an extent, the identification of the lines of inquiry could be viewed as somewhat subjective. However, my identification of lines of inquiry and research questions had a validity as they arose out of my substantial active engagement with the issues in this research. A further issue to be considered is that I am a non-disabled researcher researching a concern for many disabled people. I was alert to this and to

Figure A.1: Sample analytical memo

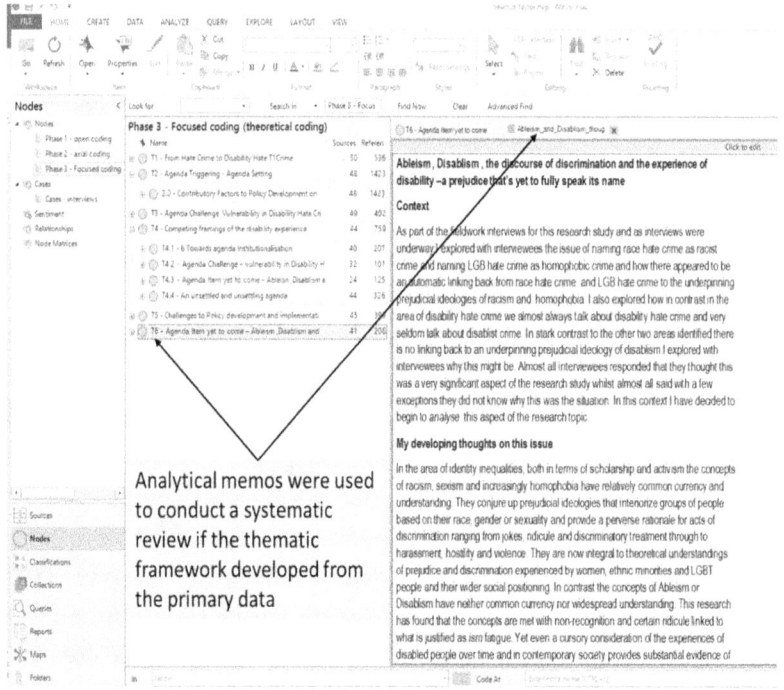

debates within the disability movement regarding this phenomenon. In some instances, 'rejection of non-disabled researchers occurred at the beginning of the British disability movement' (Shakespeare, 2000, p 195). This earlier rejection has been revisited recently. It is increasingly acknowledged that, because someone is disabled, they do not have 'automatic insight into the lives of other disabled people' (Shakespeare, 2006, p 195). There is also a recognition that the rejectionist stance risks adopting an essentialist position where only disabled people can contribute to disability issues. The social progressive perspective on disability acknowledges the role that non-disabled researchers can play and views ways forward in terms of alliances between disabled and non-disabled people. There is recognition that non-disabled researchers can make a positive contribution to the social situation of disabled people (Shakespeare, 2000, p 196). This is the committed and critically reflexive position from which I, as a researcher, approached this topic.

Bibliography

Abberley, P. (1987a) *Disability and Oppression*, Warwick Working Papers on Sociology, Coventry: University of Warwick: Department of Sociology.

Abberley, P. (1987b) 'The concept of oppression and the development of a social theory of disability', *Disability, Handicap and Society*, 2(1), 4–13.

Abberley, P. (1999) 'The significance of work for the citizenship of disabled people' [Paper], Conference. Dublin: University College Dublin.

Abrams, D. and Houston, D.M. (2006) *Equality, Diversity and Prejudice in Britain: Results from a 2005 National Survey, Report for Cabinet Office Equalities Review October 2006*, Canterbury: University of Kent.

Adam, R., Reiss, B. and Serlin, D. (2015) *Keywords for Disability Studies*, New York: New York University Press.

Adams, M., Bell, L.A. and Griffin, P. (eds) (2007) *Teaching for Diversity and Social Justice*, New York: Routledge.

Adams, M., Blumenfeld, W.J., Casaneda, C., Hackman, H., Peters, M. and Zuniga, X. (eds) (2013) *Readings for Diversity and Social Justice*, New York: Routledge.

Albrecht, G.L., Seelman, K.D. and Bury, M. (eds) (2001) *Handbook of Disability Studies*, Thousand Oaks, CA: Sage.

Alcoff, L., Homes-Garcia, M., Mohanty, S. and Moya, P.M.L. (eds) (2006) *Identity Politics Reconsidered*, New York: Palgrave Macmillan.

Allport, G. (1954) *The Nature of Prejudice*, Reading: Addison-Wesley.

Althusser, L. (1969) *Lenin and Philosophy and Other Essays*, New York: Monthly Review Press.

Asquith, N.L., Barthowiak, T.I. and Roberts K.A. (eds) (2017) *Policing Encounters with Vulnerability*, Cham: Palgrave Macmillan.

Association of Chief Police Officers (ACPO) (2005) *Hate Crime in Delivering a Quality Service – Good Practice and Tactical Guidance*, London: Home Office Police Standards Unit.

Association of Chief Police Officers (ACPO) (2010) *ACPO Hate Crime Manual 2010*, London: Home Office Police Standards Unit.

Association of Chief Police Officers (ACPO) (2014) *ACPO Hate Crime Manual 2014*, London: Home Office Police Standards Unit.

Attorney General's Office (AGO) (2006) *Race for Justice Taskforce*, London: Attorney General's Office.

Bacchi, C. (1999) *Women, Policy, and Politics – The Construction of Policy Problems*, London: Sage.

Bacchi, C. (2009) *Analysing Policy: What's the Problem Represented to Be?* French Forest, New South Wales: Pearson.

Bacchi, C. (2012) 'Why study problematisations? Making politics visible', *Open Journal of Political Science*, 2(1), 1–8.

Bacchi, C. and Eveline, J. (eds) (2010) *Mainstreaming Politics: Gendering Practices and Feminist Theory*, Adelaide: University of Adelaide.

Bagihole, B. (2009) *Understanding Equal Opportunities and Diversity*, Bristol: Policy Press.

Balderston, S. (2012) 'After Disablist Hate Crime: which interventions really work to resist victimhood and build resilience with survivors?', in A. Roulstone and H. Mason-Bish (eds) *Disability, Hate Crime and Violence*, London: Routledge, pp 182–97.

Balderston, S. (2013) 'Victimised again? Intersectionality and injustice in disabled women's lives after hate crime and rape', *Advances in Gender Research*, 18, 17–51.

Barbehon, M., Munch, S. and Lamping, W. (2015) 'Problem definition and agenda setting in critical perspective', in F. Fischer, D. Torgerson, A. Durnova and M. Orsini (eds) *Handbook of Critical Policy Studies*, Cheltenham: Edward Elgar Publishing, pp 241–58.

Barnes, C. and Mercer, G. (2003) *Disability, Key Concepts*, Cambridge: Polity Press.

Barnes, C. and Mercer, G. (2010) *Exploring Disability* (2nd edn), Cambridge: Polity Press.

Barnes, C. and Oliver, M. (1998) *Disabled People and Social Policy – from Exclusion to Inclusion*, Harlow: Longman.

Batavia, A.I. (2001) 'The new paternalism: portraying people with disabilities as an oppressed minority', *Journal of Disability Policy Studies*, 12(2), 107–13.

Beadle-Brown, J., Richardson, L, Guest, C., Malovic, A., Bradshaw, J. and Himmerich, J. (2014) *Living in Fear: Better Outcomes for People with Learning Disabilities and Autism*, Canterbury: Tizard Centre University of Kent.

Bennett, A.E. (2017) 'Live streamed hate crime against disabled man prompts national outrage', *Family and Intimate Partner Violence Quarterly*, 9(4), 47–52.

Beresford, P., Fleming, J., Glynn, M., Bewley, C., Croft, S., Branfield, F. and Postle, K. (2011) *Supporting People – Towards a Person-Centred Approach*, Bristol: Policy Press.

Berger, P. and Luckmann, T. (1967) *The Social Construction of Reality: A Treatise in the Sociology of Knowledge*, New York: Anchor.

Best, J. (1999) *Random Violence – How We Talk about New Crimes and New Victims*, Los Angeles, CA: University of California Press.

Best, J. (ed) (2001) *How Claims Spread: Cross-national Diffusion of Social Problems*, New York: Aldine De Gruyter.

Best, J. (ed) (2009) *Images of Issues* (2nd edn), Piscataway, NJ: Aldine Transaction.

Blackabay, D., Leslie, D. and Murphy, P. (1999) *Earnings and Employment Opportunities of Disabled People*, Research Report, London: DFEE.

Bletsas, A. and Beasley, C. (eds) (2012) *Engaging with Carol Bacchi – Strategic Interventions and Exchanges*, Adelaide: University of Adelaide.

Boffey, D. (2013, September 21) 'Labour to create new offence of disability hate crime', *The Guardian*.

Borsay, A. (2005) *Disability and Social Policy in Britain since 1750*, Basingstoke: Palgrave Macmillan.

Bowling, B. (1999) *Violent Racism*, Oxford: Oxford University Press.

Braddock, D.L. and Parish, S.L. (2001) 'An institutional history of disability', in G. Albrecht, K.D. Seelman and M. Bury (eds) *Handbook of Disability Studies*, Thousand Oaks, CA: Sage, pp 11–68.

British Criminology Society (2020) *British Society of Criminology Vulnerability Research Network*. https://criminology.research.southwales.ac.uk/bsc_vrn/

Brown, K. (2011) 'Vulnerability: handle with care', *Ethics and Social Welfare*, 5(3), 313–21.

Brown, K. (2014a) 'Questioning the vulnerability zeitgeist: care and control practices with "vulnerable" young people', *Social Policy and Society*, 13(3), 371–87.

Brown, K. (2014b) 'Beyond protection: "the vulnerable" in the age of austerity', in M. Harrison and T. Sanders (eds) *Social Policies and Social Control: New Perspectives on the 'Not-So-Big Society'*, Bristol: Policy Press, pp 39–52.

Brown, K. (2016) *Vulnerability and Young People – Care and Control in Policy and Practice*, Bristol: Policy Press.

Bryant, A. and Charmaz, K. (eds) (2007) *The Sage Handbook of Grounded Theory*, London: Sage.

Bryman, A. (2012) *Social Research Methods* (4th edn), Oxford: Oxford University Press.

Burawoy, M. (1998) 'The extended case method', *Sociological Theory*, 16(1), 4–33.

Burch, L. (2018) 'You are a parasite on the productive classes: online disablist hate speech in austere times', *Disability and Society*, 33(3), 392–415.

Burstein, P. (1991) 'Policy domains: organization, culture and policy outcomes', *Annual Review of Sociology*, 17(1), 327–50.

Burton, F. and Carlen, P. (2006) 'Official discourse', in J. Scott (ed) *Documentary Research (4 volumes)*, London: Sage.

Butler, J., Gambetti, Z. and Sabsay, L. (eds) (2016) *Vulnerability in Resistance*, Durham, NC: Duke University Press.

Byrne, L. MP (2013) 'Labour's commitments on disability', *Labour Party Conference*, September 2013. Brighton.

Cairney, P. (2012) *Understanding Public Policy, Theories and Issues*, Basingstoke: Palgrave Macmillan.

Cairney, P. (2013) 'Standing on the shoulders of giants: how do we combine the insights of multiple theories in public policy studies?' *Policy Studies Journal*, 41(1), 1–21.

Cameron, C. (2014) *Disability Studies*, London: Sage.

Campbell, F.K. (2008) 'Refusing able(ness): a preliminary conversation about ableism', *M/C Journal*, 11(3), 1–12.

Campbell, J. and Oliver, M. (1996) *Disability Politics, Understanding Our Past, Changing Our Future*, London: Routledge.

Capewell, C., Ralph, S. and Bonnett, L. (2015) 'The continuing violence towards disabled people', *Journal of Research in Special Educational Needs*, 15(3), 211–21.

Chakraborti, N. (2010) 'Crimes against the "other": conceptual, operational and empirical challenges for hate studies', *Journal of Hate Studies*, 8(1), 9–28.

Chakraborti, N. and Garland, J. (2009) *Hate Crime – Impact, Causes and Responses*, London: Sage.

Chakraborti, N. and Garland, J. (2012) 'Reconceptualising hate crime victimization through the lens of vulnerability and "difference"', *Theoretical Criminology*, 16(4), 499–514.

Chaplin, E. and Mukbopadhyay S. (2018), 'Autism spectrum disorder and hate crime', *Advances in Autism*, 4(1), 30–36.

Charmaz, K. (2006) *Constructing Grounded Theory*, London: Sage.

Charmaz, K. (2014) *Constructing Grounded Theory* (2nd edn), London: Sage.

Chouniard, V. (1997) 'Making space for disabling difference: challenges of ableist geographies', *Environment and Planning D: Society and Space*, 15, 379–87.

Clapham, A. (2007) *Human Rights*, Oxford: Oxford University Press.

Clement, S., Brohan, E., Sayce, L., Pool, J. and Thorncroft, G. (2011) 'Disability hate crime and targeted violence and hostility: a mental health and discrimination perspective', *Journal of Mental Health*, 20(3), 219–25.

Cohen, M.D., March Jones, G. and Olsen, J.P. (1972) 'A garbage can model of organizational choice', *Administrative Service Quarterly*, 17(1), 1–25.

Coleman, N. and Sykes, W. (2016) *Crime and Disabled People: Measures of Disability Related Harassment*, London: Equality and Human Rights Commission.

Collins, J. (1992) *When the Eagles Fly: A Report on the Resettlement of People with Learning Difficulties from Long-Stay Institutions*, London: Values into Action.

Collins, J. (1993) *The Resettlement Game: Policy and Procrastination in the Closure of Mental Handicap Hospitals*, London: Values into Action.

Collins, J. (1994) *Still to Be Settled: Strategies for the Resettlement of People from Mental Handicap Hospitals*, London: Values into Action.

Conrad, R. (ed) (2014) *Against Equality, Queer Revolution Not Mere Inclusion*, Oakland, CA: AK Press.

Cresswell, J. (2007) *Qualitative Inquiry and Research Design: Choosing Among Five Approaches*, Thousand Oaks, CA: Sage.

Cresswell, J. (2009) *Research Design, Qualitative, Quantitative and Mixed Methods Approaches* (3rd edn), London: Sage.

Crown Prosecution Service (CPS) (2001) *The Denman Report into Racial Discrimination in the Crown Prosecution Service*, London: Crown Prosecution Service.

Crown Prosecution Service (CPS) (2002) *Racist and Religious Crimes Policy*, London: Crown Prosecution Service.

Crown Prosecution Service (CPS) (2003) *Race for Justice Report*, London: Crown Prosecution Service.

Crown Prosecution Service (CPS) (2004) *Homophobic Crime Policy*, London: Crown Prosecution Service.

Crown Prosecution Service (CPS) (2006) *Single Equality Scheme*, London: Crown Prosecution Service.

Crown Prosecution Service (CPS) (2007a) *CPS Legal Guidance on Disability Hate Crime*, London: Crown Prosecution Service.

Crown Prosecution Service (CPS) (2007b) *CPS Policy for Prosecuting Cases of Disability Hate Crime*, London: Crown Prosecution Service.

Crown Prosecution Service (CPS) (2008) *Hate Crime Report 2007–08*, London: Crown Prosecution Service.

Crown Prosecution Service (CPS) (2009a) *Hate Crime Report 2008–09*, London: Crown Prosecution Service.

Crown Prosecution Service (CPS) (2009b) *Public Policy Statement on Victims and Witnesses Who Have Learning Disabilities*, London: Crown Prosecution Service.

Crown Prosecution Service (CPS) (2009c) *Public Policy Statement on Victims and Witnesses Who Have Mental Health Issues*, London: Crown Prosecution Service.

Crown Prosecution Service (CPS) (2010a) *Victims and Witnesses Who Have Mental Health Issues and/or Learning Disabilities – Prosecution Guidance*, London: Crown Prosecution Service.

Crown Prosecution Service (CPS) (2010b) *Disability Hate Crime – Guidance on the Distinction Between Vulnerability and Hostility in the Context of Crimes Committed Against Disabled People*, London: Crown Prosecution Service.

Crown Prosecution Service (CPS) (2010c) *Hate Crime and Crimes Against Older People Report, 2009–10*, London: Crown Prosecution Service.

Crown Prosecution Service (CPS) (2011) *Hate Crimes and Crimes Against Older People Report, 2010–11*, London: Crown Prosecution Service.

Crown Prosecution Service (CPS) (2012) *Hate Crimes and Crimes Against Older People Report, 2011–12*, London: Crown Prosecution Service.

Crown Prosecution Service (CPS) (2013) *The Code for Crown Prosecutors*, London: Crown Prosecution Service.

Crown Prosecution Service (CPS) (2015) *Revised Draft Public Policy Statement on Crimes Against Disabled People for Consultation*, London: Crown Prosecution Service.

Crown Prosecution Service (CPS) (2015) *Annual Hate Crime Report*, London: Crown Prosecution Service.

Crown Prosecution Service (CPS) (2016) *Annual Hate Crime Report*, London: Crown Prosecution Service.

Crown Prosecution Service (CPS) (2017) *Public Policy Statement on Disability Hate Crimes and Other Crimes Against Disabled People*, London: Crown Prosecution Service.

Crown Prosecution Service (CPS) (2021) *CPS Data Summary Quarter 4 2020–2021*, 22 July, London: Crown Prosecution Service.

De Vaus, D. (2001) *Research Design in Social Research*, London: Sage.

Department of Health (2001) *No Secrets*, London: Department of Health.

Department of Health (2009) *Valuing People Now: A New Three-Year Strategy for People with Learning Disabilities*, London: Department of Health.

Department for Work and Pensions (2002) *Disabled for Life? Attitudes Towards and Experiences of Disability in Britain*, Research Report No. 173, Norwich: HMSO.

Digranes, C. (2016) *Disabled Justice: A Qualitative Case Study on the Barriers to Registration of Disability Hate Crime Within the Norwegian Criminal Justice System*, Oslo: University of Oslo.

Dimock, S. and Al-Hakim, M. (2012) 'Hate as an aggravating factor in sentencing', *New Law Review*, 15(4), 572–611.

Disability Now (2007) *The Hate Crime Dossier*, London: Disability Now Magazine.

Disabled People's Council (2010a) *The Bigger Picture – UK Disabled People's Council's Report to the EHRC*, London: UKDPC.

Disabled People's Council (2010b) *Snapshot of Targeted Hostility Towards Disabled People in the UK*, London: UKDPC.

Disability Rights Commission (DRC) (2005) *Shaping the Future of Equality*, London: Disability Rights Commission.

Disability Rights Commission (DRC) (2007a) *Creating an Alternative Future*, London: Disability Rights Commission.

Disability Rights Commission (DRC) (2007b) *Changing Britain for Good: Putting Disability at the Heart of Public Policy*, London: Disability Rights Commission.

Disability Rights Commission England and Wales (2006) *Equal Treatment: Closing the Gap: A Formal Investigation into Physical Health Inequalities Experienced by People With Learning Disabilities and/or Mental Health Problems*, London: Disability Rights Commission.

Disability Rights Commission Scotland and Capability Scotland (2004) *Hate Crime Against Disabled People in Scotland*, Edinburgh: Disability Rights Commission and Capability Scotland.

Disability Rights UK (in association with Office for Disability Issues) (2012a) *Let's Stop Hate Crime – A Guide for Setting Up Third Party Reporting Centres*, London: Disability Rights UK.

Disability Rights UK (in association with Office for Disability Issues) (2012b) *Let's Stop Disability Hate Crime – A Guide for Disabled People*, London: Disability Rights UK.

Disability Rights UK (in association with Office for Disability Issues) (2012c) *Let's Stop Disability Hate Crime – A Guide for Non-Disabled People*, London: Disability Rights UK.

Disability Unit (2021) *UK Disability Survey Research Report, June 2021*, London: Cabinet Office.

Dole, B., Senator (1994) 'Are we keeping America's promises to people with disabilities?', *Iowa Law Review*, 79(3), 925–33.

Donnelly, J. (2003) *Universal Human Rights in Theory and Practice*, New York: Cornell University Press.

Drake, R.F. (1999) *Understanding Disability Policies*, Basingstoke: Palgrave Macmillan.

Driedger, D. (1989) *The Last Civil Rights Movement: Disabled Peoples' International*, London: Hurst.

Dunn, M.C, Clare, I.C. and Holland, A.J. (2008) 'To empower or to protect? Constructing the vulnerable adult in English law and public policy', *Legal Studies*, 28(2), 234–53.

Durant, R.F. and Diehl, P.F. (1989) 'Agendas, alternatives and public policy: lessons from the US foreign policy arena', *Journal of Public Policy*, 9(2), 179–205.

Dye, T.R. (2011) *Understanding Public Policy* (13th edn), London: Pearson.

Eisenhardt, K.M. (1989) 'Building theories from case study research', *The Academy of Management Review*, 14(4), 532–50.

Eller, W. and Krutz, G. (2009) 'Policy process, scholarship and the road ahead: an introduction to the 2008 policy shootout', *Policy Studies Journal*, 37(1), 1–4.

Emerson, E. and Roulstone, A. (2014) 'Developing an evidence base for violent and disablist hate crime in Britain', *Journal of Interpersonal Violence*, 29(17), 3086–104.

Equality and Human Rights Commission (EHRC) (2009) *Disabled People's Experiences of Targeted Violence and Hostility*, London: Equality and Human Rights Commission.

Equality and Human Rights Commission (EHRC) (2011a) *Disability-Related Harassment: the Role of Public Bodies*, Research Report 78, London: Equality and Human Rights Commission.

Equality and Human Rights Commission (EHRC) (2011b) *Hidden in Plain Sight, Inquiry into Disability-Related Harassment*, London: Equality and Human Rights Commission.

Equality and Human Rights Commission (EHRC) (2012) *Out in the Open, Tackling Disability Related Harassment, a Manifesto for Change*, London: Equality and Human Rights Commission.

Equality and Human Rights Commission (EHRC) (2013) *Crime and Disabled People, Baseline Statistical Analysis of Measures from the Formal Legal Inquiry into Disability-Related Harassment*, Research Report 90, London: Equality and Human Rights Commission.

Equality and Human Rights Commission (EHRC) (2016) *EHRC Response to the Report of the House of Lords Select Committee on the Equality Act 2010 and Disability: The Impact on Disabled People*, London: Equality and Human Rights Commission.

Equality and Human Rights Commission (EHRC) (2017a) *Being Disabled in Britain: A Journey Less Equal*, London: Equality and Human Rights Commission.

Equality and Human Rights Commission (EHRC) (2017b) *Tackling Disability Related Harassment: Final Progress Report*, London: Equality and Human Rights Commission.

Evans, S.E. (2004) *Forgotten Crimes – The Holocaust and People with Disabilities*, Chicago, IL: Ivan R. Dee.

Faye Waxman, B. (1991) 'Hatred: The Unacknowledged Dimension in Violence Against Disabled People', *Sexuality and Disability*, 9(3), 185–99.

Ferrier, L. and Muller, V. (2008) 'Disabling able', *M/C Journal*, 11(3), 1–6.

Fineman, M. (2008) 'The vulnerable subject: anchoring equality in the human condition', *Yale Journal of Law and Feminism*, 20(1), 1–23.

Fineman, M. (2010) 'The vulnerable subject and the responsive state', *Emory Law Journal*, 60(251), 255–6.

Fineman, M. (2012) 'Elderly as vulnerable: rethinking the nature of individual and societal responsibility', *The Elder Law Journal*, 20(2), 71–111.

Fineman, M. (2017), 'Vulnerability and inevitable inequality', *Oslo Law Review*, 4(3), 133–49.

Fineman, M. (2019), 'Vulnerability and social justice', *Valparaiso University Law Review*, 53(2), 341–70.

Fineman, M. (2020), 'Beyond equality and discrimination', *SMU Law Review Forum*, 73, 51–62.

Fischer, F., Torgerson, D., Durnova, A. and Orsini, M. (eds) (2015) *Handbook of Critical Policy Studies*, Cheltenham: Edward Elgar.

Flick, U. (2009) *An Introduction to Qualitative Research*, London: Sage.

Flick, U., von Kordoff, E. and Stienke, I. (2004) *A Companion to Qualitative Research*, London: Sage.

Flyvbjerg, B. (2006) 'Five misunderstandings about case-study research', *Qualitative Inquiry*, 12(2), 219–45.

Foucault, M. (1973) *The Birth of the Clinic*, London: Penguin.

Foucault, M. (1981) 'Questions of method: an interview with Michel Foucault', *Ideology and Consciousness*, 8, 3–14.

Foucault, M. (1997) 'The birth of biopolitics', in M. Foucault and P. Rainbow (ed) *Ethics: Subjectivity and Truth: Essential Works of Michel Foucault 1954–1984*, New York: New Press, pp 73–80.

Fraser, N. (1997) *Justice Interruptus, Critical Reflections on the Post Socialist Condition*, Abingdon: Routledge.

Fraser, N. (1999) *Adding Insult to Injury*, New York: Verso Press.

Fraser, N. (2003) *Recognition or Redistribution*, New York: Verso Publishers.

Fraser, N. and Olsen, K. (eds) (2008) *Adding Insult to Injury: Nancy Fraser Debates Her Critics*, New York: Verso.

Fredman, S. (2000) *Discrimination Law*, Oxford: Oxford University Press.

Fredman, S. (2008) 'Making a difference: the promises and perils of positive duties in the equality field', *European Anti-Discrimination Law Review*, 6, 43–52.

Fredman, S. and Spencer, S. (2006) 'Delivering equality: towards an outcome focused positive duty'. *Submission to the Cabinet Office Equality Review and to the Discrimination Law Review*.

Freeman, M. (2002) *Human Rights*, Cambridge: Polity Press.

Fundamental Rights Agency (2015a) *Equal Protection for All Victims of Hate Crime – The Case of People with Disabilities*, Vienna: Fundamental Rights Agency.

Fundamental Rights Agency (2015b) *Violence Against Children with Disabilities: Legislation, Policies and Programmes in the EU*, Vienna: Fundamental Rights Agency.

Furedi, F. (2004) *Therapy Culture: Cultivating Vulnerability in an Uncertain Age*, Abingdon: Routledge.

Gallagher, H. (2001) 'What the Nazi "Euthanasia Program" can tell us about disability oppression', *Journal of Disability Policy Studies*, 12, 96–9.

Galtung, J. (1969) 'Violence, peace and peace research', *Journal of Peace Research*, 6(3), 167–91.

Galtung, J. (1990) 'Cultural violence', *Journal of Peace Research*, 27(3), 291–305.

Garthwaite, K. (2011) 'The language of shirkers and scroungers? Talking about illness, disability and coalition welfare reform', *Disability and Society*, 26(3), 369–73.

Gates, T. (2010) 'The problem, policy and political streams of the Employment Non-Discrimination Act of 2009: implications for social work practice', *Journal of Gay and Lesbian Social Services*, 22(3), 354–69.

Gerring, J. (2007) *Case Study Research, Principles and Practice*, Cambridge: Cambridge University Press.

Giannasi, P. (2015a) 'The criminal justice system response to disability hate crime', in R. Shah and P. Giannasi (eds) *Tackling Disability Discrimination and Disability Hate Crime: A Multidisciplinary Guide*, London: Jessica Kingsley, pp 231–246.

Giannasi, P. (2015b) 'The narrative for change', in R. Shah and P. Giannasi (eds) *Disability Hate Crime*, London: Jessica Kingsley, pp 54–68.

Gilbert, N. (ed) (2008) *Researching Social Life* (3rd edn), London: Sage.

Glaser, B.G. and Strauss, A.L. (1967, 1979 printing) *The Discovery of Grounded Theory: Strategies for Qualitative Research*, Chicago, IL: Aldine Publishers.

Gomm, R. (2008) *Social Research Methodology, A Critical Introduction* (2nd edn), Basingstoke: Palgrave Macmillan.

Goodley, D. (2014) *Dis/Ability Studies: Theorising Disablism and Ableism*, London: Routledge.

Goodley, D. (2016) *Disability Studies: An Interdisciplinary Introduction*, London: Sage.

Goodley, D. and Runswick-Cole, K. (2011) 'The violence of disablism', *Sociology of Health and Illness*, 33(4), 602–17.

Government Equalities Office (GEO) (2010) *Equality Strategy*, London: Government Equalities Office.

Government Statistics Collective (2006) 'How official statistics are produced: views from the inside', in J. Scott (ed) *Documentary Research*, Vol. 4, London: Sage.

Grattet, R. and Jenness, V. (2001a) 'Examining the boundaries of hate crime law: disabilities and the "dilemma of difference"', *Iowa Journal of Criminal Law and Criminology*, 91(3), 653–97.

Grattet, R. and Jenness, V. (2001b) 'The birth and maturation of hate crime policy in the United States', *American Behavioural Scientist*, 45, 668–96.

Grattet, R., Jenness, V. and Curry, T.R. (1998) 'The homogenization and differentiation of hate crime laws in the United States', *American Sociological Review*, 63(2), 286–307.

Gravell, C. (2012) *Loneliness and Cruelty: People with Learning Disabilities – Their Experience of Harassment, Abuse and Related Crime in the Community*, London: Lemos and Crane.

Gray, V. and Lowery, D. (2000) 'Where do policy ideas come from? A study of Minnesota legislators and staffers', *Journal of Public Administration Research and Theory*, 10(3), 573–97.

Greenwood, R. and Hinings, C.R. (1996) 'Understanding radical organizational change: bringing together the old and new institutionalism', *Academy of Management Review*, 21(4), 1022–54.

Grewal, I., Joy, S., Lewis, J., Swales, K. and Woodfield, K. (2002) *Disabled for Life*, Research Report no. 173, Leeds: Department of Work and Pensions.

Grover, C. and Piggott, L. (2007) 'Social security, employment and incapacity benefit: critical reflections on a new deal for welfare', *Disability and Society*, 27(7), 733–46.

Haines, S. and Ruebain, D. (2011) *Education, Disability, and Social Policy*, Bristol: Policy Press.

Hakim, C. (2006) 'Research based on administrative records', in J. Scott (ed) *Documentary Research*, Volume 4, London: Sage.

Hall, N. (2013) *Hate Crime* (2nd edn), Abingdon: Routledge.

Hall, N. (2014) 'The adventures of an accidental academic in "policy-land": a personal reflection on bridging academia, policing and government in a hate crime context', in N. Chakraborti and J. Garland (eds) *Responding to Hate Crime: The Case for Connecting Policy and Research*, Bristol: Policy Press, pp 13–26.

Hall, N., Corb, A., Giannasi, P. and Grieve, J. (2015) *The Routledge International Handbook on Hate Crime*, Abingdon: Routledge.

Hamilton, P. and Trickett, L. (2015) 'Disability hostility, harassment, and violence in the UK: a "motiveless" and "senseless" crime?', in N. Hall, A. Corb, P. Giannasi and J. Grieve (eds) *The Routledge International Handbook on Hate Crime*, Abingdon: Routledge, pp 207–55.

Hanimaki Jussi, M. (2008) *The United Nations*, Oxford: Oxford University Press.

Hansard (HL) Deb (5 November 2003). Vol. 654, Col. 801.

Harpur, P. (2012) 'From disability to ability: changing the phrasing of the debate', *Disability and Society*, 27(3), 325–37.

Healy, J. (2018) 'On the periphery of hate crime: disability at the intersections of marginalization, vulnerability and difference', PhD thesis, *Department of Criminology and Sociology*, Middlesex University, London, UK.

Healy, J. (2020) 'It spreads like a creeping disease, experiences of victims of disability hate crime in austerity Britain', *Disability and Society*, 35(2), 176–200.

Heilporn, A., Andre, J.M, Didier, J.P. and Chamberlain, M.A. (2006) 'Violence and maltreatment of people with disabilities, a short review', *Journal of Rehabilitative Medicine*, 38, 10–13.

Her Majesty's Crown Prosecution Service Inspectorate (HMCPSI), Her Majesty's Inspectorate of Constabulary (HMIC), Her Majesty's Inspectorate of Probation (HMIP) (2013) *Living in a Different World: Joint Review of Disability Hate Crime*, London: Her Majesty's Crown Prosecution Service Inspectorate.

Her Majesty's Crown Prosecution Service Inspectorate (HMCPSI), Her Majesty's Inspectorate of Constabulary (HMIC), Her Majesty's Inspectorate of Probation (HMIP) (2015) *Joint Review of Disability Hate Crime Follow-Up*, London: Her Majesty's Crown Prosecution Service Inspectorate (HMCPSI), Her Majesty's Inspectorate of Constabulary (HMIC), Her Majesty's Inspectorate of Probation (HMIP).

Her Majesty's Crown Prosecution Service Inspectorate (HMCPSI), and Her Majesty's Inspectorate of Constabulary and Fire and Rescue Services (HMICFRS) (2018) *Joint Inspection of the Handling of Cases Involving Disability Hate Crime*, London: Her Majesty's Crown Prosecution Service Inspectorate (HMCPSI), and Her Majesty's Inspectorate of Constabulary and Fire and Rescue Services (HMICFRS).

Her Majesty's Government (2009–10) *Hate Crime – The Cross-Government Action Plan*, London: Her Majesty's Government.

Her Majesty's Government (2010) *Challenge It, Report It, Stop It – Delivering the Government's Hate Crime Action Plan*, London: Her Majesty's Government.

Her Majesty's Government (2012a) *Challenge It, Report It, Stop It: The Government's Plan to Tackle Hate Crime*, London: Her Majesty's Government.

Her Majesty's Government (2012b) *Government Response to Hidden in Plain Sight, The Equality and Human Rights Commission Report on Disability Related Harassment*, London: Her Majesty's Government.

Her Majesty's Government (2016) *Action Against Hate 2016–2020*, London: Her Majesty's Government.

Herek, G.M. and Berrill, K.T. (1992) *Hate Crimes – Confronting Violence Against Lesbians and Gay Men*, Thousand Oaks, CA: Sage.

Hilgartner, S. and Bosk, C.L. (1988) 'The rise and fall of social problems: a public arena model', *American Journal of Sociology*, 94(1), 53–78.

Hill, M. (2013) *The Public Policy Process* (6th edn), Harlow: Pearson.

HM Government (1999) *Youth Justice and Criminal Evidence Act*, London: Her Majesty's Government.

HM Government (2003) *The Criminal Justice Act*, London: Her Majesty's Government.

HM Government (2014) *The Care Act*, London: Her Majesty's Government.

Hollomotz, A. (2013) 'Disability and the continuum of violence', in A. Roulstone and H. Mason-Bish (eds) *Disability, Hate Crime and Violence*, Abingdon: Routledge, pp 52–63.

Holloway, I. and Todres, L. (2003) 'The status of method: flexibility, consistency and coherence', *Qualitative Research*, 3(3), 345–57.

Home Office (1997a) *Racial Violence and Harassment: A Consultation Document*, London: Home Office.
Home Office (1997b) *Responses to the Home Office Consultation Paper: Racial Violence and Harassment*, London: Home Office. United Kingdom.
Home Office (2007) *Learning Disability Hate Crime: Good Practice Guidance for Crime and Disorder Reduction*, London: Home Office.
Home Office (2010) *Home Office Structural Reform Plan*, London: Home Office.
Home Office (2012) *Hate Crime, Cyber Security and the Experience of Crime among Children. Findings from the 2010/11 British Crime Survey*, London: Home Office.
Home Office (2018) *Hate Crime, England and Wales*, 2017/18 Statistical Bulletin 20/18, 16 October, London: Home Office.
Home Office and Association of Chief Police Officers (2008) *The Agreed Definition of Monitored Hate Crime for England, Wales, and Northern Ireland*, London: Home Office.
Home Office, Office for National Statistics (ONS) and Ministry of Justice (MOJ) (2013) *Crime Survey for England and Wales 2011–12*, London: Home Office.
House of Commons Justice Committee (2009) *The CPS – Gatekeeper of the Criminal Justice System. Ninth report*, London: The Stationery Office.
House of Lords and House of Commons Joint Committee on Human Rights (2008) '*A Life Like Any Other? Human Rights of Adults with Learning Disabilities*', Session 2007–08. Seventh report. Volume 1, London: The Stationery Office.
Howlett, M. (2002) 'Do networks matter? Linking policy network structure to policy outcomes: evidence from four Canadian policy sectors 1990–2000', *Canadian Journal of Political Science*, 35(2), 235–67.
Hudson, J. and Lowe, S. (2009) *Understanding the Policy Process*, Bristol: Policy Press.
Hughes, K., Bellis, M.A., Jones, L., Wood, S., Bates, G., Eckley, L., McCoy, E., Mikton, C., Shakespeare, T. and Officer, A. (2012) 'Prevalence and risk of violence against adults with disabilities: a systematic review and meta-analysis of observational studies', *The Lancet*, 379(9826), 1621–9.
Iganski, P. (1999) 'Why make "hate" a crime?', *Critical Social Policy*, 19(3), 386–95.
Iganski, P. (ed) (2002) *The Hate Debate: Should Hate Be Punished as a Crime?*, London: Profile Books.
Iganski, P. (2008) *'Hate Crime' and the City*, Bristol: Policy Press.
Iganski, P. (2010) 'Hate crime', in F. Brookman, M. Maguire, H. Pierpoint and T. Bennett (eds) *Handbook on Crime*, London: Willian Publishing, pp 351–65.
Iganski, P. and Levin, J. (2015) *Hate Crime: A Global Perspective*, New York: Routledge.

Iganski, P., Botcherby, S., Glen, F., Jochelson, K. and Lagou, S. (2011b) *Equality Groups Perceptions and Experience of Crime: Analysis of the British Crime Survey 2007–08 and 2009–10*, London: Equality and Human Rights Commission.

Iganski, P., Nicon, A. and Lagou, S. (2011a) *Disabled People's Experiences and Concerns about Crime: Analysis of the British Crime Survey 2007–08, 2008–09, and 2009–10*, London: Equality and Human Rights Commission.

Inclusion London (2020) *Still Getting Away with Murder*, London: Inclusion London.

Independent Police Complaints Commission (IPCC) (2011) *Report into the Contact between Fiona Pilkington and Leicestershire Constabulary, 2004–07*, Final Report, London: Independent Police Complaints Commission.

Institute of Conflict Research (ICR) (2009) *Disability and Hate Crime in Northern Ireland*, Belfast: Office of the First Minister and Deputy First Minister, Northern Ireland Executive.

Independent Policy Complaints Commission (IPCC) (2009) IPCC Report into the Con Pilkington Tact between Fiona and Leicestershire Constabulary 2004–2007. Independent Investigation Final Report. 2009/016872, London: Independent Policy Complaints Commission.

Jacobs, J.B. and Potter, K. (1998) *Hate Crimes – Criminal Law and Identity Politics*, Oxford: Oxford University Press.

Jenness, V. and Broad, K.L. (1997) *Hate Crimes, New Social Movements, and the Politics of Violence*, Piscataway, NJ: Aldine Transaction.

Jenness, V. and Broad, K. (2005) *Hate Crimes – New Social Movements and the Politics of Violence*, Piscataway, NJ: Aldine Transaction.

Jenness, V. and Broad, K.L. (2007) 'The emergence, content and institutionalization of hate crime law: how a diverse policy community produced a modern legal fact', *Annual Review of Law and Social Science*, 3, 141–60.

Jenness, V. and Grattet, R. (1996) 'The criminalization of hate: a comparison of structural and polity influences and the passage of "bias-crime" legislation in the United States', *Sociological Perspectives*, 39(1), 129–54.

Jenness, V. and Grattet, R. (2001) *Make Hate a Crime*, New York: Russell Sage Foundation.

John, P. (2003) 'Is there life after policy streams, advocacy coalitions and punctuations: using evolutionary theory to explain policy change?', *Policy Studies Journal*, 31(4), 481–98.

Jones, T. and Newburn, T. (2002) 'Policy convergence and crime control in the USA and the UK: streams of influence and levels of impact', *Criminology and Criminal Justice*, 2(2), 173–203.

Jones, T. and Newburn, T. (2007) *Policy Transfer and Criminal Justice*, Maidenhead: McGraw Hill.

Jones, L., Bellis, M.A., Wood, S., Hughes, K., McCoy, E., Eckley, L., Bates, G., Mikton, C., Shakespeare, T. and Officer, A. (2012) 'Prevalence and risk of violence against children with disabilities: a systematic review 199 and meta-analysis of observational studies', *The Lancet*, 380(9845), 899–907.

Joseph Rowntree Foundation (JRF) (2020) *UK Poverty 2018/19*, York: JRF.

Judicial College (2018) *Equal Treatment Bench Book*, London: Judicial College.

Judicial Studies Board (2008) *Equal Treatment Bench Book*, London: Judicial Studies Board.

King Braydon, G., Bentele, K.G. and Soule, S.A. (2007) 'Protest and policymaking: explaining fluctuation in congressional attention to rights issues 1960–1986', *Social Forces*, 80(1), 137–63.

Kingdon, J.W. (2001) 'A model of agenda setting with applications', *The Law Review, Michigan State University*, 2, 331–7.

Kingdon, J.W. (2011) *Agendas, Alternatives, and Public Policies* (updated 2nd edn), Springfield, IL: Pearson.

Knill, C. and Tosun, J. (2012) *Public Policy: A New Introduction*, Basingstoke: Palgrave Macmillan.

Koppelman, K. and Lee, R. (2010) *Understanding Human Differences, Multicultural Education for a Diverse America*, Cambridge, MA: Allyn and Bacon.

Kristiansen, K., Vehmas, S. and Shakespeare, T. (2010) *Arguing about Disability, Philosophical Perspectives*, Abingdon: Routledge.

Kumari Campbell, F. (2001) 'Inciting legal fictions – disability's date with ontology and the ableist body of law', *Griffith Law Review*, 10(1), 42–62.

Kumari Campbell, F. (2005) 'Legislating disability: negative ontologies and the government of legal identities', in S. Tremain (ed) *Foucault and the Government of Disability*, Ann Arbor, MI: University of Michigan Press, pp 108–32.

Kumari Campbell, F. (2008) 'Refusing able (ness): a preliminary conversation about ableism', *M/C Journal of Media and Culture*, 11(3).

Kumari Campbell, F. (2009) *Contours of Ableism – The Production of Disability and Ableness*, Basingstoke: Palgrave Macmillan.

Kumari Campbell, F. (2012) 'Stalking ableism: using disability to expose "abled" narcissism', in D. Goodley, B. Hughes and L. Davis (eds) *Disability and Social Theory, New Developments and Directions*, Basingstoke: Palgrave Macmillan, pp 212–32.

Kumari Campbell, F. (2015) 'Ability', in R. Adams, B. Reiss and D. Serlin (eds) *Keywords for Disability Studies*, New York: New York University Press, pp 46–51.

Kvale, S. (2007) *Doing Interviews*, London: Sage.

Kvale, S. and Brinkmann, S. (2009) *Interviews, Learning the Craft of Qualitative Research Interviewing* (2nd edn), Thousand Oaks, CA: Sage.

Labour (1997) *The Labour Party Manifesto*, London: Labour.

Labour (2013) *Making Rights a Reality for Disabled People: A Report by the Shadow DWP Team to Labour's National Policy Forum*, London: Labour.

Landman, R.A. (2014) 'A counterfeit friendship: mate crime and people with learning disabilities', *Journal of Adult Protection*, 16(6), 355–66.

Lane, F.J. (2006) *Law Enforcement Officers' Endorsement of the Bias Categorization of Crime Scenarios: A Prospective Study of Differences Between Disability and Other Protected Statuses*, PhD Thesis, Gainesville, FL: University of Florida.

Law Commission (2013) *Hate Crime: The Case for Extending the Existing Offences*, Consultation Paper Number 213, London: Law Commission.

Law Commission (2014) *Hate Crime: Should the Current Offences be Extended?* Report number 348, London: Law Commission.

Law Commission (2020) *Hate Crime Laws: A Consultation Paper*, Consultation Paper number 250, London: Law Commission.

Law Commission (2021) *Hate Crime Laws: Final Report*, HC 942, Law Com No 402, London: House of Commons.

Lawrence, F.M. (1999) *Punishing Hate, Bias Crimes Under American Law*, Cambridge, MA: Harvard University Press.

Levin, B. (2009) 'The long arc of justice: race, violence, and the emergence of hate crimes law', in B. Levin (ed.) *Hate Crimes Volume 1: Understanding and Defining Hate Crime*, Westport, CT: Praeger, pp 1–22.

Levin, J. and McDevitt, J. (2002) *Hate Crimes Revisited – America's War on Those Who Are Different*, New York: Perseus Books Group.

Levin, J. and Nolan, J. (2011) *The Violence of Hate* (3rd edn), Boston: Allyn and Bacon.

Levitas, R. (2005) *The Inclusive Society? Social Exclusion and New Labour* (2nd edn), Basingstoke: Palgrave Macmillan.

Liberal Democrats (2010) *Liberal Democrats Manifesto*, London: Liberal Democrats.

Lincoln, Y. and Guba, E. (1985) *Naturalistic Inquiry*, Beverly Hills, CA: Sage.

Lipsky, M. (2010) *Street-Level Bureaucracy*, New York: Russell Sage Foundation.

Lister, R. (2010) *Understanding Theories and Concepts in Social Policy*, Bristol: Policy Press.

Liu, X., Lindquist, E., Vedlitz, A. and Vincent, K. (2010) 'Understanding local policy making: policy elites' perceptions of local agenda setting and alternative policy selection', *Policy Studies Journal*, 38(1), 69–91.

Macciarone, G. (1992) 'The garbage can model and the study of policy making: a critique', *Polity*, 24(3), 459–82.

Macdonald, K., DPP and Queen's Counsel (2008) 'Prosecuting disability hate crime', *Joint Bar Council and Equality and Diversity Forum Seminar*, Keynote speech by Director of Public Prosecutions, London, October 2008: Crown Prosecution Service.

MacDonald, S.J., Donovan, C. and Clayton, J. (2017) 'The disability bias: understanding the context of hate in comparison with other minority populations', *Disability and Society*, 32(4), 483–99.

Marley, J.A. and Biula, S. (2001) 'Crimes against people with mental illness: types, perpetrators and influencing factors', *Social Work*, 46(2), 115–24.

Marshall, T.H. (1950) *Citizenship and Social Class and Other Essays*, Cambridge: Cambridge University Press.

Martin, P.Y. and Turner, B.A. (1986) 'Grounded theory and organisational research', *The Journal of Applied Behavioural Science*, 22(2), 141–57.

Mary, P.J., Sapotichne, J. and Warkman, S. (2006) 'Policy coherence and policy domains', *Policy Studies Journal*, 34(3), 381–403.

Mason, G. (2015) 'Legislating against hate', in N. Hall, A. Corb, P. Giannasi and J. Grieve (eds) *Routledge International Handbook on Hate Crime*, London: Routledge, pp 59–68.

Mason-Bish, H. (2009) *Establishing, Exploring, and Expanding Hate Crime as a Policy Domain*. PhD Thesis. Colchester: University of Essex.

Mason-Bish, H. (2012) 'Examining the boundaries of hate crime policy: considering age and gender', *Criminal Justice Policy Review*, 20(10), 1–20.

Mason-Bish, H. (2013) 'Conceptual issues in the construction of disability hate crime', in A. Roulstone and H. Mason-Bish (eds) *Disability, Hate Crime and Violence*, London: Routledge, pp 11–24.

May, T. (2001) *Social Research, Issues, Methods and Process* (3rd edn), Buckingham: Oxford University Press.

McCrudden, C. (1999) 'Mainstreaming equality in the governance of Northern Ireland', *Fordham International Law Journal*, 22(4), 1696–741.

McDonnell, P. (2007) *Disability and Society – Ideological and Historical Dimensions*, Dublin: Blackhall Publishing.

McLaughlin, E. (2007) 'From negative to positive equality duties: the development and constitutionalisation of equality provisions in the UK', *Social Policy and Society*, 6(1), 111–21.

McLaughlin, E. and Muncie, J. (2006) *The Sage Dictionary of Criminology*, London: Sage.

McLaughlin, E. and Newburn, T. (2010) *The Sage Handbook of Criminological Theory*, London: Sage.

McMahon, B.T., West, S.L., Lewis, A.N., Armstrong, A.J. and Conway, J.P. (2004) 'Hate crimes and disability in America', *Rehabilitation and Counselling Bulletin*, 47(2), 66–75.

McVeigh, R. (2017) 'Hate and the state: Northern Ireland, sectarian violence and perpetrator-less crime', in A. Haynes, J. Schweppe and S. Taylor (eds) *Critical Perspectives on Hate Crime: Contributions from the Island of Ireland*, Basingstoke: Palgrave Macmillan, pp 393–417.

Mencap (1999) *Living in Fear*, London: Mencap.
Mencap (2007) *Bullying Wrecks Lives: The Experiences of Children and Young People with a Learning Disability*, London: Mencap.
Mencap (2010) *Don't Stand By – Hate Crime Research Report*, London: Mencap.
Messerschmidt, J.W. (1997) *Crime as Structured Action, Gender, Race and Class in the Making of Crime*, Thousand Oaks, CA: Sage.
Metropolitan Police Service (MPS) (2006) *Disability Equality Scheme*, London: Metropolitan Police Service.
Millar, S. (2010) 'Disability and inequality', in P. Thane (ed) *Unequal Britain*, London: Continuum, pp 163–88.
Miller, P., Parker, S. and Gillinson, S. (2004) *Disablism – How to Tackle the Last Prejudice*, London: Demos.
Mind (2007) *Another Assault*, London: Mind.
Moran, M., Rein, M. and Goodin, R.E. (2006) *The Oxford Handbook of Public Policy*, Oxford: Oxford University Press.
Morris, J. (1991) *Pride Against Prejudice, Transforming Attitudes to Disability*, London: The Women's Press.
Nacro (2002) *Community Safety Guidance for Crime and Disorder Reduction Partnerships*, London: Nacro.
Nathwani, A., Schneider, R., Ollereanshaw, S., Angoy, S., McLellan, J. and Walmsley, A. (2007) *The Public Sector Equality Duties: Making an Impact*, Andover: Schneider Ross.
National Disability Authority (2006) 'Literature review on attitudes towards disability', *Disability Research Series*, 9, Dublin: National Disability Authority.
Nario-Redmond, M.R. (2010) 'Cultural stereotypes of disabled and non-disabled men and women: consensus for global category representations and diagnostic domains', *British Journal of Social Psychology*, 49(3), 471–88.
Nario-Redmond, M.R. (2019) *Ableism: The Causes and Consequences of Disability Prejudice*, London: Wiley Publishers.
Nario-Redmond, M.R., Gospodinov, D. and Cobb, A. (2017) 'Crip for a day: the unintended negative consequences of disability simulations', *Rehabilitation Psychology*, 62(3), 324–33.
Neier, A. (2012) *The International Human Rights Movement – a History*, Princeton, NJ: Princeton University Press.
Nocon, A., Iganski, P. and Lagou, S. (2011) *Disabled People's Experiences and Concerns about Crime, Analysis of the British Crime Survey, 2007–2008, 2008–2009*, Briefing Paper 3, London: Equality and Human Rights Commission.
O'Connor, M.K. and Netting, F.E. (2011) *Analyzing Social Policy*, Hoboken, NJ: Wiley and Sons.
Office for Criminal Justice Reform (OCJR) (2009) *Victims and Witnesses: Early Special Measures Meetings Between CPS and Vulnerable or Intimidated Witnesses*, London: Office for Criminal Justice Reform.

Office for Disability Issues (ODI) (2008) *Experiences and Expectations of Disabled People*, London: Office for Disability Issues.

Office for Disability Issues (ODI) (2012) *Government Response to Hidden in Plain Sight*, London: Office for Disability Issues.

Office for Disability Issues (ODI) (2017) *Disabled People's Rights: Information for the UK's First Periodic Review*, London: Office for Disability Issues.

Office for Security and Co-Operation in Europe (2009) *Hate Crime: A Practical Guide*, Warsaw: Office for Security and Co-Operation in Europe.

Office for Security and Co-Operation in Europe (2012) *Hate Crimes in the OSCE Region: Incidents and Responses Annual Report for 2011*, Warsaw: Office for Security and Co-Operation in Europe.

Office for Security and Co-operation in Europe (2017) *Hate Crime Against People with Disabilities*, Warsaw: Office for Security and Co-Operation in Europe.

Ogden, C.A. (2016), 'Disability Hate Crime', in K. Corten, S. Moxley, P. Taylor and J. Turner (eds) *A Companion to Crime, Harm and Victimisation*, Bristol: Policy Press, pp 51–3.

Oliver, M. (2009) *Understanding Disability – from Theory to Action* (2nd edn), Basingstoke: Palgrave Macmillan.

Oliver, M. and Barnes, C. (2012) *The New Politics of Disablement*, Basingstoke: Palgrave Macmillan.

Ollereanshaw, S., Schneider, R., Jackson, G. and Iqbal, K. (2003) *An Evaluation of the Public Duty to Promote Race Equality and Good Race Relations in England and Wales*, London: CRE.

Outshoorn, J. (2004) 'Pragmatism in the polder: changing prostitution policy in the Netherlands', *Journal of Contemporary European Studies*, 12(2), 165–76.

Palacio, R.J. (2012) *Wonder*, London: Corgi Books.

Palmer, M. (2011) 'Disability and poverty: a conceptual overview', *Journal of Disability Studies*, 21(4), 210–18.

Pearson, C., Watson, N., Stabler, K., Lerpinere, J., Patersen, K. and Ferree, J. (2011) 'Don't get involved: an examination of how public sector organisations in England are involving disabled people in the disability equality duty', *Disability and Society*, 26(3), 255–68.

Perry, B. (2001) *In the Name of Hate – Understanding Hate Crimes*, New York: Routledge.

Perry, B. (ed) (2003) *Hate and Bias Crime, A Reader*, New York: Routledge.

Perry, B. (ed) (2009a) *Hate Crimes, Volumes 1 to 5*, Westport, CT: Praeger.

Perry, B. (2009b) 'The sociology of hate: theoretical approaches', in B. Levin (ed) *Hate Crimes Volume 1: Understanding and Defining Hate Crime*, Westport, CT: Praeger, pp 55–76.

Perry, J. (2008) 'The perils of an identity politics approach to the legal recognition of harm', *Liverpool Law Review*, 29(1), 19–36.

Perry, J. (2013) 'The wrong war? Critically examining the fight against disability hate crime', in A. Roulstone and H. Mason-Bish (eds) *Disability, Hate Crime and Violence*, Abingdon: Routledge, pp 47–58.

Petersilla, J.R. (2000) 'Invisible victims: violence against persons with developmental disabilities', *Human Rights*, Chicago, IL: American Bar Association.

Piggott, L. (2011) 'Prosecuting disability hate crime: a disabling solution?', *People, Place and Policy Online*, 5(1), 25–34.

Powell, W. and DiMaggio, P. (eds) (1991) *The New Institutionalism in Organizational Analysis*, Chicago, IL: University of Chicago Press.

Pring, J. (2017) 'Welfare reforms and the attack on disabled people', in V. Cooper and D. Whyte (eds) *The Violence of Austerity*, London: Pluto Press, pp 51–8.

Pump, B. (2011) 'Beyond metaphors: new research on agendas in the policy process', *Policy Studies Journal*, 39(51), 1–12.

Putnam, M. (2005) 'Conceptualizing disability', *Journal of Disability Policy Studies*, 16(3), 188–98.

Quarmby, K. (2010) *A Tipping Point for Disability Hate Crime?*, London: Prospect.

Quarmby, K. (2011) *Scapegoat – How We are Failing Disabled People*, London: Portobello Books.

Quinn, G. (2015) 'Current research on disability seminar', Keynote address, 16 October, University College Dublin, Dublin.

Quinn, S. and Redmond, B. (2007) *Disability and Social Policy*, Dublin: UCD Press.

Quinney, R. (1970) *The Social Reality of Crime*, New York: Transaction Publishers.

Ragin, C. (1992) *What Is a Case?*, Cambridge: Cambridge University Press.

Ralph, S., Capewell, C. and Bonnett, E. (2016) 'Disability hate crime: persecuted for difference', *British Journal of Special Education*, 43(3), 209–23.

Ramesh, M. and Howlett, M. (1996) *Studying Public Policy: Policy Cycles and Policy Sub Systems*, Oxford: Oxford University Press.

Rees, T. (2002) *The Changing Politics of Gender Equality in Britain*, Basingstoke: Palgrave.

Richardson, N. and Locks, A. (2014) *Body Studies*, Abingdon: Routledge.

Riddle, V. (2009) 'Policy implementation in an African state: an extension of Kingdon's multiple-streams approach', *Public Administration*, 87(4), 938–54.

Robinson, S.E. and Eller, W. (2010) 'Participation in policy streams: testing the separation of problems and solutions in subnational policy systems', *Policy Studies Journal*, 38(2), 199–215.

Rollock, N. (2010) *The Stephen Lawrence Inquiry Report – Ten Years On*, London: The Runnymede Trust.

Roulstone, A. (2019) 'Disability, hate crime and citizenship', in B. Watermeyer, J. McKenzie and L. Swartz (eds) *The Palgrave Handbook of Disability and Citizenship*, Basingstoke: Palgrave Macmillan, pp 339–57.

Roulstone, A. and Mason-Bish, H. (eds) (2013) *Disability, Hate Crime and Violence*, Abingdon: Routledge.

Roulstone, A. and Prideaux, S. (2012) *Understanding Disability Policy*, Bristol: Policy Press.

Roulstone, A. and Sadique, K. (2013) 'Vulnerable to misinterpretation', in A. Roulstone, P. Thomas and S. Balderstone (2011) 'Between hate and vulnerability: unpicking the British criminal justice system's construction of Disablist Hate Crime', *Disability and Society*, 26(3 May), 351–64.

Roulstone, A., Thomas, P. and Balderstone, S. (2011) 'Between hate and vulnerability: unpicking the British criminal justice system's construction of Disablist Hate Crime', *Disability and Society*, 26(3 May).

Russell, M. (2001) 'Disablement, oppression and the political economy', *Journal of Disability Policy Studies*, 2(2), 87–95.

Ryan, F. (2019) *Crippled: Austerity and the Demonization of Disabled People*, London: Verso Books.

Ryan, G.W. (2003) 'Techniques to identify themes', *Field Methods*, 15(1), 85–109.

Sabatier, P.A. (1991) 'Towards better theories of the policy process', *Political Science and Politics*, 24(2), 147–56.

Sabatier, P.A. (1998) 'The advocacy coalition framework: revisions and relevance for Europe', *Journal of European Policy*, 5(1), 98–130.

Sabatier, P.A. (2007) *Theories of the Policy Process*, Cambridge, MA: Westview Press.

Sabatier, P. and Weible, C. (eds) (2014) *Theories of the Policy Process* (3rd edn), Boulder, CO: Westview Press.

Schmied Blackman, V. (2005) 'Putting policy theory to work: tobacco control in California', *Policy, Politics and Nursing Practice*, 6(2), 148–55.

Schneider, A. and Ingram, H. (1993) 'Social construction of target populations: implications for politics and policy', *American Political Science Review*, 87(2), 334–47.

Schweppe, J. and Walters, M. (2016) *The Globalisation of Hate: Internationalizing Hate Crime?*, Oxford: Oxford University Press.

Scope (2007) *Unequal Citizenship: The Personal is Political*, London: Scope.

Scope (2008) *Getting Away with Murder*, London: Scope.

Scotland, P. Baroness (2007) 'Tackling Disability Hate Crime', *European Hate Crime Conference*, November 2007, London.

Scott, J. (1990) *A Matter of Record*, Cambridge: Polity Press.

Scott, J. (ed) (2006) *Documentary Research Volumes 1–4*, London: Sage.

Sentencing Guidelines Council (SGC) (2004) *The Sentencing Council's Overarching Principles, Seriousness*, London: Sentencing Guidelines Council.

Shah, R. and Giannasi, P. (eds) (2015) *Tackling Disability Discrimination and Disability Hate Crime – A Multidisciplinary Guide*, London: Jessica Kingsley Publishers.

Shakespeare, T. (2000) *The Disability Reader: Social Sciences Perspectives*, London: Bloomsbury.

Shakespeare, T. (2005) 'Disability studies today and tomorrow', *Sociology of Health and Illness*, 27(1), 138–48.

Shakespeare, T. (2006) *Disability Rights and Wrongs*, Abingdon: Routledge.

Shakespeare, T. (2010) *Disability Rights and Wrongs*, Oxford: Routledge.

Shakespeare, T. (2012) 'Blaming the victim: Disability Hate Crime', *The Lancet*, 380(9845), 878.

Shakespeare, T. (2017) *Disability, The Basics*, Abingdon: Routledge.

Sherry, M. (2000a) 'Hate crimes and disabled people', *Social Alternatives*, 19(4), 23–30.

Sherry, M. (2000b) *Hate Crimes against People with Disabilities*, Brisbane: Women with Disabilities Australia.

Sherry, M. (2003) *Don't Ask, Tell or Respond: Silent Acceptance of Disability Hate Crime*, Montreal: Disabled Women's Network.

Sherry, M. (2004) 'Exploring Disability Hate Crimes', *Review of Disability Studies*, 1(1), 51–9.

Sherry, M. (2010) *Disability Hate Crimes, Does Anyone Really Hate Disabled People?*, Burlington: Ashgate Publishing.

Sherry, M., Olsen, T., Solstad, V.J. and Erikson, J. (eds) (2020) *Disability Hate Speech: Social, Cultural and Political Contexts*, Abingdon: Routledge.

Siebers, T. (2006) 'Disability studies and the future of identity politics', in L. Alcoff, M. Homes-Garcia, S. Mohanty and P.M.L. Moya (eds) *Identity Politics Reconsidered*, New York: Palgrave Macmillan, pp 10–30.

Sin, C.H. (2013) 'Making Disablist Hate Crime visible: addressing the challenges of improving reporting', in H. Mason-Bish and A. Roulstone (eds) *Disability, Hate Crime and Violence*, Abingdon: Routledge, pp 147–65.

Sin, C.H. (2014a) 'Hate crimes against people with disabilities', in N. Hall, A. Corb, P. Giannasi and J. Grieve (eds) *The Routledge International Handbook on Hate Crime*, Abingdon: Routledge, pp 193–206.

Sin, C.H. (2014b) 'Using a layers of influence model to understand the interaction of research, policy and practice in relation to disablist hate crime', in N. Chakraborti and J. Garland (eds) *Responding to Hate Crime: The Case for Connecting Policy and Research*, Bristol: Policy Press, pp 99–112.

Sin, C.H., Hedges, A., Cook, C. and Comber, N. (2010a) 'Targeted violence and hostility against people with mental health conditions', *Mental Health Today*, 26–30. PMID: 20073110.

Sin, C.H., Hedges, A., Cook, C. and Comber, N. (2010b) 'Targeted violence, harassment and abuse against people with learning disabilities in Great Britain', *Tizard Learning Disability Review*, 15(1), 17–27.

Sin, C.H., Hedges, A., Cook, C., Mgini, N. and Comber, N. (2011) 'Adult protection and effective action in tackling violence and hostility against disabled people: some tensions and challenges', *Journal of Adult Protection*, 13(2), 63–75.

Slorach, R. (2016) *A Very Capitalist Condition – A History and Politics of Disability*, London: Bookmarks Publications.

Smith, K. (ed), Lader, D., Hoare, J. and Lau, I. (2012) *Hate Crime, Cyber Security and the Experience of Crime Among Children: Findings from the 2010/11 British Crime Survey, Supplementary Volume 3 to Crime in England and Wales 2010/11*, Home Office statistical bulletin, London: Home Office.

Smith, M. (2015) 'Disability Hate Crime – A Call for Action', in R. Shah and P. Giannasi (eds) *Tackling Disability Discrimination and Disability Hate Crime*, London: Jessica Kingsley Publishers, pp 36–53.

Sobsey, D. (1994) *Violence and Abuse in the Lives of People with Disabilities, The End of Silent Acceptance?*, Baltimore, MD: Paul H Brookes Pub Co.

Sorensen, D.D. (2001) *Hate Crimes Against People with Disabilities*, California: Coalition on Crime against People with Disabilities.

Spalek, B. (2006) *Crime Victims – Theory, Policy and Practice*, Basingstoke: Palgrave Macmillan.

Spalek, B. (2008) *Communities, Identities and Crime*, Bristol: Policy Press.

Spicker, P. (2006) *Policy Analysis for Practice – Applying Social Policy*, Bristol: Policy Press.

Spicker, P. (2008) *Social Policy: Themes and Approaches*, Bristol: Policy Press.

Stake, R.E. (1995) *The Art of Case Study Research*, London: Sage.

Stake, R.E. (2005) 'Qualitative case studies', in N.K. Denzin and Y.S. Lincoln (eds) *The Sage Handbook of Qualitative Research* (3rd edn), Thousand Oaks, CA: Sage, pp 443–66.

Stanton-Ife, J. (2013) 'Criminalising conduct with special reference to potential offences of stirring up hatred against disabled or transgendered persons', London: Law Commission.

Starmer, K., DPP and Queen's Counsel (2011) 'Prosecuting Disability Hate Crime: the next frontier', Keynote speech by Director of Public Prosecutions, 2 March 2011, University of Sussex, Brighton.

Stone, D.A. (1989) 'Casual stories and the formation of policy agendas', *Political Science Quarterly*, 104(2), 281–300.

Strauss, A. and Corbin, J. (1998) *Basics of Qualitative Research: Techniques and Procedures for Developing Grounded Theory*, Thousand Oaks, CA: Sage.

Sunsklere, E. (2017) 'Disability Hate Crime: the overlooked consequence of the deinstitutionalization of care', *Social Theory, Empiricism, Policy and Practice*, 15, 70–9.

Swain, J., French, S., Barnes, C. and Thomas, C. (2004) *Disabling Barriers – Enabling Environments* (2nd edn), London: Sage.

Swinbourn, P. (2010) *Case Study Research*, London: Sage.

Switzer Vaughn, J. (2003) *Disabled Rights, American Disability Policy, and the Fight for Equality*, Washington, DC: Georgetown University Press.

Taylor, C. (1994) 'The politics of recognition', in A. Guttmann (ed) *Multiculturalism*, Princeton, NJ: Princeton University Press, pp 25–74.

Taylor, S. (2009) 'The Crown Prosecution Service and race equality', in H. Bhui Singh (ed) *Race and the Criminal Justice System*, London: Sage, pp 66–82.

Taylor, S.J. and Bogdan, R. (1984) *Introduction to Qualitative Research Methods: The Search for Meanings*, New York: Wiley.

Thane, P. (ed) (2010) *Unequal Britain*, London: Continuum.

Thomas, G. (2011) *How to Do Your Case Study, A Guide for Students and Researchers*, London: Sage.

Thomas, G. and James, D. (2006) 'Reinventing grounded theory: some questions about theory, ground and discovery', *British Educational Research Journal*, 32(6), 767–95.

Thompson, N. (2011) *Promoting Equality* (3rd edn), Basingstoke: Palgrave Macmillan.

Thornberg, R. (2012) 'Informed grounded theory', *Scandinavian Journal of Educational Research*, 56(1), 243–59.

Thorneycroft, R. (2017) 'Problematising and reconceptualising "vulnerability" in the context of disablist violence', in N.L. Asquith, T.I. Barthowiak and K.A. Roberts (eds) *Policing Encounters with Vulnerability*, Cham: Palgrave Macmillan, pp 27–45.

Thorneycroft, R. (2020) *Reimagining Disablist and Ableist Violence as Abjection*, Abingdon: Routledge.

Thorneycroft, R. and Asquith, N. (2015) 'The dark figure of disablist violence', *Howard Journal of Criminal Justice*, 54(5), 489–507.

Thorneycroft, R. and Asquith, N (2017) 'Figurehead hate crime cases: developing a framework for understanding and exposing the "problem" with "disability"', *Journal of Media and Cultural Studies*, 31(3), 482–94.

Torrance, H. (2008) 'Building confidence in qualitative research', *Qualitative Inquiry*, 14(4), 507–27.

Travis, R. and Zahariadis, N. (2002) 'A multiple streams model of US foreign aid policy', *Policy Studies Journal*, 30(4), 495–514.

Turpin-Petrosino, C. (2009) 'Historical lessons: what's past may be prologue', in B. Perry and B. Levin (eds) *Hate Crimes: Understanding and Defining Hate Crime (Vol. 1)*, Westport, CT: Praeger, pp 23–40.

Tyson, J. and Hall, N. (2015) 'Perpetrators of Disability Hate Crime', in R. Shah and P. Giannasi (eds) *Tackling Disability Discrimination and Disability Hate Crime: A Multi-Disciplinary Guide*, London: Jessica Kingsley Publishers, pp 69–89.

Tyson, J., Giannasi, P. and Hall, N. (2014) 'Johnny come lately? The international and domestic policy context of Disability Hate Crime', in R. Shah and P. Giannasi (eds) *Tackling Disability Discrimination and Disability Hate Crime: A Multi-Disciplinary Guide*, London: Jessica Kingsley Publishers, pp 20–35.

Values into Action (1999) *Living with Fear*, London: Values into Action.

Values into Action (2001) *Just Gateways*, London: Values into Action.

Values into Action (2002) *Opening the Gateways*, London: Values into Action.

Walters, M.A. (2011) 'A general theory of hate crime? Strain, doing difference and self-control', *Critical Criminology*, 19(4), 313–30.

Walters, M.A., Wieldlitzka, S. and Owusu-Bempah, A. (2017) *Hate Crime and the Legal Process: Options for Law Reform*, Project Report, Brighton: University of Sussex.

Watermeyer, B. (2013) *Towards a Contextual Psychology of Disablism*, Abingdon: Routledge.

Weimer, D.L. (2008) 'Theories of and in the policy process', *Policy Studies Journal*, 36(4), 489–95.

West, C. and Fenstermakers, S. (1995) 'Doing difference', *Gender and Society*, 9(1), 8–37.

Wilkin, D. (2020) *Disability Hate Crime: Experiences of Everyday Hostility on Public Transport*, London: Palgrave Macmillan.

Williams, F. (1989) *Social Policy: A Critical Introduction*, Cambridge: Polity Press.

Wolff, S. (2004) 'Analysis of documents and records', in U. Flick, E. von Kordorff and I. Stienke (eds) *A Companion to Qualitative Research*, London: Sage, pp 284–90.

Wood, D. and Doan, A. (2003) 'The politics of problem definition: applying and testing threshold models', *American Journal of Political Science*, 47(4), 640–53.

World Health Organization (WHO) (2011) *World Report on Disability*, Geneva: World Health Organization.

Yin, R.K. (2009) *Case Study Research: Design and Methods* (4th edn), Thousand Oaks, CA: Sage.

Young, I.M. (1990) *Justice and the Politics of Difference*, Princeton, NJ: Princeton University Press.

Zahariadis, N. (1996) 'Selling British Rail, an idea whose time has come?', *Comparative Political Studies*, 29(4), 400–22.

Zahariadis, N. (2008) 'Ambiguity and choice in European public policy', *Journal of European Public Policy*, 15(4), 514–30.

Zahariadis, N. and Allen C. (1995) 'Ideas, networks and policy streams: privatization in Britain and Germany', *Review of Policy Research*, 14(1–2), 71–98.

Zizek, S. (2008) *Violence*, London: Profile Books.

Index

References to figures appear in *italic* type; those in **bold** type refer to tables.

A

Abberley, P. 50
ableism 12, 181, *189*, 199–200
 and institutional discrimination 175–8
 in literature 51, 186–91
 and Social Model of Disability 12–14, 185–6
 see also disablism
ableist abuse 179, 180
ableist crime 169, 200
abuse 29
 ableist 179, 180
 physical 31
 targeted 32, 179
 verbal 26, 27, 28, 36, 37, 109, 180; *see also* name-calling
abusive language 31
 see also abuse: verbal; name-calling
activism
 challenges to Disability Hate Crime policy 104–8, 113–14
 early days 67–73
 evidence building 78–9
 momentum building 73–8
 political stream 80–4
 strategic alliance 79–80
 see also Mencap; Values into Action (VIA)
activism stream 9–10, 95, 117
agenda development 89–114, *115*
 challenges by activists 104–8, 113–14
 Disability Equality Duty 93–7
 Lawrence Inquiry 90–2
 Pilkington case 109–12, 114
 policy stream 92–4
  monitored hate crime 101–4
  Policy for Prosecuting Cases of Disability Hate Crime (CPS, 2007b) 97–100
agenda institutionalization 116–42, *143*, 197–201
 coalition government 131–4
 EHRC Inquiry 123–8
 failings in 129–31
 Law Commission Review 2014 132–4, 141
 manifest differences within hate crime domain 120–3
 role of judiciary 134–40
agenda setting 86, 196–7
agenda triggering 65–88, *87*, 195–6, 202
 background 66–7
 early activism 67–73
 evidence building 78–9
 momentum building 73–8
 political stream 80–4
 strategic alliance 79–80
aggravated offences 14–15, 85–6, 132
Alli, W. 81
Annual Hate Crime Reports, CPS 118–19, **121**
anti-social behaviour 37, 38, 109, 110, 124
Anti-Terrorism, Crime and Security Act 2001 14
assault *see* common assault; physical assault; sexual assault
Association of Chief Police Officers (ACPO) 3, 81, 102
austerity 6

B

Bacchi, C. 9, 149, 187, 191, 202
Balderston, S. 158
'Being disabled in Britain' (EHRC, 2017a) 170, 171, 172
benevolent prejudice 198, 200
Best, J. 57, 118
Blunkett, D. 72–3, 75–8, 82
British Crime Survey 119
British Criminology Society 166–7
bullying 48, 66–7, 68, 109

C

campaigning *see* activism
Campbell, K. 187–8

INDEX

care 53–4
Care Act 2014 147
care home case 29–30, 137
'Challenge it, report it, stop it' (HM Government 2012) 131–2
Changing Britain for Good (DRC, 2007b) 123
Charaborti, N. 55–6
church warden case 32
citizenship 151
civil rights era 96
common assault 25–6, 27–8
community living 3, 48, 54, 67
community sector organizations 62
Conservative-Liberal Democrat coalition government 4, 131
conviction rates 131
Crime and Disorder Act 1998 14
crime recognition 150–1, 154
Crime Survey for England and Wales 43, 119, 171
criminal damage 24
Criminal Justice Act (CJA) 2003 2–3, 86
 activism 80–4
 David Blunkett 75, 76
 enhanced sentencing 15
 Section 146 66, 68, 117, 135, 139, 148, 149–50, 166
criminal justice inspectorates 129–31
criminal justice system (CJS) 3, 4, 6, 198
 impact of vulnerability on 147–9
 responses to Disability Hate Crime 129–31
criminal offences 14–15, 67
Crown Prosecution Service (CPS) 5
 Annual Hate Crime Reports 118–19, **121**
 Denman Inquiry 101–2
 Disability Hate Crime Guidance 122
 hate crime assurance system 129
 hate crime monitoring 128
 Policy for Prosecuting Cases of Disability Hate Crime (2007b) 56, 97–100, 150
 Public Policy Statement on Disability Hate Crimes and Other Crimes Against Disabled People (2017) 160, 161, 196
 Revised Draft Public Policy Statement on Crimes Against Disabled People (2015) 4, 159
 Single Equality Scheme (2006) 47
 skate park case 181

D

Davies, K. 105
deinstitutionalization 3, 54, 67
dementia 30–1
Denman Inquiry 101–2
Dholakia, N. 81
Director of Public Prosecution (DPP) 3–4, 101, 108, 159
Dis/Ability studies 187
disability construction 52–6

Disability Discrimination Act 53
disability equality 45
Disability Equality Duty 3, 59–60, 89, 93–7, 113, 123, 196, 202
Disability Hate Crime 1–2, 43–4, 79
 agenda development 89–114, *115*
  challenges by activists 104–8, 113–14
  Disability Equality Duty 93–7
  Disability Hate Crime policy, CPS 97–100
  Lawrence Inquiry 90–2
  monitored hate crime 101–4
  Pilkington case 109–12, 114
  policy stream 92–4
 agenda institutionalization 116–42, *143*, 197–201
  coalition government 131–2
  EHRC Inquiry 123–8
  failings in 129–31
  Law Commission Review 2014 132–4, 141
  manifest differences within hate crime domain 120–3
  role of judiciary 134–40
 agenda setting 196–7
 agenda triggering 65–88, *87*, 195–6, 202
  background 66–7
  early activism 67–73
  evidence building 78–9
  momentum building 73–8
  political stream 80–4
  strategic alliance 79–80
 conviction rate 131
 and disablism 51–2
 and identity politics 47–9
 legal and policy recommendations 203–4
 policy development 5–6
 policy making 57–8, 59–63
 and prejudice 160
 public milestones 2–5
 research recommendations 203
 and vulnerability 55–6
 see also ableist crime
Disability Hate Crime cases 21–40, **212–13**
 analysis 210–11
 Disability Now 105
 flagged but not raised in court 30–2
 'Getting away with murder' (Scope, 2008) 106–7
 no-crime cases 35–8
 not recognized at all 32–5
 recorded cases 43, 171–2
 rejected by the court 28–30
 with successful sentence uplift 22–8
 vulnerability focus 155–9
Disability Hate Crime Network 3, 104, 105
Disability Hate Crime policy, CPS 56, 97–100, 150

245

disability hostility 6, 9, 41, 43, 49
  as aggravating factor 53
  background 66–7
  David Blunkett 76
  enhanced sentencing 15
  including vulnerability 199, 201
  policy recommendations 204
  skate park case 181
  versus vulnerability 83, 84, 99, 149, 150, 153, 157, 161–5, 198
  see also targeted hostility
disability literature 49–52
disability motivated crimes 43
disability movement 47–8, 50, 105, 146, 183–5
Disability Now 105
disability pay gap 170
disability prejudice 178–82, 185–6, 190–1, 195, 199–200
  see also ableism; disablism
Disability Pyramid of Hate *190*, 192
disability related bullying and harassment 66–7
'Disability-related harassment' (EHRC, 2011a) 112, 121–2, 133, 157, 172, 176
Disability Rights Commission (DRC) 3, 61–2
  activism 68, 70, 72–3, 78, 104
  Changing Britain for Good (2007b) 123
  disability hostility 74
  vulnerability 84
disability violence 4
disabled people 43
'Disabled people's experiences of targeted violence and hostility' (EHRC, 2009) 4, 62–3, 120, 121
disablism *189*
  and institutional discrimination 175–8
  in literature 51–2, 186–91
  and Social Model of Disability 12–14, 185–6
  see also ablism
disadvantage 169–73, 200
discrimination 45
  and disadvantage 169–73
  institutional 96, 125, 173–5
  disablism and ableism 175–8
  racial 101
documentary analysis 209–10
domestic violence 30–1
Downtown case 23–4

E

education 170
employment 170
enhanced sentencing 15, 22–3
enslavement 33–4
Equal Treatment Benchbook (Judicial College, 2018) 138–9

Equality and Human Rights Commission (EHRC)
  'Being disabled in Britain' (2017a) 170, 171, 172
  'Disability-related harassment' (2011a) 112, 121–2, 133, 157, 172, 176
  'Disabled people's experiences of targeted violence and hostility' (2009) 4, 62–3, 120, 121
  'Hidden in plain sight' (2011b) 55, 63, 123–8
equality duties 59–60, 92–3, 202
  see also Disability Equality Duty
equality policy 52–3, 57–63
European Convention on Human Rights 45
European Union (EU) 45
evidence building 78–9

F

Fineman, M. 11
focusing events 110–11, 112
Fulford Taskforce 102

G

Garland, J. 55–6
gender equality 53
gender identity 15
general election 1997 2
'Getting away with murder' (Scope, 2008) 106–7
Giannasi, P. 63
Goodley, D. 51–2, 186, 187
Grattet, R. 44, 58, 65, 70, 117, 118, 134, 135
grooming 32

H

Hall, N. 61, 182
harassment 23–5, 26–8, 34, 66–7, 109, 110, 122
Harpur, P. 187
hate crime 2, 14, 42, 186
  conceptions and definitions 44–6
  conviction rates 131
  legal provisions 14–16, 44
  minimum charges 128
  monitored 3, 81, 101–4
  policy development 57–63
  principle offence categories **121**
  Public Policy Statement on Disability Hate Crimes and Other Crimes Against Disabled People (CPS, 2017) 160
  scholarship 46–7
  United States 42, 49, 65, 118
  see also Disability Hate Crime
hate crime assurance system 129
hate crime data 118–19, **121**
hate crime law review 134

INDEX

'Hate crime laws: a consultation paper' (Law Commission, 2020) 128, 134
hate crime movement 47
hate crime policing 61, 148–9
hate crime policy domain 168–9
'Hate crime: should the current offences be extended?' (Law Commission, 2014) 132–3, 141
hate Crime studies 201
'Hate crime: the case for extending existing offences' (Law Commission, 2013) 49, 86
'Hidden in plain sight' (EHRC, 2011b) 55, 63, 123–8
Home Office Counting Rules (HOCR) 22
homeless hostel case 27
Homophobic Crime 3, 76
hostility *see* disability hostility; targeted hostility
House of Lords 2, 68, 80, 81
housing 171
  see also supported housing

I

identity 155
  see also gender identity
identity politics 47, 65
identity recognition 151
ill-treatment 29–30
Incitement to Hatred offences 15–16
Independent Police Complaints Commission (IPCC) 4, 63
inequality 155
informant interviews 207
  NVivo analysis 211–16
    Codebook 214, **215–16**, 217
    sample analytical memo **218**
informants **207–9**
institutional discrimination 96, 125, 173–5
  disablism and ableism 175–8
institutional racism 59, 90, 92, 101, 176
institutionalization 101
  see also agenda institutionalization

J

Jenness, V. 44, 58, 65, 70, 117, 118, 134, 135
John, G. 101
Judicial College 138, 204
judiciary 134–40, 148
'Just gateways' (VIA, 2001) 69

K

key informant interviews 207
  NVivo analysis 211–16
    Codebook 214, **215–16**, 217
    sample analytical memo **218**
key informants **207–9**
Kingdon, J.W.
  agenda setting 86
  civil rights agenda 96

focusing events 110–11, 112
policy emergence 67–8
policy entrepreneurs 71
policy making 77, 97
policy solutions 95
public policy model 7–8, 117, 202, 213–14
window of opportunity 91

L

Labour government 2
Labour Party 2, 4
Labour Party conference 74, 76
Law Commission 4, 203
  'Hate crime laws: a consultation paper' (2020) 128, 134
  hate crime legal provisions 14–16
  'Hate crime: should the current offences be extended?' (2014) 132–3, 141
  'Hate crime: the case for extending existing offences' (2013) 49, 86
Lawrence case 111, 112
Lawrence Inquiry 59, 60, 70–1, 90–3, 101, 173
Lawrence, S. 2
legal recommendations 203–4
lesbian, gay, bisexual (LGB) equality 80, 81
lesbian, gay, bisexual (LGB) hate crime 52, 68, 200
lesbian, gay, bisexual (LGB) lobby *see* Stonewall
Levin, B. 45
Lipsky, M. 61, 156, 182
'Living in fear' (Mencap, 1999) 48, 68

M

Macdonald, K. 108, 159
Martin, B. 22, 34–5, 39, 179
Mason-Bish, H. 6, 32, 49, 52, 60, 63–4, 66, 93, 201
mediation 36
Medical Model of Disability 12, 42–3, 53–4, 172
  see also Welfare Model of Disability
Mencap 48, 68, 104
Mental Health Act 29–30
Ministry of Justice (MOJ) 101, 102, 132, 133
monitored hate crime 3, 81, 101–4
murder 22, 34–5, 39, 55, 62, 157, 179
murder charges 128

N

name-calling 24–5, 26–7, 109
  see also verbal abuse
Nario-Redmond, M. 188
National Schizophrenia Fellowship 68–9
neighbour harassment 23–5
neighbours' dispute 35–6
New Labour 75, 77, 147
no-crime cases 22, 35–8

noise nuisance 36–7
normalization 53–4
NVivo analysis 211–16
  Codebook **214, 215–16, 217**
  sample analytical memo **218**

O

offence categories **121**
Office for Criminal Justice Reform (OCJR) 97, 101, 102
Office for Public Management (OPM) 62–3
'Opening the gateways' (VIA, 2002) 69, 70
opportunistic crimes 163
Organization for Security and Co-operation in Europe 45

P

Perry, B. 14, 186
Perry, J. 52
physical abuse 31
physical assault 28–9, 34, 181
  see also common assault
Pilkington case 22, 37–8, 109–12, 114, 123, 179–80, 197
Pilkington Inquiry 4, 38, 63
policing 61, 148–9, 173–4
policy development 57–63, 80
policy domains 58
policy emergence 67–70
  see also agenda triggering
policy entrepreneurs 7, 8, 71–2
Policy for Prosecuting Cases of Disability Hate Crime (CPS, 2007b) 56, 97–100, 150
policy institutionalization analysis 117–18
policy making 57–63, 97, 127
policy recommendations 203–4
policy silence 149
policy stream 7–8, 95, 117, 202
  agenda development 92–4, 108, 150, 196
  Policy for Prosecuting Cases of Disability Hate Crime (CPS, 2007b) 97–100
  monitored hate crime 101–4
  politics of recognition 103–4
politics stream 8, 80–4, 95, 104, 117
post-World War II rights settlement 45
poverty 170
power relations 157, 158
prejudice *see* disability prejudice
prison population 171
problem representation 9, 54–5, 83, 99, 123, 123–5, 150, 152
problematization 8, 9, 200–1, 202
  see also Social Model of Disability; Welfare Model of Disability
problematization and activism stream *see* activism stream
problems stream 7, 8

public milestones 2–5
public policy
  Bacchi's analysis framework for 9
  construction of disability 52–6
  Kingdon's model of 7–8
  literature 50
  policy making 57–63
  vulnerability focus 54–6, 145–7, 149–55
    case analysis 155–9
    impact on criminal justice system 147–9
    moving away from 158–65
Public Policy Statement on Disability Hate Crimes and Other Crimes Against Disabled People (CPS, 2017) 160, 161, 196
public transport 6
Pyramid of Hate 45, *190*, 192

R

race equality 53
Race Equality Duty 59, 90, 92–3
Race for Justice Taskforce 102
Race Relations Act 53
racial discrimination 101
racial hostility 15
racially aggravated offences 14
racism, institutional 59, 90, 92, 101, 176
racist crime 2, 43, 200
recognition
  of crimes 150–1, 154
  politics of 103–4
recognition-based justice 154–6
redistributive justice 154–6
religious hostility 15
religiously aggravated offences 14
research design and methods 206–18
research recommendations 203
researcher issues 216–18
Revised Draft Public Policy Statement on Crimes Against Disabled People (CPS, 2015) 4, 159
Rights Model of Disability 43, 172, 182, 183, 184
  see also Social Model of Disability
Roulstone, A. 55, 64, 100, 171
Royal National Institute of Blind People (RNIB) 73, 74, 78, 82
Runswick-Cole, K. 51–2

S

Sentencing Act 2020 14, 15
  policy recommendations 204
sentencing guidelines 147–8
Sex Discrimination Act 53
sexual assault 32, 34
sexual orientation 2, 3, 15, 79, 81
Sherry, M. 49, 190
Single Equality Scheme (CPS, 2006) 47
skate park case 28–9, 39, 137, 180–1

INDEX

Smith, Sir D. 101
social care policy 146–7, 148
social issues 5
Social Model of Disability 12–13, 43, 50–1, 172, 176–7, 183, 184, 185
    Equality and Human Rights Commission (EHRC) 55
social movements 58, 65
    see also activism; disability movement; hate crime movement
social oppression 50
societal responses to disability 49–50
South London activism 70–1
spitting cyclist case 25–6
Stephen Lawrence Inquiry *see* Lawrence Inquiry
stirring up offences 15–16
Stonewall 74, 78, 79–80, 81
strategic alliance 79–80
    political stream 80–4
street-level bureaucracy 60–1, 182
suicide 38, 63, 110
Sunset View care home case 29–30
supported housing 24

T

targeted abuse 32, 179
targeted hostility 9, 23, 37, 42, 43, 66–7
Thomas, G. 163
Thorneycroft, R. 51
transport 170–1

U

United Nations (UN) 45
United States
    civil rights movement 47
    disability legislation 53
    hate crime 42, 49, 65, 118, 164
    judiciary 135
    vulnerability 55

V

Valetown case 24–5
Values into Action (VIA) 48, 66–7, 69–70, 78, 82, 104
verbal abuse 26, 27, 28, 36, 37, 109, 180
    see also abusive language; name-calling
victimization 6, 55–6
victims of crime 171
visiting mates case 26–7
vulnerability 10–12, 49, 144–67
    'Hidden in plain sight' (EHRC, 2011b) 124–5
    versus hostility 83–4, 99–100
    and hostility 198–9, 201
    impact on criminal justice system 147–9
    institutional focus on 137
    in public policy 54–6, 145–7, 149–55
        case analysis 155–9
        impact on criminal justice system 147–9
        moving away from 158–65
Vulnerability Research Network 166–7
vulnerable victims 23, 24, 26, 27, 29, 31, 32, 34, 35

W

Walters, M. 164, 203
Watermeyer, B. 51
Waxman, F. 49, 54–5
Welfare Model of Disability 12, 42–3, 172, 173, 182, 183, 184, 185
    see also Medical Model of Disability
'What's the problem represented to be?' (WPR) 9
window of opportunity 8, *10*, 74, 91
women 125, 158
World Health Organization 43

Y

Youth Justice and Criminal Evidence Act 1999 147

www.ingramcontent.com/pod-product-compliance
Lightning Source LLC
Chambersburg PA
CBHW051534020426
42333CB00016B/1930